BONES
of the
TIGER

BONES of the TIGER

Protecting the MAN-EATERS OF NEPAL

HEMANTA MISHRA
with **JIM OTTAWAY JR.**

LYONS PRESS
Guilford, Connecticut
An imprint of Globe Pequot Press

Lyons Press is an imprint of Globe Pequot Press.

Text design: Sheryl P. Kober

Project editor: Julie Marsh

Map updated by Daniel Lloyd © Morris Book Publishing, LLC

Library of Congress Cataloging-in-Publication Data is available on file.

ISBN 978-1-59921-491-7

Printed in the United States of America

10 9 8 7 6 5 4 3 2 1

*To Suriya and Sophia. With prayers that,
when you reach my age, the tigers in the wild continue
to be born free and to roam free.*

CONTENTS

PREFACE

THE FIRST YEAR OF THE TIGER IN THIS MILLENNIUM STARTED ON February 14, 2010. It was kicked off with two weeks of joyous celebrations stretching from Shanghai to San Francisco and other major Chinese and Tibetan population centers. Yet the tiger, the iconic symbol of this lunar new year, ironically may become a tragic footnote to a failed international conservation effort and may be extinct by the next Year of the Tiger in 2022.

I celebrated the last Year of the Tiger in 1998 in Dallas by giving a keynote speech at a gathering of distinguished tiger conservationists from all over the world. Then I believed that the Year would awaken people to the plight of the tiger, particularly political leaders and decision makers in tiger countries. Consequently, I hoped to see increased measures for protection of the tiger against poaching and habitat destruction. Tragically, the opposite happened. The past ten years have been a decade of destruction for tigers in the wild. Illicit but lucrative trade in tiger bones, tiger skins, and other body parts for human consumption has decimated the tiger population of the wild. Furthermore, human encroachment deep into its territory has engendered increasing conflicts between man and tiger.

As an aging warrior who has won a few battles to save the tiger, I hope that this Year of the Tiger will begin a better decade for both humans and tigers. Like those who believe that the positions of the moon, the planets, and the stars in the universe have the power to influence living beings on Earth, I also believe that the fate of the tiger is linked to the fate of mankind. After all, the tiger is a key zodiac sign of our ancient civilization. Therefore, like many Asians, I believe in the ancient prophecy that the tiger protects human homes on Earth from fire, theft, destruction, and evil spirits. Modern science indicates that there may be truths in these legends. Protection of tigers in the wild also helps maintain clean air and protect soil and water, the lifelines of humanity. The tiger's habitat also provides natural sinks to sequester carbon dioxide and offset greenhouse gases in the atmosphere. Consequently, saving the tiger plays a vital role in climate change in the twenty-first century.

The tiger has survived many prophesies of doom that they would be extinct by the end of the twentieth century. There is no reason why they cannot survive beyond the end of the twenty-first century. All the tiger needs is a bit of space, food, and cover and protection from poaching to enable it to continue to be born free and roam free in the wild on our planet—even in an era of man-eating tigers and tiger-eating men, as narrated in this book.

I would not have been able to complete this book without the support of my friend Jim Ottaway Jr., my partner in my previous book (*The Soul of the Rhino*, also published by Lyons Press), a philanthropist, and a comrade in arms in campaigns for conservation. Jim spent days with me painstakingly reworking, rewording, and editing my initial drafts. I am also indebted to Drs. Mahendra Shrestha, John Seidensticker, Chris Wemmer, Dave Smith, Bhim Gurung, and Ambassador Philip Trimble. They reviewed key sections of the book and provided constructive criticism. Dr. Bhim Gurung provided some of the baseline data on man-killing tigers. Likewise, Dr. Anup Joshi helped with double-checking facts and figures. Dr. Chuck McDougal helped me in updating information on some of the man-eating tigers. Some of the statistical information on tigers in the wild is based on country reports of tiger countries and the Web site of the World Conservation Union (IUCN) and information provided by Save the Tiger Fund. Data on trade in tiger parts are mostly derived from the publications of Trade Record Analysis of Fauna & Flora in Commerce (TRAFFIC), Convention on Trade in Endangered Species of Wild Flora & Fauna (CITES), Environmental Investigation Agency (EIA),

International Fund for Animal Welfare (IFAW), and others cited in the bibliography.

Mr. Masahiro Iijima—a friend and a partner in the making of several tiger documentary films, and a coauthor of our coffee-table book *Tiger—the King of the Jungle* (Newton Books, Tokyo, in Japanese) provided most of the photographs used in this book. Other photos were provided by Sushma Mishra, Chris Wemmer, Lisa Choegyal, and Dave Smith. JaVonne Pope, Binayak Mishra, and Alita Mishra reviewed the first draft. They did not hesitate to give some of the initial harsh but constructive criticism, which only close family members can do without any intimidation. In addition, I got support from Rashed Sultan, Pragya Mishra, and Sushma Mishra to meet my deadline with the publisher. I am also grateful to Bonnie Burgoyne, who patiently retyped and formatted the manuscript as she did meticulously for *The Soul of the Rhino*. Karna Jung Thapa of WWF–Nepal provided map information on Chitwan, and the cover was designed by Georgiana Goodwin. Holly Rubino, my editor at Lyons Press, worked with me constantly to get the book into shape, and Paulette Baker copyedited the final draft, while Julie Marsh, the project editor, pulled it all together. I am grateful to all of them.

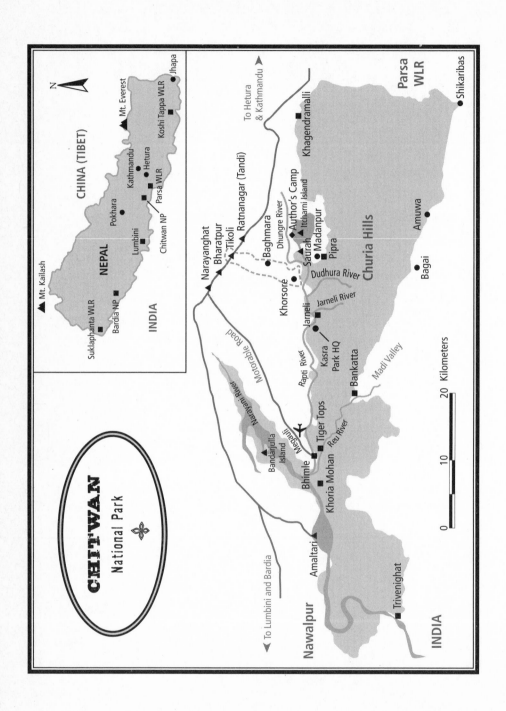

1
THE CALL OF THE TIGER

MY FIRST INTRODUCTION TO THE TIGER WAS ON A NIPPY NOVEMBER night in 1950 as I lay cuddled between my parents in their bed. I was a five-year-old brat born to an affluent Nepalese Brahmin family, and we were at our home in Kupondole near the banks of the Bagmati River in Kathmandu.

An eerie *aauuoom-aauuoom* call broke my sleep. The ghostly sound swished from the south, across a sea of lush wheat fields that surrounded our brick house. The sound in the middle of the night made me shiver with fear. I nudged my mother gently. She was snoring softly on my right side. Lost in deep sleep and unaware of the sound, she looked beautiful and peaceful. I rolled over in the bed and elbowed my father, who was sleeping to my left. He sat up on the bed and stared at me with an annoyed "Why are you bothering me" look in his face. I pointed toward the dark night outside a big glass window and whispered with a quivering voice. "What is that sound?"

"What sound?" he snapped with a tone of mild irritation. Clearly he had not heard the *aauuoom-aauuoom* that had awakened me. I did not have to answer him. The rhythmic *aauuoom-aauuoom* call again sailed through the air and caught my father's attention. He paused and gazed outside the window, his grumpy face becoming smiley. *"Laata,"* he lovingly called me a "dumb kid." "That is the roar of a tiger from the Jwalakhel Zoo. The beast is either hungry or is calling its mate tucked in a separate cage in the zoo."

The zoo was a mile from our house. In those days, there were hardly any paved roads, cars, or concrete buildings in Kathmandu. Fertile farmland dotted with a few hamlets stretched from the Bagmati River to the zoo and beyond. Sound traveled freely over long distances through the clean and cool air of the night.

My father's words reassured me that it was not a ghost. Nevertheless, the tiger's *aauuoom-aauuoom* continued to ring in my ears as I fell back asleep.

Next morning, appreciating my persistence, my father sent me to the zoo with Kaila, our housekeeper. Kaila took me directly to the tiger's cage at the northwest corner of Nepal's only zoo. It was the first time I saw a live tiger, and it was a very disappointing sight. The tiger was merely a big cat that was confined behind thick iron rods in a narrow cage. I had imagined the tiger to be majestically prowling over a wide-open space stretched across the zoo calling *aauuoom-aauuoom*. The animal I saw was a sluggish beast that stretched on a cement floor, lazily chewing a dusty bone of a dead water buffalo.

Lost in my thoughts, I kept milling outside the sturdy cage. Suddenly the tiger stood erect over the half-chewed buffalo bone and stared at us with its large, black, menacing eyes. Frightened, I grabbed Kaila's hand tightly. The tiger strolled stealthily toward us, displaying its huge black-on-yellow-striped body that carried a large head and sinewy limbs. The beast was big and scary, even inside a well-built cage. I stepped back to hide behind Kaila's back, but curiosity soon conquered my fear. I stretched my neck around Kaila's body and peered inside the tiger's cage.

The tiger, a large male, brushed its big head against the iron bars of the cage, prominently displaying a set of black stripes. The markings on the tiger's forehead reminded me of a Chinese calligraphic painting that I had seen in my uncle's living room. Seventeen years later, as a wildlife officer in Nepal in 1967, I learned from Dr. Grame Caughley—a wildlife expert from the United Nations—that this marking on the tiger's forehead represents the symbol of the "Wang'" or "King" to the Chinese. Indeed, this pictogram has earned the tiger the title of the "King of the Jungle."

Slowly my fears faded as I continued to watch the captive tiger. The huge cat captivated me as I watched it waltz in a circle inside its cage. Absorbed by this gorgeous but deadly beast, I began to stretch my imagination. *What would it be like to meet a tiger in the forest?* I wondered. If a tiger imprisoned in a zoo was so fascinating, what would my reaction be to the sights and sounds of a freely roaming wild tiger? Would the animal be quiet and docile like this zoo tiger? Or would it be aggressive and attack me?

I became fixated with a deep desire to see a tiger in the wild, but I had to wait sixteen years to see my first wild tiger. That happened not in the steaming jungles of southern Nepal but in northern India's Phanduwala Forests.

In 1966 I was in my senior year at the Indian Forest College in Dehra Dun. As part of my training I was with a group of fellow students, camping deep in the forests of Phanduwala about thirty miles from our college. Our assignment was to survey the forests and write a forestry management plan. One of my tasks was to estimate the extent of commercially viable timber. Consequently, on a misty December morning I was measuring trees along a forest road in a patch of sal tree forest.

It was a cold but pleasant morning. The sun had just penetrated through the evaporating mist, and the air was warming. The jungle was alive with twittering bulbuls, hopping from tree to tree to feed on insects that were emerging from their burrows to catch the warmth of the morning sun. Dressed in my khakis and a warm woolen jersey, I measured the diameter of a sal tree using a big wooden caliper. As I bent down to pick up my notebook, I saw a flash of movement about twenty yards west of my tree. Ignoring my notebook, I stood erect and looked toward the motion that had caught my attention. I had been warned to keep my eyes and ears open for wild elephants that roamed the Phanduwala Forests. No one had said anything about wild tigers, but to my horror I saw a huge tiger standing in the middle of the forest road. I was too nervous to figure out if it was a male or a female.

The tiger glowered at me with its menacing eyes. My hairs stood up; my body trembled with fear. I was certain that I was about to be eaten. The tiger and I stared at each other. My nerves buzzed with anxiety, my mind terrorized by tales of man-eating tigers. I feared the tiger would soon sprint and pounce on me.

Nothing that I imagined happened. The tiger remained cool and composed. It gave me a last look and quietly crossed the road to melt into the thick bush. But I could not overcome my fears. Believing that, under the cover of the forest, the beast would circle back to devour me, I ran to a nearby amala tree and scrambled to the treetop to hide in the branches fifteen feet above the ground. I hung on the tree for an hour, on the lookout for any sight or sound of the tiger.

The tiger did not come back to attack me. The jungle remained peaceful. Gathering my courage, I climbed down from the tree, collected my gear, and raced about a mile down the road to the safety of our camp.

Later that evening I had the story of my lifetime to tell my colleagues. Some of them said enviously that I had been extremely lucky to see a wild and free-ranging tiger and wished they had been with me. Others argued that I didn't need to fear the tiger: Unless provoked, it had no reason to attack me, since humans are not a tiger's natural prey. These words were comforting, but I never ventured alone into the Phanduwala Forests again. I teamed up with my good friend Subba Rao—a tall and tough graduate student in my class. He watched me and I watched him as we continued our fieldwork of measuring trees. Over the next four weeks, we saw a few deer and many wild boars. But we never saw any elephants or tigers.

My close encounter with the tiger in the Phanduwala Forests left a deep impression. I am not sure what drew me toward the tiger. I often ask myself, *What caused me to become a professional tiger conservationist?* Was it the thrill of dealing with danger? Or was I mesmerized by the beauty of the beast? Perhaps it was both. To me the tiger symbolized a noble and gentle savagery. Gracious and dignified, yet wild and bloodthirsty. A calm and composed cat and yet a dangerous and cruel carnivore that sometimes devours innocent men and women. Revered in myth and religion, yet killed for pleasure and for the supposed magic powers of its bones and body parts, the tiger has survived in contradictions for centuries.

The paradox of the tiger mirrors our own species. The contradiction rooted in tigers symbolizes the philosophy of Yin-Yang—that there can be no virtue on Earth without vice; no kindness without cruelty or good without evil. This Chinese philosophy dating back to 2100–1600 B.C. is equally applicable to tigers and humans. History has repeatedly demonstrated that mankind's cruelty is counteracted by kindness and compassion toward other fellow humans and animals. However, while I believe that mankind will survive the disruptions of the twenty-first century, sadly I cannot be so certain that the tigers will.

In 1900, just fifty years before I was first fascinated by the *aauuoom-aauuoom* calls of a captive tiger, there were more than one hundred thousand tigers roaming freely on Earth. Then the human population was less than two billion people. By 2009, forty-three years had passed since my close encounter with a wild tiger in the Phanduwala Forests of India. During these four decades, the number of tigers on the planet has plummeted to fewer than 3,500. In contrast, the human population has soared from 3 billion in 1966 to more than 6.5 billion in 2009. The Balinese, Javan, and Caspian tigers became extinct in the twentieth century. The fate of the South China tiger is at best uncertain. In the last one hundred years, wild tiger habitat has shrunk by 95 percent. Consequently, the tiger is marginalized in a few wildlife reserves that endure as islands in a sea of humanity. Will these remaining tigers survive the twenty-first century—a century that commenced with civil wars and civil unrest; a period marked by unprecedented destruction of forests and wildlands; an era besieged by environmental pollution, which is triggering unparalleled impacts on our atmosphere and climate?

I have been a student of the tiger since I graduated from the Indian Forest College in Dehra Dun in April 1967. My studies focused not on captive zoo tigers but on wild tigers in the Himalayan foothills of Nepal. Over a decade stretching from 1978 to 1992, I studied the habits, habitat, and behavior of tigers. These studies were often jointly undertaken with a team of like-minded colleagues from Nepal and other parts of the world under the aegis of a program supported by the Government of Nepal, the King Mahendra Trust for Nature Conservation, the Smithsonian Institution, and the World Wildlife Fund.

Over the years I have studied what tigers eat; how they hunt; when and how they mate and produce offspring; how big an area they need to ensure a viable breeding population; and, above all, what the prerequisites are to preserving wild tigers in perpetuity in their natural habitats. As part of my studies I have also been fascinated by the role of tigers in religion, mythology, and folklore throughout human history.

I have journeyed for four decades on my quest to find the right answers to avoid the extinction of this magnetic Asian mammal. Revered for its beauty, strength, and magical supremacy and yet killed mercilessly for fun, fur, and bones and other body parts for their alleged psychopharmacological powers, the problem of saving the tiger is complex and the solution seldom obvious. Yet hope keeps me energetic in pursuing my goal to ensure that tigers still live in the wilds of Asia when my two-year-old granddaughters, Sophia and Suriya, reach my age—and when *their* granddaughters reach their own golden years.

The paths of my journey to save the tiger have been paved with anxiety and uncertainty. They have led me to places both beautiful and intimidating in the world of the tiger. Some sights were pretty; a few were ugly. Along the way I have met many scholarly and fascinating people from all over the world. I also have lived a life of fun even in times of uncertainty and adventure as I learned a lot about the ecology and behavior of tigers.

It is not only about tigers that I learned. I also became aware of the history and culture of the people who dwell in the land of the tiger. I benefitted by living with the Tharu people—Nepal's foremost indigenous people—listening to and admiring their ancient wisdom. Studying the tiger also taught me how to blend Western science with Eastern tradition and mythology. I also discovered that any efforts to save Asia's large wild mammals will fail unless the needs and aspirations of the people in the tiger-land are integrated into our nature conservation programs. I believe that, for the tigers to survive in perpetuity, they cannot be perceived as a problem animal, but as a solution for human welfare.

All these experiences would not have been possible without the vision of a few American scientists working for the Smithsonian Institution and helping me save the tiger in Nepal.

2

The Smithsonian Nepal Tiger Ecology Project

Dr. S. Dillon Ripley was an American and a man of vast vision. He passionately believed in education through fieldwork, a theme he pursued throughout his life. The Smithsonian Nepal Tiger Ecology Project (STEP) was his brainchild.

Ripley was over six feet tall, well built, and handsome; calm and composed; and as regal as a tiger. Indeed, as secretary of America's prestigious Smithsonian Institution, he was also "King of the Mall"—the Smithsonian's complex of museums and art galleries in Washington, D.C. Ripley was a power player in the world of science and nature conservation. Against all odds, four decades ago he had the clout to create the one and only tiger research outpost in Asia.

In the beginning, Ripley wanted to establish the project not in Nepal but in India. In the 1960s, with the exception of Ripley, tiny Nepal was not on the radar of American scientists at the Smithsonian Institution. Many Americans viewed Nepal as a shadowy Himalayan kingdom—home of the yak and the Yeti, or abominable snowman. They perceived Nepal as a land of mountains, monks, and mystery—a playground for wandering Western hippies searching for their souls. But not the land of the tiger.

When Americans thought tiger, they thought India—the big carnivore had been identified with the country throughout its history. Most Americans knew more about the larger and mightier Republic of India than the small, isolated Kingdom of Nepal.

It was natural that the Smithsonian Institution initially targeted India for its first project to study the ecology and behavior of wild tigers. Furthermore, the United States owned millions of dollars in Indian rupees. This huge amount was accumulated over the years through a Food for Peace program under Public Law 480—an act of Congress signed in July 1954 by President Dwight D. Eisenhower. The aim of this act was to win friends and influence countries like India that were facing severe food crises.

Under PL-480 the United States sold three million tons of American wheat to India at a subsidized rate. Since the Indians were acutely short of dollars or any other convertible currency, they paid the American government in Indian rupees. The United States had also agreed to spend the PL-480 rupees within India. Key American science and educational institutions had access to these funds for their programs in India, and the Smithsonian topped the list.

Armed with ideas, cash, and a missionary zeal, Ripley kicked off a proposal for tiger research in the Indian city of Bombay (Mumbai) in May 1967. Addressing a gathering of eminent scientists, naturalists, and civil servants, he highlighted the plight of the Indian tiger. The venue and the theme of the meeting dovetailed with the mission of the Smithsonian Institution. Aptly named the Indo-American Cooperation on Nature Science and Environmental Conservation, the conference was organized by the Bombay Natural History Society—a prestigious body in the Indian subcontinent.

At the conference Ripley warned that tigers had reached the limit of their capacity to survive and that they could become extinct within twenty-five years. He also articulated four basic factors contributing to the tiger's path toward extinction: (1) the failure to curb habitat destruction by agricultural encroachments; (2) poaching, mostly stemming from laxity in law enforcement; (3) the decision of the provincial governments to promote tiger hunting as a source of revenue; and (4) most important, the lack of baseline data and a scientific approach to tiger conservation in India.

Ripley's message was refreshingly candid. The nature conservation fraternity in India praised it, but a few members of the Indian bureaucracy condemned Ripley. These critics were a proud group who detested any outside criticism, particularly from Americans, who they viewed as arrogant, aloof, and self-serving. The timing was also bad. The cold war was at its peak. The geopolitics of the Indian subcontinent were confused. India tilted toward the Soviet Union, and it was widely believed that the United States was blatantly favoring Pakistan—India's archenemy.

A few Indians even saw a sinister plot behind the American proposal to establish a tiger research center in a remote part of the Indian forest. Murmurs behind closed doors connected the Smithsonian Institution with hidden motives of the U.S. government to undermine India, and Ripley's past patriotic services for his country were distorted to give credence to this rumor.

During World War II Ripley had been a field operative of the Office of Strategic Services (OSS)—the precursor of the Central Intelligence Agency (CIA)—coordinating Anglo-American intelligence gathering in Southeast Asia. The truth that Ripley was not an American spy but a globally recognized scientist was ignored. His detractors dismissed the fact that Ripley had written a dozen scholarly books on the birds of India with his friend Dr. Salim Ali, India's eminent ornithologist. It was an era of paranoia about American foreign policy in India. National tabloids propelled anti-American sentiments with screaming headlines such as "CIA Jamboree in New Delhi," "Coca Cola Colonialism," and other sensational claims about CIA plots in India.

Ripley was an ardent advocate of banning tiger hunts in the Indian subcontinent. Working against him, however, was a hunting fraternity in cahoots with high-powered Indian officials. A few safari outfitters, who profited from their wealthy American and European clients, were against any ban on hunting tigers. They may have plotted behind the scenes to demonize Ripley's recommendations. In addition, Ripley was critical of state forest departments of the Indian Union, specifically their command and control–style management of tiger-reserves. He saw the system as a vestige of colonial British India that needed radical changes.

The Indian authorities had opposite views. The entrenched bureaucracy was mostly run by the Indian Administrative Services (IAS). Modeled after the British administrative system, it was too powerful and too rigid for change. The bureaucrats also viewed Ripley as a chauvinistic neocolonialist who believed that only the Americans had the technological ingenuity to undertake tiger research in India.

But Ripley was determined. He kept fighting for the cause of tiger conservation and got his first major break during the tenth general assembly of the International Union for Conservation of Nature and Natural Resources (IUCN) in New Delhi in 1969. There Ripley played a pivotal role in getting the tiger globally recognized as a rare and endangered species. The International Union for Conservation of Nature (IUCN) is the largest conservation organization on Earth, and the government of India is one of its founding members. Headquartered in Switzerland, this international body's membership consists of governments, nongovernmental organizations, and the world academic community. This global wildlife watchdog also produces the *Red Data Book,* an inventory of Earth's most endangered species of plants and animals.

With an overwhelming majority, the IUCN General Assembly in New Delhi adopted a resolution to include the tiger in the *Red Data Book.* This decision was a major victory for the battle to save the tiger, resulting in a total ban on tiger hunting in India. The IUCN resolution was also motivation for the World Wildlife Fund to launch Operation Tiger—a global effort to save the tiger and its habitat. I was not a part of the program. Operation Tiger largely focused on India. However, it provided an impetus to ban tiger hunting in Nepal by 1972 and later to create tiger sanctuaries in collaboration with the World Wildlife Fund.

Ripley and the Smithsonian scientists believed that there was too little baseline data to implement Operation Tiger successfully. They believed good science must be an integral part of any good conservation and management of large carnivores. They knew that detailed studies of large predators in North America revealed sobering insights and that systematic field research nullified conventional management prescriptions that were largely based on hunters' or ranchers' experiences and opinions.

The Smithsonian scientists believed that knowledge of elusive predators like the tiger could only be attained though sustained scientific research in their natural habitat. Yet their efforts to sell hard science as an integral tool to save the tiger misfired in India. The scientists even offered the Indian authorities $1 million from U.S.-owned PL-480 funds to support the protection and management of tiger reserves. But the Indians were adamant and kept the Smithsonian's proposal on the shelf.

Privately Indian authorities said that the Smithsonian's intentions were noble but their approach was naïve. They pointed out that India had welcomed George Schaller to study tigers in Kanha National Park in central India. Schaller, an American scientist from the New York Zoological Society, is recognized as the world's preeminent field biologist.

The Indians felt that the Smithsonian had failed to recognize that a proposal based solely on hard science was not enough. It also had to integrate the social, political, and administrative culture of India. They argued that from the onset the Americans had failed to consult key Indians or bring them on board. Apparently the Smithsonian had pushed its tiger project intensely with an all-American "our way or no way" attitude. Consequently the Smithsonian's tiger proposal was firmly resisted, both at the federal level in New Delhi and at the affected state capitals.

Back in Nepal, I was unaware of the Smithsonian's battle for tiger science in India. I was a midlevel civil servant in the Forest

Department seeking to create Nepal's first national park in Chitwan. I knew nothing about the Smithsonian Institution. However, I did know about S. Dillon Ripley through his voluminous books on birds of the Indian subcontinent. I also knew about Ripley from his book *Search for the Spiny Babbler, an Adventure in Nepal*. In the early seventies there were hardly ten books on the natural history of Nepal—I read them all.

Ripley was one of the first foreigners allowed to visit the forbidden Kingdom of Nepal. He became fixated on Nepal during his bird collection trip to India in 1946–47. He was searching for the Himalayan quail (*Ophrysia superciliosa*), a bird belonging to the pheasant family. Ranked among the rarest of the rare birds of Asia, it was last sighted in 1876 in northwestern India near the Nepalese border. Ripley believed that this bird could have survived in the Karnali region of western Nepal.

No ornithological expeditions were mounted in Nepal in the twentieth century. A century before, Brian Hodgson had been the last person to study the birds of Nepal. As a resident to the British Legation (Embassy) in Nepal from 1821 to 1843, the Briton studied birds in his free time. But he had not been to the remote areas where Ripley wanted to search for the Himalayan quail.

In the winter of 1947, when Ripley was in India probing for a permit to visit Nepal, he befriended Col. Daman Shamsheer Rana, the chargé d'affaires in the Embassy of Nepal in Delhi. The colonel was a relative of the prime minister of Nepal, and Ripley sweet-talked the diplomat regarding his proposal to launch an ornithological expedition to Nepal. Colonel Daman was impressed by Ripley's grace and knowledge of Asia but told Ripley that the chance of getting approval was slim. Although the Government of Nepal had a rigid policy of keeping foreigners out of the country, Colonel Daman duly passed Ripley's request to the office of the prime minister in Kathmandu. As a trusted Nepalese official in Delhi, he strongly recommended approval—a rarity in Nepalese diplomacy.

To Ripley's delighted surprise, he received permission to visit Nepal, but his permit was restricted to travel within a fifteen-mile radius inside the Kathmandu Valley. The valley was rich with wild birds and kept Ripley busy for days, but he was nowhere near the Karnali Valley—the area in far west Nepal where he believed he would find his elusive bird. Being in Kathmandu did, however, provide him with opportunities to kowtow to the Nepalese authorities and promote his quest for the mysterious Himalayan quail.

Ripley, a New York–born aristocrat, was well versed in the art of diplomacy. He managed to get an audience with Maharaja Padma Shamsheer—the ruling Rana prime minister and Nepal's most powerful man. In those days, it was not the Shah kings but the Rana prime ministers who governed Nepal. They had a firm autocratic grip on all matters of state, and their words dictated the law of the land. Kept in total isolation in the royal palace compound in Kathmandu, the king was merely a figurehead.

At the meeting, Ripley tried to impress the prime minister with language describing the "ornithological significance of Nepal" in the "bio-geographical realm" of the world. Prime Minister Padma had no clue about what Ripley was talking about. Totally bored with Ripley's jargon, he did not utter a word. If Ripley had been a Nepali, he would have been summarily dismissed with harsh warnings for wasting the prime minister's time. Ripley was smart enough to read Prime Minister Padma's body language and soon realized that the prime minister was neither amused nor interested in conversing about the birds of Nepal.

Since Ripley had rubbed shoulders with nobility from all over the world, he recognized his mistakes and changed his strategy. Instead of talking about birds, he talked about regional politics. Politics was a passionate subject for the prime minister, who was impressed by Ripley's knowledge of political events in the Indian subcontinent. Ripley also subtly engaged the prime minister with several leading questions that gave the prime minister an opportunity to boast about the glory of Rana rule in Nepal.

The meeting ended with a gloating Nepalese prime minister and an American scientist with his coveted permit. Prime Minister Padma consented to Ripley's request to launch a bird-collection expedition in Nepal the following year. He also assured Ripley that there would be no restrictions on his travels in Nepal.

When Ripley returned to the United States, he persuaded Yale University, the National Geographic Society, and the Smithsonian Institution to sponsor his bird-collection trip to the Kingdom of Nepal in 1948. Alas, while Ripley was hustling for sponsors for his expedition to Nepal, Prime Minister Padma was forced out of power by his cousin Mohan. The change in regimes cast doubts on the viability of Ripley's permit. The key question: Would he be allowed to travel outside Kathmandu? Ripley decided to take his chances and in the fall of 1948 reached Kathmandu with his team of bird collectors.

Immediately upon his arrival, he requested an audience with the new prime minister, Mohan Shamsheer. His request was immediately granted. Like his predecessor, Prime Minister Mohan had no interest in birds. But, to Ripley's relief, Mohan honored his cousin's commitment, giving Ripley open-ended permission to travel and collect birds anywhere in Nepal.

Ripley traveled throughout Nepal on elephants, in bullock carts, and mostly on foot. He had five dozen porters and a Nepalese army lieutenant at his disposal. The lieutenant was his liaison officer for travel in the Karnali Valley. The army officer had two roles—one overt; the other, covert. His first duty was to ensure that Ripley's travels were not questioned by local administrators in the provinces. His second job was to keep an eye on Ripley, just in case the American had hidden motives while masquerading as a bird collector.

For four months Ripley meandered from Kathmandu to the southern Terai before heading north to the Himalayas, shooting and collecting hundreds of prize birds—he was content. He bagged a few rare specimens, including a bird even more rare than the Himalayan quail. The spiny babbler (*Acanthoptila nepalensis*) had never been collected before by any European or American ornithologist. Discovery of this bird inspired Ripley to write his classic book *Search for the Spiny Babbler, an Adventure in Nepal.*

During his travels to Nepal, Ripley fell in love with the country. He discovered that the small Kingdom of Nepal matched India as home to large oriental mammals such as rhinos and tigers. He was also touched by Nepal's scintillating beauty and the warmth of its people, despite their poverty and harsh economic conditions.

The idyllic sights and sounds of Nepal stirred him with new visions. One of them was to stimulate American involvement in wildlife research in the biologically pristine Himalayan kingdom. His dreams remained dormant for two decades. But they germinated again in 1972 when India rejected his tiger research proposal.

By the beginning of 1972, the Smithsonian's mission to forge Indo-American cooperation on tiger research was headed toward a dead end. In September 1972 the Americans made their last pitch. They intensively lobbied a high-level Indian delegation that was visiting the United States to participate in the Second World Congress on National Parks at Yellowstone in Wyoming. Again the Smithsonian's effort proved futile. After failing for five years, the Smithsonian Institution gave up on India and recommended that Ripley shift his focus to Nepal.

In September 1972 Ripley approved a new proposal from his staff at the Smithsonian Institution's Office of the Assistant Secretary for Science. This proposal targeted Chitwan National Park as the venue for the Smithsonian's tiger research.

Ripley's goals were consistent with the Smithsonian's mission in the advancement of science, but he found that there was a large gap in the science of big-carnivore ecology. Most members of his staff were small-mammal experts who focused on the biology of bats and rats—and not on large carnivores, such as leopards or tigers. Thus, upon deciding to choose Nepal as the venue of the tiger project, he asked David Challinor, the Smithsonian's assistant secretary of science, to find an American big-cat specialist to lead the effort.

Challinor approached Dr. Maurice Hornocker, one of the world's leading wild cat specialists, at the University of Idaho. In turn, Hornocker found John Seidensticker, a brilliant scientist and young rising star on elusive carnivores. Seidensticker had pioneered a study on the mountain lions in remote areas of Idaho. Having just earned his doctoral degree, he wanted to expand his horizons in Asia. The wild tiger was his choice.

It was a happy coincidence that I was also at Yellowstone to attend the conference on national parks in September 1972. My boss, Birendra Bahadur Shah, was heading our two-member Nepalese delegation. He was the head of the newly created National Parks and Wildlife unit in the Forest Ministry of His Majesty's Government of Nepal, where I was then working.

Few people called Shah by his real name. He went by his half-Nepali and half-English nickname—Love Raja, or Love King. In keeping with his nickname, Shah was a loveable middle-aged man with a good sense of humor. The grandson of former Prime Minister Juddha Shamsheer Jung Bahadur Rana, he also was distantly related to Nepal's royal family on his mother's side. Consequently, he was well connected. He was also well versed on the inner workings of His Majesty's Government of Nepal. A perpetual optimist, Love Raja had a can-do attitude. He was also an adventurous fellow, open to new ideas.

At Yellowstone, Love Raja and I met an old Nepalese colleague, Kirti Man Tamang. Kirti was a former civil servant in Nepal's Ministry of Forest—a body that had jurisdiction over all matters related to wildlife. He had friends in high places and an unimpeachable reputation for integrity within Nepal's forestry and wildlife community.

During the peak of his career, Kirti fell in love with an American girl who worked with the Peace Corps program in Nepal. He resigned from the Forest Ministry to marry his American sweetheart and took the job of a general manager at Tiger Tops—a deluxe jungle lodge in Royal Chitwan National Park—before he immigrated to the United States.

In the USA he enrolled in a PhD program in the Department of Fisheries and Wildlife at Michigan State University in Lansing. His professor was George Petrides, a faculty member who had supervised other Nepali students enrolled in the university. Professor Petrides was well-traveled, with a passion for engaging his faculty in international wildlife conservation efforts in developing countries. He advised Kirti to select Nepal as a field site for his doctoral research. Homesick for Nepal, Kirti needed little persuasion.

Kirti was attending the Yellowstone conference with a specific agenda: to network and find sponsors for his field studies in Nepal. He managed to link up with Michael Huxley, administrator of the proposed Smithsonian Tiger Ecology Project, and John Seidensticker, the specialist from Idaho. A reformed tiger hunter, Kirti had given up his guns and aspired to help save tigers in his homeland.

Kirti brokered our meeting with Michael Huxley and John Seidensticker at the Old Faithful Inn in Yellowstone. My boss and Kirti's friend, Love Raja, presided at the meeting. He and Kirti had worked hard and played hard together for years as senior members of the Nepalese Forestry Ministry. Love Raja was moved by Kirti's desire to return to Nepal. He took him as a prodigal son who had come to his senses and wished to return home to help his country's wildlife conservation program.

At our meeting, Michael Huxley directly expressed the Smithsonian's desire to create a tiger ecology project in Nepal. He also preached to us regarding the value of field research and described the project's benefits to Nepal. Being less educated and unexposed to modern American scientific terminology, we were flabbergasted by his long-winded oration. His punditry was overkill, and it made us skeptical.

Later that evening it took Kirti an hour and three shots of Jack Daniels Old Tennessee Whiskey to explain the project to us in layman's language. Kirti did a better job—and convinced us of the project's merits.

We also consulted Peter Jackson, an Englishman who was also attending the Yellowstone conference. Director of Information at the World Wildlife Fund (WWF) international headquarters in Morges, Switzerland, Peter was also coordinating the organization's "Operation Tiger."

A former correspondent for Reuter's News Agency, Peter was a friend and a frequent visitor to Nepal. He had fallen in love with Nepal when he first reported the successful 1953 ascent of Mount Everest by Norgay Tenzing Sherpa and Edmund Hilary. He also ranked among the few Europeans my boss trusted.

Peter Jackson briefed us on the background of the project, including the discords between the Indian government and the Smithsonian Institution. He urged us to be opportunistic and "grab" this opportunity because it would provide our program with sound scientific and credible expertise. He believed that our association with the Smithsonian Institution would enhance Nepal's image in the global conservation community. It would also help generate international support for wildlife conservation in Nepal.

Between Kirti and Peter, we were sold on the idea of creating a tiger research project in Chitwan. But we had no authority to make any commitment to permit foreigners to undertake wildlife research in Nepal.

As a follow-up to our meeting, we invited John Seidensticker and Kirti Tamang to visit Nepal. We asked them to submit a project proposal for approval by the government. We also urged them to keep the language straight, simple, and easily understandable. We were optimistic that the project would be approved by His Majesty's Government of Nepal. But, unknown to us, an Anglo-American battle was brewing on the future of the proposed Smithsonian Nepal Tiger Ecology Project.

In 1971 the government of Nepal had requested the Food and Agricultural Organization (FAO) of the United Nations to help Nepal create a network of national parks and wildlife reserves. The FAO assigned a team of advisors to Nepal, all British—and all the old East African colonial kind. But they were seasoned experts who had successfully developed a network of wildlife reserves in Africa, without spending any time or money on field research. They also had a poor opinion of "starry-eyed" American academics running loose with their own agendas in developing countries.

Through their British counterparts at the World Wildlife Fund in Switzerland, they knew all the details of the Smithsonian project. They were also aware that India had rejected the original project and they agreed with that decision. They believed the project to be an impractical study driven by American academics that had no relevant application.

"Protection is 99 percent of conservation," asserted Frank Poppleton, an FAO technical adviser in Nepal, at a meeting in Kathmandu seven months after the Yellowstone conference. He had worked all his previous professional life in East Africa combating poaching and agricultural encroachment. He believed in wild animal conservation with guns, guards, and barbed wire.

"The Americans will baffle you with their scientific jargon," complained Frank, "and the end result of this project will be a series of ivory-tower papers in American journals that none of you will ever read in Nepal. They will be of no use to your job of building national parks and saving wildlife in Nepal."

I was surprised by Frank's strong words. I could not understand why he was so biased against the project. However, I kept quiet.

"What Nepal needs now is a good management plan that combats poaching and agriculture encroachment," he continued. "These are the two critical issues for developing national parks and wildlife reserves to save tigers and other species."

"Frank," I argued, "what harm can this project do? It is costing us nothing. The Americans are covering all the costs, including hiring a dozen new staff members that will give jobs to a few Nepalese. Furthermore, any publication on Nepal's wildlife is a plus for us. We also have no information at all about tigers. We need to expand our international partnership beyond the UN systems. You people are not going to be here forever. All we need to give the Americans is a piece of paper permitting them to establish the Tiger Ecology Project in Chitwan. They pay and we do the rest. I do not see any harm from this project."

"A large part of the project," Poppleton countered, "is being funded by the World Wildlife Fund. These funds are better used for building infrastructure. Your office needs money for building guard posts and buying vehicles and equipment to fight poaching and grazing encroachment. These are Nepal's priorities. Not ivory-tower research driven by publish-or-perish paradigms of the American academics. Furthermore, Nepal gets what Nepal wants. You people are in the driver's seat. I urge you to write formally to WWF rejecting this project. You must also make a strong appeal to them to divert the funds to your priority for antipoaching and grazing control. We will use the FAO's influence and do the rest. We know the WWF's mandate is to help Nepal and not to support the hobbyhorses of misty-eyed American biologists. But first you must categorically decline the Smithsonian project."

Obviously, the FAO experts in Nepal were many steps ahead of us. They had good links with WWF headquarters in Switzerland. A few experts at the WWF headquarters agreed with them that anti-poaching efforts and habitat protection, not research, was Nepal's priority. In contrast, the WWF national organization in the United States (WWF-US) held a different view. They had thoroughly parsed the project and had committed to fund it for at least the first three years. They had no qualms about the long-term benefit of the project's research emphasis. These benefits included generating baseline data for park management and creating a cadre of trained personnel in Nepal. Furthermore, their funding was earmarked as matching funds for the Smithsonian's own commitments.

The proposed Tiger Ecology Project got entangled in a feud within the WWF family for a few months. We were caught in between. However, we knew that the WWF-US was not going to give us money for building guard posts or equipping our anti-poaching units, even if we rejected the project. Furthermore, WWF headquarters in Switzerland wanted their support to Nepal to be a component of their "Operation Tiger" proposal in India. This idea was unacceptable to the Nepalese authorities, who resented India's unsolicited big-brotherly attitude toward her neighbors.

Besides concerns that the Smithsonian project would misdirect Nepal's much-needed resources, the FAO also had concerns about the research methodology of putting radio collars on tigers. This concern was prompted by Tiger Tops, which specialized in showing wild tigers to their clients. The deluxe jungle lodge was the only tourism franchise in Chitwan. It was also a big generator of revenue to the government coffers and the largest source of local employment in the private sector in Chitwan.

The lodge management believed that the sightings of a tiger with a collar might make their guests feel cheated. They teamed up with Frank Poppleton's boss, John Blower—a tall, smooth Briton with a pleasant English accent and powerful contacts in high places. Blower offered an alternative proposition to move the Smithsonian Tiger Ecology Project to Bardia, a wildlife reserve in western Nepal.

Tiger Tops management agreed with Blower's proposal. I disagreed. Bardia was too isolated and remote. Compared with Chitwan, it also lacked the basic infrastructures to support the project.

I was at odds with my friends at Tiger Tops—people with whom I had collaborated in building Chitwan National Park. A few members of their staff believed that their competition in India could spread rumors that Tiger Tops was a sham operation where tourists were fooled by collared pets or trained animals instead of wild tigers. I considered their concerns to be unfounded.

I approached my good friend Dr. Charles "Chuck" McDougal, a top naturalist and a shareholder of Tiger Tops. He came to our rescue, supporting our argument that the dark-band of a radio collar would blend with the tiger's black stripes and would be well camouflaged behind the beast's huge head. However, we agreed not to conduct any tiger-capture operations within two miles of the lodge.

This commitment proved meaningless. Our radio-collared tigers did not recognize man-made geographical boundaries, and a few of our tigers often wandered close to the lodge. However, as Chuck McDougal had aptly predicted, few visitors saw or complained about sighting a radio-collared tiger.

Another concern was about the use of drugs to immobilize wild tigers. This was a legitimate issue. The drugs had been tested on captive tigers in the secure environment of a modern American zoo, never on wild free-ranging tigers in primitive conditions in the jungle of Nepal. Consequently, project critics raised several valid questions. What were the chances of a tiger dying from the effects of the drugs? Who would be responsible or liable for any mishaps during the capture operations? Given the low numbers of tigers in Chitwan, were the risks justified?

I knew that accidents could happen in the wild. Any tiger could die from the effects of the drug. But I firmly believed that the chance of losing a tiger from the effects of the drug was slim.

The drug had been tested by the world's top veterinarians in the best zoos in the United States. Years later we were proved right. Out of the two dozen darted tigers, only one died—not from the direct effects of drugs but from drowning as it wandered off from our ring of elephants and collapsed into a pool of water.

Tiger Tops and FAO joined forces to stop the Smithsonian project. They exerted immense international pressure on me to abandon the idea, but I was hardheaded. I resented the patronizing and self-serving attitude of the FAO and Tiger Tops. Later our relationship changed for the better, but then it exemplified the mercurial nature of conservation organizations. The more pressure they exerted on me, the more I was determined to move this project forward.

While these conflicts were brewing, my old boss was transferred from the Ministry of Forests to a different department in Biratnagar—a town in southeastern Nepal. I felt like an orphan. I alone was left to guide the Smithsonian proposal and get approval from the government of Nepal.

I was adamant in my belief that Nepal had more to lose without the Smithsonian project in Chitwan than with it. I believed it would provide us with basic data for management plans to combat poaching and habitat destruction. Furthermore, it would also provide my colleagues and me with training opportunities in field techniques and conservation biology. To compound my problem, my new boss, P. B. S. Pradhan, was a seasoned bureaucrat. He detested controversy. He was also a master in the art of CYA— "Cover Your Ass"—practiced by bureaucrats worldwide.

However, Pradhan perfected CYA with a three-pronged mantra that he openly preached, albeit poking fun at the working of the Nepalese government: First, "No matter how mundane, do not make any decisions without approval from your immediate supervisor and without consultation with an immediate subordinate in the governmental pecking order." Second, "The best safeguard strategy against any unforeseeable consequences is not to make any decision at all." Third, "Saying No is a safer option than saying Yes."

Like any rule maker, Pradhan was not immune to finding exceptions to his own rules. Furthermore, in Nepal rules are never rigidly adopted; they are always flexible. "Who you know" overrides "What you know" in the decision-making processes. Favors are remembered and bartered among friends. Pradhan knew Kirti Tamang. He was his old friend—a colleague who had given up his good life in America to return home. Pradhan also knew that Kirti had a great influence with his supervisor, Emerald Jung Rana—the Chief Conservator of Forests—who favored the project.

As Pradhan's immediate subordinate, I had signed off on the proposal, so his ass was covered. But that was not the only reason Pradhan supported this project. He, too, was offended by the pressure from outsiders to kill the Nepal Tiger Ecology Project—a project promoted by Love Raja, his predecessor. He agreed with me that the Britons in FAO could use fresh competition and an injection of new ideas. Nepal was not East Africa. The British did not have a monopoly on foreign collaboration to enhance Nepal's wildlife and conservation program.

Despite objections from FAO, we got the government's approval. The Nepal Tiger Ecology Project was finally established in Nepal's Royal Chitwan National Park in 1973—a long six years after it was first proposed in Bombay, India, by Dr. S. Dillon Ripley. Dr. David Challinor, Assistant Secretary of Science at the Smithsonian Institution, took full control of the project. Challinor had a delicate task of balancing the differing expectations of the Nepalese and American sides. Maximum participation, including at least one Nepalese counterpart for every one American field researcher, was the only acceptable arrangement for the Nepalese. Hard science driven by their publish-or-perish imperative drove the Americans. Working with both bottom-up and top-down approaches, Challinor kept the funds flowing into Nepal to the satisfaction of both parties.

He assigned Ross Simons to oversee the project in Washington, D.C. Ross was an enthusiastic young American from Alexandria, Virginia. A good listener and an effective manager, he knew how to keep the tone simple and not baffle us in Nepal with the scientific gibberish then in vogue in America. Ross soon earned our respect. We also kidded him with the title of "Viceroy" for his administrative skills and his commanding tones in resolving internal conflicts among field workers in Nepal on sharing elephants or motor vehicles.

The Smithsonian also assigned Dr. Chris Wemmer as our scientific supervisor. Chris was chief curator at the Smithsonian's Conservation and Research Center in Front Royal, Virginia. He was a brilliant scientist who knew the art of simplicity when it came to hard science. He was a frequent visitor to Nepal and helped us with our field operations. He also trained a few Nepalese staff of the National Parks Department in field research techniques at the Conservation and Research Center in Front Royal. I was one of his students.

One of Chris's hardest tasks was to avoid friction between field researchers, particularly among the American scientists. They were competitive and aggressive and zealously protected their turf, particularly when it came to sharing data and information with fellow American researchers. Chris often took the role of a therapist in conflict resolution.

Dr. Thomas Lovejoy also played a vital—albeit behind-the-scenes role—to ensure that the Tiger Ecology Project was established in Nepal. At that time, he did not work for the Smithsonian Institution, but directed global conservation for the World Wildlife Fund (WWF-US). A globally recognized scientist, he is credited with coining the term *biological diversity* in the scientific lexicon. He also masterminded the recognition and role of tropical rain forests in the global environmental map, particularly in linking biodiversity conservation with climate change. A protégé of S. Dillon Ripley, he remained a strategic thinker with skills to reach out to those who even vehemently opposed the creation of the Tiger Ecology Project in Nepal, including the harsh critics at the WWF's international headquarters in Switzerland. A man with a good sense of humor and a good listener with diplomatic skills, he played a central role in smoothing all ruffled feathers. Ironically, he has never been to Nepal. Yet, without Dr. Lovejoy's ardent but subtle and largely anonymous contributions, I doubt that I could have succeeded in enticing the Smithsonian Institution and the World Wildlife Fund to support our endeavors in Nepal for all these years.

Over the years, the Smithsonian Nepal Tiger Ecology Project had its ups and downs. However, thanks to David Challinor, Ross Simons, Tom Lovejoy, and Chris Wemmer, the program survived for two decades to emerge as one of Asia's premier field stations for American and Nepalese scientists. By 1980 its activities were expanded to include rhinos and other large mammals and the dynamics of saving large Asian wild mammals in a sea of growing human population and poverty. The name of the project was changed to the Nepal Terai Ecology Project. By 1990 it was totally managed by Nepalese who had been trained by the Smithsonian Institution. Today the project runs under a new name, the Biodiversity Conservation Center. It operates under the aegis of the Nepal Trust for Nature Conservation—formerly the King Mahendra Trust for Nature Conservation. But the project's territory in the Terai is the same—where the Smithsonian Nepal Tiger Ecology Project was established in 1973.

Back in 1973, the Smithsonian Institution assigned two experts to run the project in Nepal. Naturally they were Dr. John Seidensticker and Kirti Tamang, the two original movers and shakers of the project. They made an excellent team.

Kirti, a qualified forester, was well known and well respected in Nepal. Having hunted big game in his youth, he knew the forests and wildlife of the tiger's land. He was a traditional Nepalese forest officer. His dress, manners, and style were friendly but formal. He believed in proper protocol when it came to seniority of age and rank. Kirti also had an uncanny talent for picking the right elephant driver and game scouts for the project.

John was Kirti's opposite in both style and substance. He was a brilliant scientist. Statistical data, hard biological science, and publication in peer-reviewed journals excited him most. He was also skilled in asking the right questions to get the answers we needed to manage the newly created Royal Chitwan National Park—Nepal's first: How does the nature of the tiger's habitat affect its numbers and reproduction? What is its main prey? Is the prey density balanced to maintain a healthy population of tigers in Chitwan? What are the patterns of the tiger's behavior and dispersal? How many tigers can the park support?

The radio-telemetry technique used by John and Kirti to study the tiger was innovative. The project was also a historical benchmark for wildlife conservation. Affixing an electronic collar to a tiger's neck to study its ecology and behavior had never before been ventured in Asia. Radio telemetry was good American science, but it had to be adapted for Nepal and the tiger. Even American scientists had to first catch a wild tiger before they could affix a radio collar. That was more of an art than science—the art of knowing how to corner a tiger and keep it in its natural location. This skill required the blending of modern American science with the Nepalese traditional system of *bagh shikar* (tiger hunt) in a bygone era. I myself used these techniques to catch a tiger by its tail.

3

TIGER BY THE TAIL

"SAHIB . . . SAHIB," HUSHED LAHURAY. "THE TIGER HAS TAKEN
the bait." After a hard day's work, I was fast asleep inside my mos-
quito net. His words were music to my ears. I wiped my eyes and
jumped out of my cot. I left my wife, Sushma, in bed to doze off
the cool March morning in 1980 in the steaming jungles of the
Terai—a stretch of subtropical forest that marches east to west
along the foothills of the Himalayas.

I opened the door of our sleeping quarters—one of the small
mud-plastered wooden hut built on tall stilts that were common in
Nepal's Royal Chitwan National Park. Lahuray waved a fragrant
cup of tea under my nose. "Get dressed," he urged. "The shikaris
are waiting for you in the yard."

The shikaris were our game scouts. Along with our elephant
drivers, they worked as our field-assistants and helped us to track
rhinos, tigers, and other big game for our research.

Lahuray was a lanky forty-five-year-old migrant from the
western hills of Nepal. He had settled in the Chitwan Valley in the
early 1960s, after malaria had been eradicated. Prior to that he had
served for two decades as a *sipahi*—a foot soldier in the Nepalese
army. Now he was my all-in-one lieutenant, cook, handyman, and
babysitter for my two daughters. He was my eyes and ears about
the goings-on in our camp. As a trusted camp confidante, he was
also my drinking partner—an act for which he needed no encour-
agement. He performed his duty diligently, combining the flair of
military-like precision with a can-do attitude. Occasions when he
got drunk and grumpy were a few notable exceptions.

I grabbed the steaming cup of my breakfast tea—a luxury that
I cherished in my humble dwelling in southern Nepal, less than

twenty miles from the Indian border as the crow flies south. To me the tea ranked as the best vestige of the British, who had ruled neighboring India from 1750 to 1947. I could not start my day without my cup of Darjeeling.

I sipped my tea slowly as I pondered the morning ahead. It would be a thrilling and exciting day for a tiger hunt. But the purpose of our hunt was not to kill this magnificent beast and collect its vibrant pelt to decorate our living rooms. On the contrary, our objective was to catch a live tiger. This was not for pleasure or profit but for science.

That day our challenges were compounded by an additional task. We had to help a group of American filmmakers shoot a documentary on our tiger-capture operation. The film was being produced by a major American television network for a series entitled *The American Sportsman.*

"Lahuray," I said, sipping my tea. "Please ensure that Dave Sahib is up." Dave Sahib was my American counterpart, James L. David Smith, a researcher from the University of Minnesota. We were studying the ecology and behavior of the tiger and its prey species under the aegis of the Nepal Tiger Ecology Project— a research outpost funded by the Smithsonian Institution and the World Wildlife Fund—a project that would not have materialized without the timely intervention of S. Dillon Ripley, secretary of the Smithsonian Institution.

The technique we used in the field was called radiotelemetry. It consisted of catching a tiger and fixing a radio collar around its neck. Each collar was programmed to transmit its own signal at a set frequency. Using a handheld receiver, we picked up the signals and mapped the movement and behavior of individual tigers. Our success in catching tigers depended on the efficiency of our efforts to lure a tiger to bait. In Nepal, young Asian water buffalo were used for this purpose.

A day before, we had scouted for tiger signs along riverbanks and animal trails. Signs such as footprints, claw marks, urine, and fecal droppings indicate a tiger's territory. The claw marks were often long and deep scratches on tree trunks. To mark its domain, a tiger stands on its hind legs, claws a tree trunk, rubs its paws and face against the tree, and discharges a pungent liquid from tiny scent glands hidden in the animal's face, toes, and other parts of its body. A tiger also scratches the ground, but these scratches are often not visible. Often a tiger sprays the base of the tree or the ground with urine, leaving a strong odor. However, fresh footprints are the best indicator of the presence of a tiger.

During our reconnaissance, we found several tiger signs along the Saurah–Kasra Road in a block of riverine forest across the Rapti River. Two hours before sunset, we baited the area with five young water buffalo spaced at regular intervals along the tiger's trail. The water buffalo, averaging 150 pounds, were tethered with light jute ropes to sturdy wooden stakes that were anchored deep into the ground. The rope was strong enough to stop the buffalo from breaking loose and escaping but weak enough to allow the tiger to break the rope and drag the buffalo away once it made the kill.

It is either feast or famine for tigers in the wild. They can go hungry, not making a kill for ten days. But once a kill is made, tigers will feast on the meat for the next two to three days, alternately eating, resting, and quenching their thirst from nearby streams. A tiger is lucky if it can kill one deer a week. Consequently, the predator spends most of its time and energy prowling the forests and the tall grasslands in search of food. In contrast to its sometimes-elusive wild prey, domestic buffalo tethered to stakes are easy meals for the tiger.

After about an hour or so, I joined the shikaris in the big yard in front of my quarters. *"Sir-Nameste,"* Prem Bahadur Rai greeted me with his trademark smile shining from his handsome face. A chorus of *"Nameste Sahib"* greetings echoed from other members of the camp staff. *"Nameste"* is the traditional form of Nepalese greeting, meaning "I bow to the god within you." *Nameste,* or *Namaskar,* has a universal application. It could mean good morning, good day, good evening, good night, or even good-bye. It is usually spoken with both hands clasped in a praying posture at the chest. *Sahib* means "Sir." Its origin dates back to the colonial days of British India as a term of respect for Indians to address the colonial rulers. Now it is common all over South Asia.

Prem was our fifty-year-old chief shikari, or chief game scout. He had four elephants, each with three elephant keepers, and seven shikaris under his command. Despite my excellent college education, worldwide travels, and several publications to my credit, there was no way I would be able to catch a wild tiger without Prem and his team. Unlike other staff in our camp, Prem never used *Sahib* when he addressed Dave or me. He preferred the English *Sir*. However, he insisted that his subordinates address him as "Subedar Sahib"—a title equivalent to the highest rank of a noncommissioned officer in the Royal Nepal Army. He was proud of the title he had earned when he worked for the king of Nepal.

Prem was a short, slim man with tiny mouselike eyes. These sharp eyes made him the best tiger tracker in Nepal. Born in eastern Nepal, Prem worked for almost two decades for the king of Nepal as a *bagh-shikari* (tiger hunter) at the Royal Hunting Department in the Narayanhiti Royal Palace. After retirement from the palace, Prem joined Tiger Tops—a luxurious jungle lodge in Chitwan that caters to the world's rich and famous. His job was to find, bait, and lure the elusive wild animal to a specific point where wealthy tourists could see the carnivore in comfort and safety. Recognizing that the Smithsonian scientists could not catch and radio-collar wild tigers on their own, our project "poached" Prem from Tiger Tops. He was offered more cash, more prestige, and a chance to get international recognition for his rare talents—an offer he could not resist. As a master of jungle craft, he was our guru. Americans or Nepalese, he taught us all, without prejudice or discrimination, the art of catching wild tigers safely and expediently and without harm to humans or to tigers.

Prem was a petite man with the looks of a middle-aged Nepalese film actor. His sharp, angular, and wizened face was furrowed from years of tracking tigers in the tropical sun and monsoon rains in the jungles of Nepal. As a former ace tiger hunter for the King of Nepal, he knew the jungles like the palm of his hand. He sported well-groomed jet-black hair that he dyed often to hide his graying crown. His sharp eyes could spot game hiding in thick cover at the slightest flicker of a twig. The tiger was no exception. Unlike our elephant drivers, Prem never cursed or made obscene gestures. He was always soft spoken; yet he held the respect of the elephant drivers and shikaris under his command. He was a real gentleman, a rarity in our colorful camp.

Prem and the shikaris were standing around a wooden table when I joined them in the yard. Man Bahadur and Bishnu, two of our best tiger trackers, were unpacking a black plastic box. They took the drugs, darts, syringes, and other paraphernalia out of the box and laid them systematically on the table. Another shikari, Harkha Man, was cleaning the dart gun. Four other shikaris—Ram Krishna, Man Singh, Bal Bahadur, and Keshav Giri—were hauling bundles of *vhit* from our thatch-and-mud store to the yard. Vhit is a thin, pure-white cotton cloth that comes in segments of about one hundred feet long and three feet wide. Later we would use the cloth to drive the tiger to a strategic point, where a shooter in a treetop would dart the animal with a sedative.

"Where?" I questioned Prem without elaborating further. He knew that I was inquiring about the location of the bait taken by the tiger.

"Patch 2," he answered promptly, "between Simal Ghol Bridge and Dudhura Bridge. An adult male."

Patch 2 was a small tract of riverine forest about a mile away from our camp. Prem could identify the sex of the tiger by the size and shape of its pugmark (pawmark). Males have round toes, while females' pugmarks are smaller and a bit pointed. The pugmark size also indicates if the tiger is young, a subadult, or a mature adult.

"Sukram coffee aaunuus," yelled Dave as he stepped down the stairs of his sleeping quarter—barely fifty feet from mine. He was ordering Sukram, his cook, to bring him his morning coffee. He was also butchering the Nepali language. Instead of saying "Bring coffee," he was mistakenly calling "Come coffee." Dave's pidgin Nepali was a source of amusement in our camp, but he did not care. He was not afraid to speak out in broken Nepali as long as his message was understood.

"What time," he asked after greeting us, "is the ABC team expected to arrive?"

"Eight," I replied looking at my Japanese watch. "We have plenty of time; it is just after seven. But the question is should we wait for them or get on with our preparatory works for the jungle ritual and loading the dart gun?"

"Better to wait," suggested Dave. "We do not know what they want to film. We also need to wait for Tirtha Man Maskey."

Maskey was the thirty-year-old superintendent of Royal Chitwan National Park. He lived at Kasra, the national park head-quarters, twelve miles away from our camp and was a constant partner in our tiger-capture operations. He ensured that we had full cooperation of all the governmental staff and the government elephants, which were under his command.

It was 7:30 in the morning when Maskey roared into our camp driving his sturdy but noisy Land Rover. As though his arrival were a signal, a dozen elephants slowly marched into our yard one by one. These elephants belonged to His Majesty's Government of Nepal and had traveled from the Saurah Hathisar (Saurah Elephant Stable), less than a furlong east of our camp. They lined up in the yard with four other elephants that had arrived earlier from the elephant stable in our camp.

The ABC crews were staying at Tiger Tops Jungle Lodge, twenty-four miles west of our camp. They had flown three days earlier into the hot and humid tropical forests and grasslands of Nepal from their cold glass-and-concrete jungle in New York City. John Wilcox, ABC's film producer, prized perfection and punctuality—two traits of the fast-paced Western culture of New York. These traits were foreign to the relaxed Eastern culture of Chitwan. Yet Wilcox's expectations were clear, and none of us was tardy. That day we had beaten the ABC team by half an hour.

In addition to John Wilcox, the ABC team had five crewmembers: two cameramen, two sound recorders, and a field technician. The American team also included a major attraction—a tall, slim, and strikingly beautiful blond actress. She was Shelley Hack, one of the three stars that year of the popular American television series *Charlie's Angels.* To everyone's embarrassment, we were ignorant about Charlie or his Angels or, for that matter, about any American television series. We were sequestered in the rolling forests and grasslands of Chitwan with no electricity, no television, no newspapers, and no connection to the tinseled world of Hollywood.

The ABC team arrived sharply at eight o'clock in two open Land Rovers belonging to Tiger Tops. We served them tea and briefed them on the day's proceedings.

"We are lucky," explained Dave, kicking off the briefing. "A male tiger has made a kill just over a mile from here. If the tiger is not disturbed by humans, he will stay with the kill all day, so there is no need to rush. We will go to the site by elephants and round up the tiger when we are ready."

He paused and looked at me. It was his cue for me to take over.

"We have two preparatory tasks," I explained. "The first task is to get the blessing of the goddess of the forests by performing a *puja*—an act of worship to make a spiritual connection with the jungle deity. It is an old tradition here in Chitwan. We do not like to venture into the forest without doing our *puja*. Animal sacrifice to appease the deity is a key component of the *puja*. John," I asked Wilcox, the film producer, "do you want to film the *puja*?"

"What sacrifice?" he questioned, his eyes flashing.

"A black goat, a red rooster, and a pair of white pigeons," I responded casually. John stared at each of his fellow Americans, who kept quiet. John's face was somber and indicated that he did not find the sacrifice appealing for his film.

"The second task this morning," I continued pointing to our tiger-capture paraphernalia and the piles of vhit cloth, "is to load the dart gun, pack the vhit cloth on top of the elephants, and ride into the jungle."

"We do not want to infringe on your religious ritual," Wilcox said, "but we would like to film the elephants and the loading of the dart gun."

I knew that his words had little to do with infringement of our religious sentiments. I was sure that like most Westerners, he thought that our shamanistic ritual was both bizarre and barbaric. It would disgust his television audience back home in America. It could also create a backlash against ABC from animal-rights groups in the United States.

I left the second task to Dave. He was better at explaining the details of the drugs and our capture equipment that were imported from the United States. He also had a nice American accent. I had an accent that was jokingly called Nepenglish. The ABC's American audience might not understand me.

Dave eloquently described our tools of the trade to the video cameramen, picking each tool up from the table. Our tiger-capture equipment had three main components. The first was a rifle that shot the second component, a feathered aluminum syringe loaded with drugs. Manufactured by the Palmer Chemical and Equipment Company, it goes by the trade name Capchur Gun. We simply called it a dart gun. The dart gun comes with a few accessories, such as tiny chargers that resemble a .22 rifle bullet. The third component was the drug we used to sedate tigers. Known as CI-744, it was manufactured by the Parke-Davis Company and supplied to us by the Smithsonian Institution's National Zoo in Washington, D.C. Drug doses varied from as low as three milliliters for subadults to five milliliters for adult male tigers. This drug wore off naturally; however, the recovery time varied from two and a half hours to more than five hours.

While Dave was loading the dart gun, I followed Badai, our chief elephant driver, into a small patch of forest in front of our camp to participate in our first duty of that morning. I was among the practitioners of the traditional ritual that was to be performed. I also needed to keep our shikaris and elephant drivers happy— most of them were devotees of Ban Devi, the goddess of the forests. Badai performed the ceremony. Chanting his prayers, he coolly sacrificed a black goat, a red rooster, and two white pigeons at the base of a silk-cotton tree that symbolized our deity.

Following the ritual we returned to the camp yard to join Dave and the ABC crew. Badai garlanded us with strips of red ribbon and marked our foreheads with a mixture of rice, yogurt, and vermilion, which he had already offered to the goddess. He also blessed the dart gun. Being unsure of their reactions, he ignored the ABC filming team. Later we would feast on the meat of the sacrificed animals, chasing the meat with *rakshi*—a local drink distilled from rice. For the time being we believed that our ritual would appease the goddess of the forests and give us license to catch a wild tiger.

Our camp bustled with activity, which the ABC film crew captured for their television documentary. Under Prem's supervision, the elephant drivers packed the vhit on top of two elephants. The shikaris loaded bright-red jars of water to douse the tiger to keep its body temperature down after darting, as the drug would raise its body temperature. We also packed extra drugs and other equipment, including radio collars, on the other two elephants.

"You do the honors," said Dave as he handed me the dart gun and several chargers. Prem had taught me the tricks of the trade, and I was ready. This was not my first experience darting a tiger. I mounted Mel Kali, one of our calmest elephants—aptly named for an equally calm American scientist, Mel Sunquist, who had preceded Dave Smith on the project. We assigned each of the ABC crew his own elephant. Shelley Hack got Bahadur Kali, King Birendra's hunting elephant. The elephant was driven by Bhaggu, the king's personal elephant driver, a veteran of many tiger hunts.

"Attention please," called Prem when all of us had mounted our elephants. "I want you to maintain absolute silence once we cross the Rapti River and approach the forest."

We crossed the river single file, stopping briefly to water our elephants in the Rapti. The jungle was quiet except for a few calls of the ubiquitous peacock and chirping sounds of small birds. We dismounted from our elephants about one hundred feet away and quietly jogged to a bait stake—one of the five stakes where Prem had tethered buffalo bait. The bait was gone. Except for a broken piece of rope, the stake was empty, providing us with concrete evidence that the tiger had killed and dragged our buffalo bait into the bush. Two elephants joined us and stood next to us. They were our safeguards to prevent any close encounters with the tiger, which generally avoids the bigger beast. A pungent smell filled the air. Piles of buffalo dung formed a mosaic over a dark patch on the forest floor. The patch was a mixture of dirt, dried blood, and buffalo urine. Shrubs and grasses on the ground were trampled, and a prominent drag mark led from the dark patch into the thick bush.

"The tiger has dragged the kill southwest toward the Dudhura River," whispered Prem as he pointed to the drag mark. "I believe that the tiger is resting about one hundred yards under thick cover of the trees." His voice was serious, triggering an air of anxiety. We stood silent and still.

Prem's expertise and knowledge of the forests ensured that our plans rarely failed. "Time to lay the vhit," he murmured as he signaled the elephants to come forward. Two vhit-carrying elephants were positioned about seventy yards apart on both sides of the bait stake. The remaining elephants were spaced at periodic intervals in between. The shikaris laid down the vhit in a V shape. One shikari dropped the vhit cloth from the top of an elephant. Two shikaris on the ground tied the cloth to shrubs in an upright position to create a three-foot-high wall of cotton cloth. A funnel-shaped corral slowly emerged as the vhit-elephants moved forward. Our strategy was to position the tiger in the center of the funnel. A tiger that has just caught and eaten its fill will not leave its kill.

The erecting of the vhit cloth was soon completed. Twelve elephants stayed at their position to guard the wide end of the funnel. Later they would beat the jungle and force the tiger to move toward the narrow end of the funnel. I did not like that my wife, Sushma, was on one of the elephants. Anything can happen during the beat. I recalled a tiger jumping on the head of Sushma's elephant during one of our tiger-capture operations a year ago. The elephant simply jerked its head and threw the tiger to the ground. Except for a deep scratch on the elephant's forehead, there was no serious injury to Sushma or the elephant.

But Sushma didn't share my anxiety. "You men can do it," she often claimed obstinately, "I—a woman—can do it too." She also enjoyed and helped us in our research. With Dave Smith and Shelley Hack quietly following us on their elephants, Prem guided Peter Henning—the lead ABC cameraman—and me to a velar tree (*Trewia nudiflora*) at the narrow but open end of the V-shaped corral.

"Please climb up," he told Peter, pointing to a forked branch about fifteen feet high. "Sir," he beckoned me, "You take the lower branch. I will pass the camera and the dart gun to you after you take your position." We climbed the tree using the back of our elephants as a platform—first Peter, then me. We adjusted our positions until we felt at ease, Peter on a branch just above me. The sturdy and wide branches allowed us to stand and to lean against the tree trunk, freeing both of our hands to handle our equipment. Admiration for Prem flowed through my mind. He seemed to know every tree in tiger country.

"The tiger will stop right here," said Prem, pointing to a small opening on the edge of a thick hedge, a dozen feet from the base of my tree. "Tigers, like most wild animals, will pause before crossing a forest opening," he warned. "But you will have only a few seconds to fire the dart gun, before the tiger crosses into cover."

I nodded my head nervously at the thought of an eye-to-eye encounter with Chitwan's mightiest predator, only a dozen feet down from my tree. Prem must have noticed an edgy look on my face.

"The tiger will not spot you that high up a tree," said Prem, "as long as you do not make any noise. Keep your cool. Do not move. You will see the tiger long before it reaches your tree." He was right. Evolution and the laws of nature had given tigers no reason to look up into trees. They had no enemies or predators that attacked them from treetops.

I looked up at Peter. His feet almost touched my head, and I had to tilt backwards to see his face. He smiled and shook his head to indicate that he had gotten the message. Peter was a veteran wildlife cameraman—a calm and composed professional. He was a jovial American who, after a good day's work, often regaled us with his jokes at the bar in Tiger Tops. A few of his stories were about his primary hobby—racing World War II–era airplanes in Reno, Nevada.

Prem escorted Dave Smith and Shelley Hack to a tree about ten feet behind me. Dave was equipped with a second dart gun—just in case I missed my shot. Peter was filming them from our tree. I watched Shelley struggle to climb the tree as Dave tried to push her up the tree trunk. Shelley finally climbed up the tree from the back of an elephant. She looked nervous even when she tried to mask her uneasiness with a faint smile. Dave followed her up and perched on a branch a few feet below her. Prem waved his hand from the top of his elephant and melted into the forest. He was heading back to the wide end of the funnel. There he would beat the jungle to drive the tiger to my tree.

From my perch, I had a good a view of the vhit cloth, as it snaked through the forest floor. I shifted to look back and saw Harkha Man and Bishnu—our two shikaris—standing on the branches of two separate trees about fifteen feet behind Dave and Shelley's tree. Their job was to spot the direction of the tiger's flight after I fired my dart gun.

Almost fifteen minutes later, the jungle boomed with a chorus of "haat-haat-haat." The sound blended with a discordant choir of "hey-ho-haw-ho" and the *tang-tang* beatings of empty metal vessels. The beat had started. I cocked my dart gun and focused on the ground, but it was a good five minutes before I saw a movement in a cluster of grass some twenty yards from my tree. Suddenly I had a glimpse of black and yellow stripes moving toward my right. It was tiger heading toward me. Prem had herded the tiger to the right place. Now the onus was on me to shoot straight. I watched nervously as the tiger disappeared into the thick cover of shrubs near the vhit cloth.

"Bagh aayo!" I heard Prem screaming to warn me that the tiger was closing on my tree. My breathing getting heavier, I searched the forest floor with anxiety. I did not see a tiger, but I spotted a barking deer. The deer trotted nervously under my tree and disappeared into the thick bush.

Silly deer, I thought. *What on Earth are you doing sharing a patch of forest with the mighty tiger?* The deer sighting eased my nerves. I looked up at Peter. His face was glued to the eyepiece of his camera, which was pointed farther out on the forest floor. He was higher than I was and had spotted the tiger. I could hear the quiet buzz of his camera.

I scanned the forest floor, swaying my head left to right and right to left. Suddenly I saw the tiger in full frame. The magnificent animal, the undisputed king of the jungle, looked gigantic. I felt that my hair was standing on end. The beast got closer and louder. So did my heartbeat as I watched the tiger zigzag from one end of the vhit to the other. The tiger could easily jump over or crash through the flimsy white cloth. It could also easily crawl under it. But I knew that rarely happened.

The technique to contain a tiger inside a vhit-cloth corral was first used in Nepal in the late nineteenth century by Jung Bahadur, founder of the Rana dynasty that ruled Nepal with an autocratic grip for 104 years. From my treetop perch, I could see the elephants closing toward my tree. My stomach churned as my anxiety climaxed. I was petrified as I watched the majestic Royal Bengal tiger traverse slowly toward my tree. The tiger paused occasionally and turned his humongous head to look back at the sound of the marching elephants, but his posture was regal. He did not appear to be in a hurry or even angry at the noisy elephants that were chasing him.

The tiger finally reached the open spot and stopped directly under my tree. Just a dozen feet up the tree, I was becoming a nervous wreck. My heart pounded faster and I felt the sudden rush of adrenaline flow through my body. Palms sweating, I leaned hard against the tree trunk. I zeroed the dart gun toward my target, took a deep breath, and slowly squeezed the trigger.

Phut, the dart drove home on the tiger's right shoulder. "Hwaak," called the tiger loudly. It sprinted past my tree through the narrow opening of the vhit funnel and disappeared into thick cover. I exhaled a long sigh of relief and looked up at Peter, who had twisted his body to focus his camera on the dashing tiger. Soon he turned around and continued to film the row of elephants beating the forests.

We remained quiet and gave the tiger time to stop moving and rest. I waved my hands toward the elephant drivers to signal that I had hit the tiger. They got the message and stopped the drive. Suddenly the jungle was quiet again. So was my heartbeat as I realized that I had not missed my shot. Hardly five minutes later I heard Harkha, one of our game scouts, whistle. He was perched in a tree almost a hundred feet behind me. I waved at him. He waved back and pointed his finger in a southeasterly direction to indicate that he had the tiger in his line of sight. In the next two minutes, I waved at Prem and gestured to him to come forward. Calmly perched atop his elephant, Prem moved to our tree to fetch Peter and me. Another elephant headed toward Dave and Shelley's tree.

Peter and I passed our equipment down to the elephant driver and climbed down to the back of Prem's elephant. We moved toward Harkha's tree, where he pointed us toward the spot where we found our tiger. The beast was stretched out on the ground with its huge head resting on its sinewy shoulder bone. Our elephant driver moved us closer to the tiger. The elephant's belly rumbled nervously. Elephants carrying other members of our party moved forward and circled the tiger.

Prem threw a small stick, hitting the tiger on its back. The tiger did not budge. Clearly the drug had taken full effect. I dismounted from my elephant and moved forward to grab and jerk the tiger's tail. The tiger was unconscious. Gathering my courage, I moved forward and brushed my palms against the tiger's whiskers. The beast was breathing. His big black oval eyes were shiny and alert. The tiger was very much alive but temporarily paralyzed. We had a maximum of three hours before the tiger woke up.

Dave moved forward and covered the tiger's eyes with a piece of cloth to protect the pupils from direct sunlight. Using a pair of pliers, Prem pulled out the dart. He opened the cap and tilted the syringe upside down. It was empty, indicating that the entire contents had been injected into the tiger's body. The shikaris and the elephant handlers cleared a patch of shrubs with their *khu-kuri*—sharp Nepalese machetes—and moved the tiger under shade. Harkha stuck a thermometer up the tiger's anus to measure the animal's body temperature. The drug often caused the body temperature to rise from the normal of about 98.6 degrees Fahrenheit to as high as 105 degrees. Harkha read the thermometer and doused the tiger with a bucket of water to keep its body cool. Shelley Hack hovered around the tiger, her eyes misty and sparkling with curiosity. The ABC cinematographers rolled their cameras to film the actress with the sights and sounds of the jungle in the background. Dave captured visual images of our operational procedures.

"Tigers have only thirty teeth," explained Dave, opening the tiger's jaws to expose a set of sharp, buttery colored teeth to the actress. "In contrast, most other carnivores, including your dog or cat, have forty-two teeth. But," he added after a pause, "tigers have the biggest and most powerful canine teeth of any of the wild cats."

Shelley kneeled down and brushed her well-groomed fingers over both pairs of canine teeth on the upper and lower jaws as Dave continued explaining the tiger's dentistry.

The tiger's canines up front are its main weapon of attack. They measure up to three inches long. Tigers use their canines to stab and crush their prey's neck, killing their quarry instantly. Tucked between the canines are the smaller but sharp sets of six incisors. Tigers use their incisors to tear their prey's flesh off into chunks. A gap between the canines and the incisors enables tigers to clasp their jaws tightly and firmly hold their prey. Behind the incisors are the premolars and the molars, which are used for chewing. Anchored between powerful jaws is the tiger's raspy tongue. The tongue is covered with minuscule bristles that help the carnivore groom its body and clean the skin of its prey.

"Catch the tiger by the tail," I murmured to Maskey, the park superintendent, to get him into the shot. About three feet long on an adult, the tail is an important part of the tiger's anatomy. Like most carnivores, tigers allow their tail to sag when they are relaxed. But when they are in attack mode, tigers erect and swing their tails up in the air. Like a rudder, the tail also helps a tiger to balance its body when chasing and pouncing on its prey.

While I was talking with Maskey, Dave and Shelly were examining the tiger's paws. The paws are the tiger's all-purpose instrument. They are used as tools for hunting, for marking their territories, and even for grooming their bodies. Tigers have four oval toes protruding out of a bigger heel. Soft in texture, the toes and the heel are the most vulnerable parts of the tiger's anatomy; they often get cut or blistered during a hunt or a fight with another tiger. The front paws of the tiger are equipped with five sharp claws that measure three to four inches each. Their hind feet have only four claws. The extra claw on each of the front paws is known as a dewclaw. The dewclaw does not touch the ground when the tiger is in motion. It functions as a thumb to help the tiger clasp tightly to its prey or hold tight to a tree when marking its territory.

After Dave finished giving the film team an anatomical tour of the tiger's body, it was time to weigh the majestic cat. The shikaris rolled the animal onto a tarpaulin and then lifted and hooked the tarpaulin to a weighing scale anchored to a thick pole. The tiger weighed just under 400 pounds—the normal size for an adult male.

Dave got back into the action once the weighing was done. He affixed the black band of a radio collar around the tiger's neck and tested the radio signals by switching on one of our radio-receivers.

Several beeps emitted from our receivers, demonstrating that our electronic equipment was functional. However, our task was not yet over. CI-744, the drug we used to sedate the tiger, does not have an antidote. We had to wait for the tiger to recover from the effects of the drug and return safely to the jungle.

We took a group photo with the ABC team and Shelley Hack with the tiger in the center. This was followed by a session of individual photos with the tiger. All of us wanted our own personal snapshot with a live tiger. Presumably the photos would preserve our bragging rights to tell stories to our grandchildren about our adventure with a wild tiger and a Hollywood actress in the jungles of Nepal.

As the ABC team hovered around the sleeping tiger, Dave and I moved back to join Prem and Maskey. We all had little to do except wait for the tiger to recover. I was relaxed and in a jovial mood.

We mounted our elephants for safety and waited for the tiger to wake-up. Three hours later the tiger finally woke up and staggered drunkenly into the thick bush. We followed and tracked the tiger with our radio signal for about thirty minutes before returning to our camp.

Our mission was accomplished. We parted company with the film team, who headed for Tiger Tops Jungle Lodge. We would join them later in the evening to celebrate our success.

The radiotelemetry technique as filmed for American television was vital to our research. This technique, which is now more advanced, was the best way to track elusive mammals, such as the tiger, that dwell in thick forests. The radio collar lasted two to three years and fell off as the hinges wore out. We tracked two-dozen radio-collared tigers between 1978 and 1982 on foot or from the back of an elephant and even from the sky with a small aircraft that Dave used periodically.

Dave and I were catching, radio-collaring, and tracking tigers as a part of our research on the ecology of wild tigers and their prey species.

Our research was focused on the movement and behavior of wild tigers. We found that tigers frequently dispersed from their natal areas and established their own territories in adjacent forests outside the national park. But forests outside Royal Chitwan National Park did not receive the protection afforded those inside the park. Consequently, most of the forests had been degraded and overgrazed by domestic cattle from nearby villages. Dispersed tigers often preyed upon domestic cows and buffalo, thereby bringing tigers in direct conflict with humans. Some of these tigers even killed humans. These incidents magnified the social problems in our efforts to save the tiger. Nevertheless, our findings clearly indicated that Chitwan was unlikely to have a viable population of tigers without extending the park boundary to include the adjoining forests. But these forests, which are mostly degraded, must be protected and rejuvenated to increase the density of wild ungulates, the tiger's main prey.

Following the ABC film expedition, in early 1981, I reported our findings to Prince Gyanendra, a former hunter and an ardent conservationist. The prince was the younger brother of King Birendra, Nepal's absolute monarch. He was also chairman of the Royal Palace Wildlife Committee, a body that made all policy decisions on Nepal's national parks and wildlife conservation programs. In December 1982 the king and the prince visited our project. We gave them a live demonstration of our radiotelemetry techniques as we had done for the ABC television crew. We also surveyed the Chitwan Valley and adjoining areas in the king's French-built Puma helicopter. Subsequently the king issued an executive order declaring an additional 200 square miles forest adjacent to Chitwan as the Parsa Wildlife Reserve to form a contiguous habitat for tigers and other wildlife. By 1984 King Birendra's directives had been fully implemented, and the Parsa Wildlife Reserve promulgated in the official gazette of the Nepalese government and declared a protected wildlife sanctuary under the laws of Nepal. In addition, the government allocated budgets and deployed game wardens in the wildlife preserve.

The king's actions were a major milestone in Nepalese tiger conservation. I was pleased by the results of our endeavors—a painstaking task undertaken jointly by Nepalese and Americans and a diligent effort that meticulously combined hard work, teamwork, and networking.

Two members of the team who were critical in helping me convert our scientific findings into concrete practical and pragmatic actions were Tirtha Man Maskey, superintendent of the Royal Chitwan National Park, and Biswa Nath Upreti, director general of Nepal's National Park and Wildlife Department. Between 1981 and 1984 they arduously pushed the necessary paperwork through the maze of Nepalese bureaucracy. They turned our paper plans into concrete and legally binding actions before lumber lobbies and political forces blocked or diluted the king's 1982 directive to create the Parsa Wildlife Reserve. Maskey and Upreti saw that the extension of the tiger's range was good not only for the tiger but also good for other wild plants and animals. This extension also saved Nepal's diminishing Terai forests from the lumberman's saw or the farmer's hoe. In addition, the edict protected the watershed from erosion, stabilizing the riverbanks and helping conserve soil and water—the lifeline of the people of Chitwan and Parsa.

The radiotelemetry methods we had mastered in Chitwan also gave us an opportunity to demonstrate that good science results in good political decisions, even in an impoverished country like Nepal. It provided us with the necessary skills for dealing expeditiously with tigers that behave badly. One of them was a young tiger that had killed a well-respected schoolteacher.

4

Playing God with a Teacher Killer

The man's death was neat and sudden. The odds were solidly stacked against Trilochan Poudyal—a thirty-two-year-old schoolteacher from the village of Madanpur, a picturesque hamlet on the eastern flank of Nepal's Royal Chitwan National Park. The tiger was too quick and too strong for the man.

We were able to determine that the tiger was Son of Chuchchi (or Son of Pointed-Toe), a Royal Bengal tiger whose name referred to his mother's prominent footprint. Chuchchi was a tiger that frequented the Tiger Tops area. Unlike her son, she did not have a radio collar, Further, she was not a man-eater or a man-killer. It was our job to find out why her son became a killer. We also had to locate him and stop him from killing humans in the future.

Son of Chuchchi was also a lame carnivore. The lameness was the result of a fight with another tiger—a foe older and stronger. Two months earlier, my colleagues had saved Son of Chuchchi. They had played god and brought this tiger back from the brink of death.

In September 1979 Prem, our expert tracker, was surprised to find a badly wounded tiger in the middle of Itcharni—an island in the Rapti River near our camp. Prem knew him as Tiger 119—a number tattooed on his ears when he had been captured and radio-collared six months earlier. The tiger was just over two years old when he left his mother and his birthplace to establish his own territory.

I was curious to know why the numbering of radio-collared tigers started with three digits. Why was the first radio-collared tiger designated "Tiger 101" instead of "Tiger 1"? I learned that in 1973 my predecessor, Kirti Man Tamang, decided to designate the 100 series as the numbers of the radio-collared tigers and reserved the 200 series for leopards. Consequently, the Son of Chuchchi, the nineteenth radio-collared tiger, was also called Tiger 119. Like most humans, we field scientists have our idiosyncrasies.

In search of a new territory, Son of Chuchchi had moved eastward to prowl for prey and encroached upon the domain of another radio-collared tiger, number 126. Tiger 126 was a big adult that soon discovered a young tiger had invaded his territory. He patrolled the forest, sniffing around for Son of Chuchchi's calling cards—mostly urine and scent marks. The young and inexperienced tiger was unsuccessful in dodging Tiger 126. They met head-on at the edge of a big meadow in the middle of the jungle, and a brutal fight took place. Tiger 126 won the battle, viciously mauling his opponent. Prem found the dying tiger while radio tracking on Itcharni Island early one morning in August 1979.

Son of Chuchchi was badly injured. His body was bloodied, with cuts on his back and shoulders. The knee joint of his left leg was shattered and looked as if his attacker had chewed on it.

"There is no way this tiger will be able to move and hunt deer," said Prem to Brijlal, his elephant driver. Brijlal responded with a blank face and a nod of his head. He had no idea where Prem was going with his comment.

"Brijlal," ordered Prem, "I want you to wait here with your elephant. I will walk back to the camp and consult Maskey Sir." He was referring to Tirtha Man Maskey, the national park superintendent, who was visiting our camp at Saurah on official business. Both Dave Smith and I were away on travel.

Prem walked a mile to the camp though the rhino-infested riverine forest of Itcharni Island and fetched Maskey back to the wounded tiger. They were followed by a team of shikaris on two elephants. Prem and Maskey examined the site where the brutal battle between Tiger 126 and the Son of Chuchchi had taken place.

Maskey was in a quandary. He had been the warden of the park for five years, yet he had never seen such a sight. However, he knew he had only two options. The first option was to do nothing and leave Son of Chuchchi to die. Tigers fighting for their territory was a fact of life in the forest, where the strong survived and the weak perished. His second choice was to treat the wounds with man-made medicine and try to save the tiger's life. But this meant reversing the natural dictate of the jungles of Chitwan.

"As a custodian of Royal Chitwan National Park," reasoned Maskey, "I cannot let this beautiful beast die in vain. We must sedate him and treat his wounds." Prem agreed. His conscience did not permit him to desert the wounded tiger.

The shikaris raced back to camp to get the sedation drugs and the dart gun. Prem sedated Son of Chuchchi, and Maskey stitched the wounds and bandaged the tiger's badly battered knee.

"If he survives at all," Prem remarked, "Son of Chuchchi will not be able to make a kill for days. He will die soon if we do not feed and water him."

The shikaris agreed. They butchered a buffalo and left piles of meat in front of the tiger. They also left bowls of water. Fearing another attack from Tiger 126, Prem left two elephants to guard Son of Chuchchi.

The treatment and medicine did wonders for Son of Chuchchi. In two days he was eating the buffalo meat and drinking the water left by the shikaris. He was a resilient cat. Within a week he recovered and left the island. Under cover of night, the tiger waded the Rapti River and limped to a patch of forest near the village of Madanpur. However, his lame foot drastically changed his hunting behavior. Soon he acted more like a cunning leopard than a regal tiger. Instead of prowling deep into the jungle for his natural prey, Son of Chuchchi hung around the edges of the forest devouring domestic cattle that strayed into the jungle from nearby villages. Domestic cattle were much easier to kill than wild ungulates for this tiger with a deformed foot. He became a notorious cattle lifter but never attacked any of the villagers.

The cold and foggy morning of November 30, 1979, was a notable exception. Early that morning, Trilochan Poudyal was walking down a ravine a few yards from his house in the village of Madanpur. The schoolteacher was heading toward the Rapti River to perform his morning ablutions. The fog was thick; visibility was low. Unknown to Poudyal, Son of Chuchchi was quietly hobbling up a steep cliff to reach the top of the ravine. The tiger wanted to avoid being caught in the open and to be under cover inside the forest south of Madanpur Village long before the first rays of sunlight dispersed the heavy fog. But first he had to reach the top of the ravine and cross the village farmlands to make his way to the forest.

The man and tiger met by sheer coincidence on top of the ravine. Both were momentarily stunned by this sudden encounter. Poudyal panicked. "*Bagh!* (Tiger!)" he screamed. The tiger roared and pounced on Poudyal. Devi Lal, another villager, was a few feet behind Poudyal and witnessed the attack. He too panicked. "*Guhar, guhar* (Help, help)!" he screeched in terror. Holding on to the schoolteacher's body, the tiger growled at Devi Lal. Responding to the tiger's thundering roar and Devi Lal's terrorized screams, a dozen villagers rushed to the top of the ravine. The tiger dropped the schoolteacher and dashed back into the ravine. Alas, the schoolteacher was dead. The tiger had punctured his neck with his sharp canines and gnawed deeply into his head.

It was nearing noon when we got news of the attack at our camp in Saurah, some six miles from the kill site. We had two overseas guests in our camp. One of them was Peter Jackson, chairman of the Cat Specialist Group of the International Union for Conservation of Nature (IUCN), an association in which I am an active member. Peter, an Englishman in his forties, was a well-known photographer and author of books and articles on tigers. Our other guest was Leo Caminada, a jovial Swiss forester. Leo was visiting from Bhutan, where he worked as a technical advisor for the Bhutan Forest Department.

Our main agenda that afternoon was to take Peter and Leo for a jungle drive and treat them to dinner at Tiger Tops Jungle Lodge, some twenty-four miles on the other side of the national park. We were also looking forward to keeping their spirits high with a few stiff gin and tonics. We told them that the potion worked as a cure against malaria; an excuse we perpetuated for the sake of having a good time in the tropical and steamy jungle of Royal Chitwan National Park.

The news of the tiger attack meant that there was no way we could go frolicking at Tiger Tops. I huddled with Dave and Prem in our kitchen to plan our next line of action. We were dealing with a man-killer—for me, the first time. We were joined by Peter, Leo, and Dale Miquelle, an American research associates who was helping us in our field program. The gravity of the situation compelled us to act promptly. We had no choice but to kill or capture the Son of Chuchchi to pacify the villagers.

We decided to go to Madanpur and hunt for the killer. Peter and Leo were thrilled by the opportunity to be part of a once-in-a-lifetime hunt for a man-killing tiger, but we had to leave Leo behind. A skilled carpenter, we needed him to construct a sturdy cage to imprison the tiger—that is, if we could catch it.

We drove to the kill site along a long, windy, and bumpy bullock cart trail. We were armed with two dart guns and the vhit cloth. We would use them to trap and sedate Son of Chuchchi and haul him back to our camp unharmed.

It was almost two in the afternoon when we reached the banks of the Rapti River. A mob of villagers had gathered on the riverbank. The first person I identified was Nanda Prashad Bhattarai, the elected representative of the village of Madanpur. He was the highest-ranking politician in that area, and like most politicians he was a skilled orator. Standing on higher ground, he was castigating the national park authorities—badmouthing them for creating a sanctuary for wild animals where humans were struggling for existence. He stopped pontificating but huffed and puffed like an agitated rhino as soon as he saw us. "Your tiger," he barked in Nepali as he pointed a finger at me, "has killed our beloved schoolteacher. We demand that you find and shoot the killer beast." Raising his fist in the air, he exclaimed in a high-pitched voice, "Now!"

There was no way I could comply with his demands. I had neither a gun nor the authority to shoot a tiger, a highly endangered animal that was fully protected under Nepal's National Park and Wildlife Conservation Act. I needed a special sanction from high authorities of His Majesty's Government of Nepal to destroy a tiger—a feat that would take days in the snail-paced centralized bureaucracy of Kathmandu—Nepal's capital. Though stories of man-killing or man-eating tigers abound in Nepal, an actual occurrence is still a rarity. A few that I heard appeared to be sensational and focused on the havoc created by man-eating tigers.

"I need orders from Kathmandu to kill the tiger," I replied without realizing that I had misspoken. Clouded by anxiety, I was neither thinking clearly nor realizing the painful sentiments of the villagers who had just lost a respected member of their community to one of our radio-collared tigers. My tone sounded haughty and hardhearted.

"*Rakami mora,*" erupted in the air as the angry crowd cursed me as a "pen-pushing dead bureaucrat." Their protest did not give me a chance to explain that we were there to catch and remove the tiger from their neighborhood, even if we did not have authorization to do so.

I also heard angry voices accusing me of valuing the life of a tiger more than that of a human being. "The tiger will return and kill our brothers, sisters, and children in our village," added Bhattarai in a defiant voice. "We hold you responsible for the death of our beloved schoolteacher."

There was a veiled threat in the village leader's tone. I did not think it would be prudent for me to argue with him or the angry crowd. I was in a sticky situation, and I was nervous. This was my first experience with a man-killing tiger. *Muji Maskey,* I silently cursed the park superintendent. *He should never have played god but left the tiger to die,* I thought. Cursing Maskey made me feel a little better.

"Win by losing" is an age-old saying in Nepal that suggests losing an argument to obtain the desired objective is better than wining a verbose squabble but getting nowhere. My goal was to catch the man-killer expeditiously. I had to let the politician win the argument. At the least, I had to let him feel important in front of his constituents. I needed his help to calm the situation.

"Bhattarai-ji," I addressed him, adding the honorific "ji" to his last name. "We agree with you, precisely. We are here to capture the tiger and transport it to Kathmandu for imprisonment in Jwalakhel Zoo. But I will need your help to ensure that we can get on with the capture operation smoothly." That got his attention and also drew the attention of the crowd. It was the moment to present my case.

"We cannot afford to have angry villagers disturbing our operation or being rude to my foreign coworkers," I added, pointing toward Dave, Dale, and Peter. "I cannot capture the tiger without their help."

The trio of Westerners had wisely left me to deal with the politician and the villagers. They were heading toward the face of the ravine to search for the tiger's pugmarks.

Many Nepalese, particularly those who lived in the rural areas, often acted shy or intimidated in the presence of foreigners. They rarely spoke out in front of Americans and Europeans. Others, like Bhattarai, liked to show off their importance. Yet in front of foreigners, they also liked to be seen as less argumentative. Dave, Dale, and Peter provided me with a perfect shield against getting into a bickering debate. Bhattarai was a shrewd politician. He knew that he could win an argument with me, but he also knew that he could not get rid of the man-killing tiger without my intervention. He too was looking for a way to save face.

"Fellow villagers," he gloated, "I sent the message to Saurah on your behalf as soon as I heard about the tragedy. They heeded our call and came here immediately. We must let them remove the tiger from our neighborhood. We will deal with them later if they don't keep their word."

Relieved that we did not face a long impasse, I walked from the riverbank to join my colleagues atop the ravine, only to face an agonizing sight.

The disfigured body of the schoolteacher was lying flat on the ground, facing upward. His mutilated face was covered with dried blood. A group of the dead man's relatives squatted around his body, mourning the unprecedented tragedy. They were surrounded by a large crowd of villagers, silently lamenting the tragic loss of their only schoolteacher. The scene was somber, sorrowful, and silent. The aura of death hovered in the air. From a nearby hut, the wailing of the schoolteacher's wife weeping in pain with her two children periodically broke the silence. A white blanket of cotton and a freshly cut green bamboo bier were laid next to the body. The dead man was a Hindu. His death ritual demanded that he be wrapped in a shroud of white cotton, fastened to the bamboo bier, and transported to the cremation site on the banks of a river. The scene both heart wrenching and gruesome—reminiscent of a nightmarish movie.

"What is the future of tigers in the wild?" I asked myself, realizing that Bhattarai and his constituents had a right to be angry at our efforts to save wild carnivores in their backyards. "Marauding and terrorizing poor villagers? Killing humans and preying on their cattle?" I too became angry. I felt that the Son of Chuchchi deserved to die. No longer able to bear the scene, I walked over to Prem.

Prem was crouching along the top of the ravine searching for the tiger's footprints. He was having a hard time, as the spoor had been trampled by villagers. But he was equipped with a more precise tool—a radio receiver. He tracked the tiger, which was hiding inside a thick bush deep inside the ravine. The tiger could not have chosen a more strategic location. It was not possible for us to drive the tiger out of the ravine without taking a big risk with a killer too close to a village. Nor could we venture on foot into the narrow ravine harboring a man-killing tiger.

"How about showering the ravine with a hail of stones and rocks?" I quietly proposed to Prem. "We have no shortage of manpower," I added, pointing to the crowd of onlookers.

"Too risky," he replied. "Even if we managed to flush the tiger out of his hiding place, we would not be able to dart it. It is broad daylight. The tiger will not crawl quietly out of the ravine. It will make a lighting dash—too fast for a dart gun. Furthermore, the area is wide open and crowded with humans. The tiger could sprint in any direction."

Prem made valid points. The chances were high that the man-killer would barge into the onlookers that had gathered for the show. It could also scramble right into the village and maul or even kill more people. We did not have high-powered automatic rifles. We had only two dart guns, which fired one shot at a time. Reloading would take time.

"Sir," whispered Prem, "this is too uncertain. It is too dangerous to try anything today. We must come back early tomorrow morning."

I consulted with Dave, who agreed that we should call it a day. I went over to Bhattarai and explained to the village leader that we needed to abort the operation for the day. He was unhappy but receptive. He grudgingly agreed to our proposal and explained the risks to the villagers.

Prem and the shikaris unloaded the piles of vhit cloth from our truck and cordoned off the area. I did not know if the vhit corral would contain the tiger, particularly at night. But I knew that our actions would send the right signals to the villagers. A few of them knew about the vhit cloth technique for keeping the tigers at bay. Furthermore, the tiger was a man-killer and not a man-eater. The tiger had attacked the schoolteacher because he felt provoked or threatened by the sudden encounter with the man. The chance was remote that Son of Chuchchi would creep into the village at night to attack another human. The tiger also wore a radio collar. We could track the cat down easily and dart it early next morning, even if it sneaked out of the ravine and hid in the thick forest. "Please ask the villagers to stay indoors," I advised the village leader. "I promise that we will be back here at the crack of dawn."

We left Madanpur Village at dusk. As night fell, we reached our camp near the village of Saurah, the base for the Nepal Tiger Ecology Project. Leo was anxiously waiting for us next to a well-built cage. The cage was constructed of three-inch-thick and sturdy sal-timber planks. Five feet in length, it would be a narrow cage at two feet each in breadth and height.

Next morning we woke before daylight crept into the Rapti River Valley. It was a cloudy morning with a light drizzle of rain. We packed our gear and returned to the kill site with our elephants and our Isuzu truck. Leo also joined us with his cage. A large crowd of curious onlookers greeted us on the top of the ravine. But the tiger was long gone.

Our radio-receiver and the footprints proved that the man-killer had breeched the vhit cloth, showing that the corral did not work at night—at least not for this sly, albeit lame tiger. Prem got on top of an elephant and waved his radio antenna.

"I get no signal," he said casually in Nepali as the onlookers eyed him curiously.

"We seem to have lost the tiger," he added in a loud voice.

In our experience, signals sometimes do get lost. At times the receivers did not catch any signals from a tiger's radio collar; particularly when the animal was resting in a hollowed depression or immediately behind thick tree trunks. Though Prem's words were casual and routine, they proved to be a tactical error. His comments were totally misinterpreted by an onlooker in the crowd.

"Einiharule," yelled a villager, *"jani jani raati bagh bhagaye,"* accusing us of deliberately letting the tiger escape the vhit cloth corral while the villagers slept.

I did not know if the misinterpretation was genuine or staged. Experience had taught me that politicians and unsavory characters thrive on crisis and crowds. The setting that morning on the banks of the Rapti River was perfect for any politician to grandstand. I also did not know whether the yeller was a supporter of Bhattarai or belonged to an opposing faction. Regardless, Bhattarai, the savvy politician, could not let the yeller take central stage. He had to add fuel to the political fire and establish his authority.

"These government people," he pontificated, waving his fist in the air, "love wild bloodthirsty beasts more than they love us poor humans. Only yesterday, they promised me, your elected representative, that they would capture and remove the tiger this morning. Today they say the tiger has escaped. Clearly they do not want to deal with the man-killing beast."

The villagers converged toward him as he continued to attack us verbally. He also accused me of being a coward and of buying time to delay any action until I got orders from my "masters" in the Kathmandu bureaucracy.

I saw no point in trying to stop his oration. It was better to let him blow off steam. Soon the crowd swelled. Bhattarai's rhetoric became laced with the poignant theme of the life and death of poor rural people. He spoke about their daily struggle to survive in the midst of dangerous tigers and rhinos that the government wanted to protect at the expense of its own citizens. Clearly he was arousing the deep emotions of the crowd.

"For months, they did nothing when the tiger killed hundreds of our cows and buffalo," he accused. "It is their radio-collared tiger. We must hold them responsible. We will detain them here until they remove this man-eating tiger from the area."

The crowd was big, and we felt a riot brewing. However, I did not believe the situation would turn violent. If push came to shove, we had our elephants and shikaris to ward off an attack. I needed to calm the crowd and get on with our mission of catching Son of Chuchchi. It was just a matter of time before we located the tiger.

"Bhattarai-ji," I pleaded loudly so that the crowd could hear me. "Either you let us get on with our job or you catch the tiger by yourself. Why would we be here this early in the morning if we had no intention of removing the tiger? We know where the tiger has gone. Once we get to the edge of the forest, we will pick up the radio signal and capture the beast in no time. But if you threaten us, we will be compelled to go back to our camp. If the tiger mauls or kills any other villagers, you will be responsible, not us."

"What is the guarantee," he yelled back "that you will capture and remove the man-killer this morning?"

"Only my word," I countered. "But you can hold me hostage as long as the tiger is not caught or destroyed. You can also keep our expensive Japanese truck as guarantee of our words." The crowd was momentarily silent.

"You know we live just down the river," I began, watching the crowd. "Where can I run away to if I tell you a lie in front of the hundreds of witnesses that have gathered here?"

Bhattarai did not respond to me but looked at the crowd. "We will give him all morning," he proposed. "We will see if he is talking from his mouth or his ass. Okay with you, fellow villagers?"

His words triggered laughter among the onlookers. Bhattarai

was a clever politician. He knew how to work the crowd—when to heat them up and when to cool them down.

"*Thikcha-thikcha,*" chorused a few voices to say "Okay-okay" to their leader's proposal.

Now we were free to get on with our job without being pestered by political punditry. We left our truck on the banks of the Rapti River and headed toward the forest southeast of the village.

Prem followed the tiger's spoor on foot to the edge of the forest. Dave was atop an elephant, scanning for signals. When he did not get a radio signal, we quietly moved deeper into the forest on the back of our elephants.

We were almost a mile deep in the jungle when Dave gave me a thumbs-up to indicate that he had picked up the radio signal. He passed the radio receiver to Prem. Our chief shikari climbed up a tree from the back of an elephant and moved the antenna in a semicircle before pointing it in a southwesterly direction. I took my turn after Prem, but it was not necessary. The radio signals indicated that the tiger was within 500 yards of our location.

Prem laid out the vhit cloth with the help of the shikaris and elephant drivers. Armed with a dart gun, Dave perched in a tree at the V point of the cloth. Equipped with a second dart gun, I perched a few feet behind him in another tree, as backup in the unlikely event that Dave missed his shot. Dale, Leo, and Peter were positioned on top of our elephants at the wide end of the vhit. Their job was to join the shikaris and our elephant wranglers and beat the jungle to drive the tiger toward Dave's tree. Soon the beat started noisily as our elephants thrashed through the forest.

From my treetop I had a perfect view of the tiger as he limped toward Dave, who was waiting in his tree, dart gun at the ready. Dave nailed the tiger when it was about twenty feet from his tree. The tiger dashed straight ahead three hundred yards before crouching on the ground, stunned.

We got down from our trees. The tiger was fully sedated by the time we approached him. We examined his body methodically. The tiger's teeth were perfect and the paws were also in good shape. But the wound on his left knee was unhealed, with a thick pink lesion over the broken bones. The major part of our task was over, but we still had to get the tiger out of the forest. It was also our time to parade the predator in front of the village crowd. This would demonstrate to the denizens of Madanpur and surrounding villages that the man-killing tiger no longer prowled their neighborhood.

It was about two miles to the edge of the village. Our truck could not reach the site where we had darted the tiger because the terrain was rough and broken.

"Let's load the tiger on Mel Kali," proposed Dave. "She is the calmest." I did not like the idea. We had never loaded a tiger on the back of an elephant, and I was not sure how the elephant would react. I looked at Prem and muttered, *"Huncha?"* to ask him if that was okay. He nodded his head to signal his agreement with Dave.

Prem had loaded many tigers on the backs of elephants and transported them to the royal camp. But I was still hesitant. Prem's tigers of bygone days had been dead tigers. Our tiger was alive and breathing, even if it was sedated. I preferred to hand-carry the tiger, using the vhit cloth as an improvised stretcher—a feat that would take much longer. My anxiety was due in large part to a story I had heard a long time ago.

In the early 1960s King Mohammad Zahir Shah of Afghanistan was hunting tigers in Chitwan as the guest of King Mahendra. Like most royal hunts, this shikar was well organized. The Afghan king hunted his tiger using techniques similar to those we used to capture our tiger.

However, there were three differences. First, the vhit cloth laid out for the Afghan king was neither V shaped nor open at the narrow end. It was a big circle with no outlet, designed to confine the tiger in the ring. Second, the king did not climb a tree but shot his tiger from a sturdy wooden *machan*—a tree stand specially constructed inside the tiger ring. Third, instead of using a few elephants to drive the tiger, the Afghan king used hundreds of elephants. His elephants chased the tiger inside the ring to create the fanfare of a sporting event—and to enable the Afghan monarch to shoot the tiger at his royal pleasure.

Consequently, the king bagged his tiger with ease and flair. He was very pleased with his trophy—a big male weighing over four hundred pounds. The monarch looked forward to decorating his smoking room at the royal palace in Kabul with his trophy. The customary photograph to decorate the royal photo album was taken. Orders were issued to bring the tiger to the royal party camp near Sukhibar at the western end of Chitwan, where the tiger would be skinned after King Mahendra and his honored guest inspected the animal during cocktail hour.

The shikaris of Nepal's Royal Hunting Department decided to load the Afghan king's tiger on Prem Prasad, a veteran elephant of innumerable tiger hunts. He was a calm tusker. As they loaded the tiger on the back of this huge elephant, Prem Prasad suddenly lost his cool. The pachyderm shook his body and threw the Afghan king's tiger to the ground. Then the elephant charged the dead tiger, kicking the carcass like a soccer ball and tearing it with his sharp tusks. The prized trophy of His Majesty King Mohammad Zahir Shah was ripped into several pieces.

The royal shikaris suddenly found themselves in a shaky position. They could not figure out why Prem Prasad had gone berserk, but they knew they could not take the tattered pieces of the Afghan king's tiger to the royal camp without having to face his royal wrath. In a fix, they huddled under a tree and came up with a clever idea.

After many royal hunts, these veteran shikaris had developed the habit of not only creating a backup plan but also making provisions for a backup of a backup plan. Experience had taught them that kings' tiger hunts provided problems and opportunities that translated into rewards or punishments, depending on whether regal pleasure or anger resulted from the hunt. A happy king resulted in job promotion, prestige, good standing in the royal court, and financial rewards for the shikaris. Conversely, an angry monarch meant loss of job, loss of face, and even monetary penalties.

A tiger hunt was the biggest of any big-game hunting in Nepal. The hunt's success and the size and condition of the trophy animal were paramount to boosting royal egos. The palace shikaris knew the habits and behavior of their kings. Consequently, for the Afghan king's hunt, they had staked out not just a handful but dozens of buffalo, profusely baiting the territories of several tigers. On that day they had two back-up tiger kills.

Baiting several tigers for a royal hunt was also a routine precaution for the Kathmandu palace shikaris. They never knew if Nepal's king would decide at the last moment to compete with his guest to see who could bag the biggest trophy. Although this was rare, it was not unlikely. Like European kings and princesses, Asian monarchs were also renowned for their last-minute whims.

The shikaris knew that the two extra tigers that had taken the buffalo baits would stay put with their kill. They had time to shoot a new tiger. Unlike the Afghan king, the palace shikari did not need an elaborate *machan* to shoot the tiger. They had the vhit and the elephants handy; and they were experts who could shoot a tiger while hanging from the branch of a tree.

One of the tigers with its fresh kill was a small female—not an option because the Afghan king's tiger was a big male. The other was a male whose footprints indicated that it was slightly smaller but similar to the king's kill. The shikaris knew that no one would notice the difference.

The male had taken the bait some three miles from their current position. The palace shikaris made a pact of secrecy, and then they stalked quietly through the forest, laid out the vhit cloth, and shot the second tiger. In no time, they had a replacement for the Afghan monarch's tattered trophy.

Later in the evening, the Afghan king noticed no difference as he proudly inspected his trophy at the royal camp. He ordered the tiger to be skinned and cured for transportation to Kabul.

Mahila Dai, an ace tiger hunter and a key staff member of the Nepal's Royal Hunting Department, told me this story. It was among the many tiger hunting stories that I would hear during my thirty years of service in Nepal. I had often repeated the story in our camp to entertain visitors. But today, in the forest of Madanpur, my thoughts were far from entertainment. I feared that our elephant, Mel Kali, might rip the Son of Chuchchi into pieces, as Prem Prasad had done with the Afghan King's tiger in the early 1960s. I argued for an improvised stretcher, but Prem vetoed my suggestion. I finally conceded. Though I was Prem's boss, he was the master when it came to the crafts of the jungle. He knew his elephant and his tiger better than I did.

I anxiously watched our shikaris and elephant drivers haul the Son of Chuchchi and load his body on top of Mel Kali. To my relief, our trained elephant showed no qualms, allowing our crew to load the live, albeit unconscious, tiger on her back.

Dave and two other shikaris climbed on the back of the elephant with the tiger. As we marched out of the jungle, Dave was hanging precariously over the back of the elephant, clinging to the tiger. The sight sent chills up my spine. *What if the tiger woke up? What if the elephant panicked?* At the edge of the forest, we were warmly greeted by a cheering crowd, the relieved and thankful citizens of Madanpur Village.

"Manche khane bagh. Manche khane bagh," called out men, women, and children as they ran after Dave's elephant shouting, "Man-eating tiger. Man-eating tiger." They were wrong. The Son of Chuchchi was no man-eating tiger, merely a man-killer. But even to this day, a few questions linger in my mind. Would Son of Chuchchi have eaten the man he killed had the villagers not chased him into the ravine? Would he—an accidental killer—have lost his fear of humans and started preying on villagers, seeing them as easy kills?

We paraded through the village and reached our truck. There we transferred the tiger from the elephant to our truck. As we drove happily to our camp, all of us were filled with a sense of pride and relief for accomplishing our mission.

At our camp we locked up Son of Chuchchi in the cage that Leo Caminada, our Swiss friend, had meticulously constructed. Dave volunteered to drive the tiger to Kathmandu Zoo, with our reliable driver Kancha Lama behind the wheel. I stayed behind to take care of the paperwork, including preparation for an inquest into the death of the popular schoolteacher. I also had to take care of guests at our camp.

The capture of Son of Chuchchi established our credibility in Chitwan. While our primary job was to save tigers, we proved to the people of Chitwan that we were not going to tolerate tigers that attacked humans. It was one of my biggest accomplishments in public relations. It was also a major milestone in my efforts to understand and minimize conflicts between humans and wild beasts. However, this was the first time that a harsh reality came upon me. My mind was fogged by my own goals to understand the biology of the tiger and not the human factors involved in the issue. Until then, I was mostly indifferent on how the local people perceived the tiger, particularly when it came to tigers that behaved badly. How I would deal with man-killing tigers was something for which no amount of schooling could have prepared me. I was torn between saving an animal that I deeply respected and the tremendous sympathy I felt for those killed by a tiger and their families and friends.

Antagonism between human beings and wild animals was and is a reality in Nepal and other developing countries. There were also matters beyond biology and academic research that I had to deal with long after Dave, Leo, Dale, and Peter returned home to Europe and America. Nepal was my home. The people of Chitwan were my fellow citizens. I had to learn wildlife conservation the hard way—not only by focusing on catching animals like rhinos and tigers inside pristine forests within national park boundaries but also by understanding the needs and aspirations, fears and concerns of my fellow Nepali who lived outside the Royal Chitwan National Park. I learned to respect their fears and concerns as I learned more about the world of the tiger.

5

THE WORLD OF THE TIGER

BEFORE I CONTINUE WITH MY STORY OF THE TIGERS OF NEPAL, I'd like to share the story of how tigers came to exist in this part of the world.

Sixty million years ago, primitive carnivores called miacids lived in Europe and Asia. These small, squirrel-like creatures are believed to be the original ancestor of today's mighty tiger. Miacids looked nothing like tigers. With squat legs, long tails, and an elongated body, they resembled civets more than any cat and survived on a diet of insects rather than flesh.

Forty million years later, the miacids split into two groups. One branch formed the modern canids, whose descendants include wolves, dogs, bears, raccoons, weasels, and seals. The other group evolved into the felids, which include cats, mongooses, and hyenas. A tree-dwelling felid called *Proailurus* is the earliest ancestor of the tiger and the other thirty-six modern-day cats. *Proailurus* also was not yet close to the tiger in shape, size, or appearance. Weighing about twenty pounds, the animal resembled a big civet or a binturong (bearcat). These tree-dwelling carnivores had agile bodies with a long tail, sharp eyes, and sharp teeth that enabled them to hunt prey efficiently on the ground.

It is believed that the modern day tiger evolved seven hundred thousand years ago in Siberia. That is some three hundred thousand years before our own apelike ancestor, *Homo habilis,* learned to walk erect in the heart of Africa. However, in contrast to our ancestors, who moved north to Eurasia, the tigers migrated south from Siberia to form the eight subspecies of twentieth century tigers.

The first group did not move far. They stayed near Siberia to form the Siberian, or Amur, tiger (*Panthera tigris altaica*), which once flourished in Siberia, northeastern China, and Korea. A second group dispersed to southern China to form the South China tiger (*Panthera tigris amoyensis*). A third group migrated southwest toward the Caspian Sea to become the Caspian tiger (*Panthera tigris virgata*), settling in northern Afghanistan, Iran, Turkey, and other areas around the Caspian Sea. The fourth group streamed into the Indian subcontinent to form the Indian, or Royal Bengal, tiger (*Panthera tigris tigris*) of Bangladesh, Nepal, Bhutan, and northwest Burma. The fifth group migrated into Southeast Asia in two streams. The first subgroup occupied southern China, eastern Burma, Thailand, Vietnam, Laos, Cambodia, and the Malaya Peninsula to form the Indochinese Tiger (*Panthera tigris corbetti*). The second subgroup flowed over the islands of Indonesia to form three distinct subspecies: the Sumatran tiger (*Panthera tigris sumatrae*), the Bali tiger (*Panthera tigris balica*), and the Javan tiger (*Panthera tigris sondaica*).

Although the Beringia land bridge in the Bering Sea connected Siberia with North America, tigers never migrated to the Americas, unlike the humans who used that route. Tigers also never made it as far as Australia or Africa as they radiated south out of Siberia. (Australia's now-extinct Tasmanian tiger was a carnivorous marsupial that got its name from the tiger-like stripes on its body.)

The white tiger—a prized exhibit of zookeepers—is neither a freak nor an albino. It is not a different subspecies but a morphological variation of the Royal Bengal tiger. The normally yellow coat changed to white through a genetic mutation. However, like other members of their species, white tigers retain dark stripes on their coats. They mate with other tiger subspecies and have produced offspring.

Maharaja Martand Singh of Rewa captured a white tiger in Bandhavgarh National Park in central India in 1951. He named it Mohan, meaning "lovely." The maharaja is also credited with popularizing white tigers by breeding them in captivity and distributing them to zoos in India and in the West. Though rare, black tigers have also been reported in the wild. As with white tigers, the black color is a result of "false melanism"—a process that in the case of black tigers, increases the amount of black pigmentation in the skin. Only a few sightings have been reported in Simlipal National Park in eastern India.

The tiger is one of the thirty-seven species of wild cats in the world. These species range in size from the three-pound rusty-spotted cat (*Felis prionailuru rubiginosa*) of India and Sri Lanka to the biggest of all cats—the mighty tiger (*Panthera tigris*), weighing more than five hundred pounds.

Despite its size and might, the tiger tops the list of endangered species. The world population of tigers was estimated to be more than one hundred thousand in the beginning of the twentieth century. Their population extended from the Caspian Sea to the highlands of Bhutan, from the islands of Indonesia to the arctic tundra of Siberia. Current estimates are that no more than 3,500 tigers are left in the wilds of the world. During the past hundred years, tiger habitat has shrunk by almost 95 percent from its original range. Three of the eight subspecies of tiger have become extinct. These statistics are shocking. However, the tiger seems to be resisting extinction when compared with other species of big mammals. In contrast, the last Barbary lion (*Panthera leo leo*) was shot in the Atlas Mountains in North Africa in 1922. Likewise, Przewalski's horse (*Equus ferus przewalskii*) was last seen on the steppes of Mongolia in 1966, and the Honshu wolf (*Canis lupus hodophilax*) of Japan was extinct by the early twentieth century.

Among Asian carnivores that parallel the endangered status of the tiger are the clouded leopard, snow leopard (*Panthera uncia*), and Indian lion (*Panthera leo persica*). The clouded leopard and the snow leopard are very elusive, and their populations in the wilds of Asia are unknown. The Indian lion—the only Asian species—can be seen in the Gir Sanctuary of western India, and their number is estimated to be about 250. Like the tiger, the Indian lion is subject to poaching, largely because they also prey on domestic cattle. In addition, their habitat is facing agricultural encroachment and overgrazing by domestic cattle. Nevertheless, unlike the Caspian, Javan, and Bali tigers, the Indian lion survived extinction in the twentieth century.

The Bali tiger—the smallest tiger—was the first subspecies to become extinct. The last wild specimen was killed in the western part of the island of Bali in September 1937. There are no Bali tigers in captivity in any of the world's zoos. The second subspecies of tiger to become extinct was the Caspian tiger. It is reported that the last of this subspecies was shot in Golestan National Park in northern Iran in 1959. However, there are anecdotal reports of the Caspian tiger in Afghanistan, Turkey, and Turkmenistan. There is no solid evidence that the Caspian tiger survives. These sightings could have been leopards, an animal that is often mistaken for the tiger. Like the Bali tiger, there are no Caspian tigers in captivity.

The last official sighting of the Javan tiger was reported in 1972. However, in 1979 reports based on identification of pugmarks, or pawmarks, left on soft or muddy soil in their natural habitat indicated that there were three of these tigers left in the wild. However, by the 1980s there was no evidence that the Javan tiger had survived. In 1990 it was declared extinct by the International Union for Conservation of Nature (IUCN). Although some animals in captivity are claimed to be Javan tigers, it is thought that these animals are actually Sumatran tigers.

Of the five surviving subspecies of tigers, the South China tiger is the rarest. The IUCN estimates that there may be no more than twenty to thirty of these tigers left in the wild. Ranked among the world's ten most endangered species, the South China tiger may become extinct within a decade if the Chinese government does not take strong action to protect the animal from poaching—largely to feed the black market trade in tiger parts—and habitat destruction. Even with that, given its low numbers, this subspecies faces an uphill battle for survival in the wild.

Reports from the Russian Far East indicate that there may be 480 to 520 Siberian tigers living in the wild today. However, they are sparsely spread over vast areas of far-eastern Russia, mostly Primorsky Krai and Khabarovsky Krai, and are vulnerable to poaching. The Save the Tiger Fund—a program of the U.S.-based National Fish and Wildlife Foundation—is credited with helping double the tiger population over the past decade by funding tiger conservation programs in the field, particularly in the 1990s, when Russia was going through an economic crisis.

Current estimates of the Indochinese tiger population vary from 1,285 to 1,785, with the largest population in Malaysia. Elsewhere the subspecies has been decimated, particularly in eastern Burma, Thailand, Vietnam, Laos, and Cambodia, to meet the rising demand for tiger bones and other body parts in neighboring China. In addition, ungulates—the main food species of the tiger—are heavily poached to supply the burgeoning bush-meat market in Indochina. Yet with effective control of poaching and habitat destruction, this region, particularly the forests of the Tenasserim Range, which separates Thailand and Myanmar, has the potential to be restored into one of the biggest and healthiest blocks of unbroken tiger habitat.

As its name implies, the Sumatran tiger is found on the island of Sumatra, the last stronghold of tigers in the Indonesian archipelago. In the past two decades, its habitat has been severely fragmented by logging and agricultural encroachment. Currently its population is estimated to be between four hundred and five hundred, mostly in scattered pockets. Large numbers are concentrated in protected areas such as Gunung Leuser, Kerinci-Seblat, and Bukit Barisan Selatan National Parks. The Sumatran tiger is the smallest of the five surviving subspecies of wild tiger. A common tiger exhibited in zoos and safari parks around the world, their numbers are dwindling in the wild. Habitat loss from logging, conversion of land to plantations for commercial crops, and the rising conflicts between tigers and humans are prime reasons the Sumatran tiger is losing its battle for survival in the wild. In 2008–2009 twenty problem tigers—suspected of man-eating or cattle lifting—were captured in the Indonesian territory of Aceh alone.

The recent crash in the number of Royal Bengal (Indian) tigers demonstrates another plight of tigers in the wild. During the early part of the twentieth century, India was home to about forty thousand tigers. There could have been at least another ten thousand of this subspecies in eastern Burma, Nepal, Bhutan, and southeastern Tibet, where tiger habitats were mostly intact. By 1972 the first systematic census of tigers found that there were fewer than 1,830 tigers in India. This appallingly low number was linked to indiscriminate hunting, rampant conversion of tiger habitat to farmland, and unsustainable forestry practices that also destroyed the tiger's habitat.

This revelation shocked Indira Gandhi, India's powerful prime minister, who launched an aggressive program to save the tiger. This program, aptly named "Project Tiger," was a coordinated effort among the state and central governments of India and nongovernmental organizations (NGOs) such as the World Wildlife Fund. Prime Minister Gandhi's efforts paid off. The number of tigers in India rose from about 1,800 in the beginning of the 1970s to more than 3,500 by the mid-1980s. However, the political will she courageously generated to save the tiger waned after she was assassinated by one of her own bodyguards on October 31, 1984. Consequently, the number of tigers in India began to decline steadily into the new millennium.

The conservation community got its biggest jolt in 2004. Scientists discovered that the Sariska Tiger Reserve in Rajasthan—one of India's famous national parks—contained no tigers, even though government records indicated that there were fifteen to twenty tigers in the reserve. In addition, camera traps, pugmark surveys, and searches for other indicators demonstrated that tigers had long been gone from Sariska.

Both national and global conservation groups were dismayed at how three decades of efforts to save the tiger had not only failed but failed miserably. A comprehensive report issued in March 2008 by the National Tiger Authority of the Government of India and the Wildlife Institute of India reported that tiger numbers were the lowest ever recorded—1,165. Even an overtly optimistic estimate set the maximum number of tigers in India at just over 1,650. Despite millions of dollars poured into the World Wildlife Fund and the Government of India, the number of tigers in India had plummeted by 40 percent in twenty years.

For the past thirty years, the World Wildlife Fund and Project Tiger had been using the tiger as the flagship species of their conservation efforts. During their fund-raisers, many tiger conservation groups had been bragging about how they had brought the tiger back from the brink of extinction. Obviously, preoccupied with gloating over their own published claims, they never checked the facts in the field.

Tiny Nepal was not far behind its goliath neighbor in losing tigers to poachers. Like Indira Gandhi, Nepal's King Birendra had created a political will in the 1970s to save tigers from becoming extinct in his kingdom. Sadly, King Birendra's fate was the same as that of Indira Gandhi. He was assassinated, on June 1, 2001, by his own son, Crown Prince Dipendra.

In the years since King Birendra's assassination, the status of tigers in Nepal has become even worse than in her neighboring countries. In 2000 there were an estimated 350 to 370 tigers in Nepal, most of them concentrated in three tiger reserves. According to estimates from the Department of National Parks and Wildlife Conservation, Royal Chitwan National Park, including the adjoining Parsa Wildlife Reserve, harbored 150 to 170 tigers. Royal Bardia National Park was home to an estimated 90 to 115 tigers; while there were twenty-five to forty tigers in the Royal Suklaphanta Wildlife Reserve. Other tigers were sparsely scattered in forests outside these three tiger sanctuaries. Estimates in 2008 indicate that there may not be more than seventy-five tigers in Chitwan, thirty to forty in Bardia, and as few as five in Suklaphanta.

It must be stressed that the data on the number of tigers in the wild in Nepal and elsewhere must be considered with caution. These are more guesstimates than estimates. Counting tigers in the wild is not easy. They rank among the most elusive of the wild cats, and their habitat is densely covered jungle, where actual sightings are rare. Thus census techniques largely remain unsystematic, unscientific, and unreliable, as our team discovered while monitoring radio-collared tigers. Depending upon the condition of the soil, pugmarks are often distorted resulting in double counting or miscounting.

Rampant poaching and the ever-increasing black market in tiger bones, skins, and other body parts are pushing the tiger to extinction in Nepal. Media reports indicate that Nepal is not only losing tigers in her own national parks and wildlife reserves but is also abetting the decimation of tigers in other South Asian countries. As conservation laws to prevent poaching and habitat destruction are largely ignored, Nepal has become a haven for wildlife smugglers.

As politicians continue to bicker for power after the Maoist rebellion and end of the monarchy, Nepal has become a key transit point for smuggling tiger bones and tiger skins to China, particularly from India and Bangladesh. Consequently, Nepal plays a crucial role in the war against this illicit trade. The current government's attitude is mostly apathetic when it comes to saving Nepal's tigers and other endangered species or cooperating with her neighbors to curb illicit trade in endangered plant and animal species. Preoccupied with issues related to health, education, and poverty alleviation, the government does not rank wildlife conservation high in its national development schemes.

The official government count of tigers in Bangladesh is five hundred. This figure indicates a dramatic increase from the two hundred tigers reported in 1970, when Bangladesh was still a part of Pakistan. However, many tiger experts question this increased number, claiming that they cannot be correct, considering the rate of forest destruction, population growth, a series of military coups, and other political upheavals in the country. Bangladesh also has not been immune to rampant poaching and smuggling of tiger bones and skins. Furthermore, the density of prey species is too low to support five hundred tigers. A recent scientific study suggests that there may actually be no more than two hundred tigers in Bangladesh, the same population as the 1970 estimate.

The number of tigers estimated by government sources in Bhutan is between 115 and 150. However, some tiger experts doubt these figures. Although human population in the country is low, the density of the tiger's prey is also low to sustain 115 to 150 tigers. However, the habitat of tigers is much more varied in Bhutan than anywhere on the Indian subcontinent.

The tiger's range in Bhutan extends from the hot and humid tropical jungles of Manas at near sea level in the south to higher than 12,000 feet in the cool evergreen forests of the Himalayas near the capital of Thimpu. Most of the tiger habitat is in unbroken corridors, facilitating the dispersal of tigers. But they are subjected to heavy grazing pressures from domestic cattle. Overgrazing degrades tiger habitat by causing reduction in the wild ungulates that are the tiger's main prey species. Tigers here also prey heavily on domestic livestock, triggering human-tiger conflict.

The fate of the Royal Bengal tiger in northern Burma is at best uncertain. Its tiger country has been mostly closed because

Burma—or Myanmar, as the rulers now call their country—is paranoid about the prying eyes of outsiders. Furthermore, the country's own scientists are often censored by the ruling military junta when they release facts and figures, even those deemed harmless by the scientific community. Nevertheless, Burma has the largest tiger reserve in the world—the Hukawng Valley Wildlife Sanctuary. Created in 2004 by the Burmese government, the reserve covers an area of 2,500 square miles in one of the most isolated sites in northern Burma. Surrounded by rugged terrain, this lush green river valley once topped the list of pristine tiger habits on Earth.

In 1961 the Burmese government isolated the valley from outsiders as government forces waged a brutal war against the Kachin Independence Army (KIA)—a separatist group of guerillas seeking their own homeland. In 1994 KIA gave up their guns and signed a peace treaty with the Burmese government, and the government reopened the area to outsiders. With peace restored, poachers and gold miners soon moved into the Hukawng Valley. The tiger, its prey, and its habitat were devastated. Currently only a hundred tigers are estimated to survive in the core area. Yet the Vermont size valley has the potential to support at least three hundred to four hundred tigers. Most of the 5,580-square-mile valley still has intact forest cover.

A few Western organizations, such as the New York–based Wildlife Conservation Society, are seeking ways to make the Hukawng Valley one of the world's most pristine tiger sanctuaries. However, the relationship between the West and Burma is strained. Led by the United States, the West has imposed tough sanctions against Burma that prevent funding from such large organizations as the Global Environment Facility (GEF). Consequently, except for limited funding though small independent international organizations such as the Save the Tiger Fund, money has not been available to move this ambitious plan forward.

The tiger occupies the apex of the food chain in its habitat in the wilds of Asia. Its survival is dictated by the rule of the jungle: "Eat or be eaten." Fortunately for the tiger, it is more an eater than a species that is eaten. The tiger's culinary choices are varied. It relishes tiny termites and frogs as appetizers. For its entrée the tiger prefers young rhinoceros, elephant, and gaur (a wild ox) but mainly dines on deer and wild boar. It is even known to prey on its carnivorous cousins, such as leopards and dholes (wild dogs). The tiger also has a huge appetite. It is estimated that it needs to kill at least one animal weighing 125 to 135 pounds every week to survive. Females with cubs need more. Ulaas Karanth, an eminent Indian scientist who has been studying tigers for three decades, estimates that while a tiger needs to kill at least forty to fifty ungulates per year to survive, a tigress rearing cubs needs at least sixty to seventy such animals each year. This is not an easy task, even for the mighty tiger.

The life of common tiger prey, such as chital, sambar, and hog deer, is focused on avoiding being eaten. Consequently, they are not easy to catch. A tiger is considered extremely lucky if it can kill one deer a week. As humans have aggressively encroached on its domain, the tiger is increasingly relying on domestic cattle such as buffalo, cows, and even yaks over 12,000 feet in the highlands of Bhutan. Preying on domestic cattle that stray into the jungle is much easier than hunting wild deer and boar. In Chitwan, my own research as a key field scientist for the Smithsonian Institution's Nepal Tiger Ecology Project from 1978 to 1982 indicated that at least 30 percent of the tiger's food per annum was domestic cattle. However, most predation took place near the forest edge adjacent to human settlement. The predators of domestic cattle were mostly tigers that had been pushed out of their territory by a stronger opponent.

The tiger's body has evolved to make it an agile, solitary hunter. In addition to its sinewy claws and powerful jaws, the tiger's yard-long tail is a key hunting component of its anatomy. The tail stands erect and sways from left to right when a tiger attacks its prey, sprinting at full speed. This action enables the tiger to balance its body, particularly when it needs to turn abruptly during the chase and make the kill. The tiger has good eyesight, with the ability to see in the dark. However, its hearing ability is more important for hunting than its senses of sight or smell. With their large flaps and two prominent white spots on the back, the tiger's ears are primarily used to scout for prey. Though the function of the white spots is not clear, a tiger's ear can catch even the feeblest noise of its prey rustling in thick bush at a far distance. Its sensitive ears also allow the tiger to hear footsteps or other human sounds, enabling it to avoid encounters with humans—the tiger's worst enemy.

My experience with the radio-collared tigers of the Smithsonian Nepal Tiger Ecology Project indicates that the tiger often spots us long before we humans can make visual contact. We have located tigers by radio signal that were barely a dozen feet away, and yet we were unable to see them. However, we knew the tiger was crouching quietly in the bush, totally camouflaged and invisible even to trained human eyes.

Like that of most cats, the tiger's sense of smell is too weak to be used to search for and stalk prey. However, it uses its short nostrils to smell the telltale signs of other tigers in its territory. Although the tiger lives a solitary life, it does communicate with other tigers by marking its territory. By rubbing its face against or clawing a tree trunk, the tiger discharges a pungent liquid from tiny scent glands hidden in its face, toes, and other parts of its body. It also leaves its smelly calling card by spraying urine around the base of trees and shrubs and on the ground. The strong urine odor signals other tigers to keep out of its territory. It also indicates the tiger's readiness for reproduction. Tigers also communicate vocally, emitting an aauuoom-sounding roar as they roam their territory.

Tigers reach their sexual maturity when they are just over two years old. However, it is unlikely that they become sexually active until they leave their mothers and establish their own territories. Females always initiate courtships, which last about a week, leading to sexual union. During this period, males and females roam together, often resting no farther than fifteen or twenty feet apart. Occasionally during courtship, they also brush their heads and bodies against one another. Mating is quick, lasting only twenty to thirty seconds. However, tigers mate frequently, often as many as fifty to sixty times over a week's period.

Cubs are born after a gestation period of 90 to 110 days. Litter size varies from as low as one to as high as seven, with larger number of cubs born in captivity. The average litter size in Chitwan was two to three cubs per birth. Cubs weigh less than two pounds to three pounds at birth. As with most members of the cat family, infanticide by other tigers occurs occasionally. Thus the mothers are constantly on the move. They also lead a hard life between hunting, feeding, and protecting their cubs from other tigers and sly animals such as hyenas and jackals. In 1973 we were shocked to find that two cubs of our first radio-collared female tiger had been burnt to death in a forest fire. Tiger cubs have also drowned during the heavy monsoon flooding, even though adult tigers are excellent swimmers.

Cubs are born blind, their eyes opening up within ten to fifteen days, and require intensive nurturing from their mother. Cubs stay with their mothers for twenty to twenty-four months and learn the skills of hunting. Cubs reach their sexual maturity between two to three years, by which time they leave their mothers to establish their own territory. They defend their domain from incursion by other tigers.

In Chitwan a tiger's territory varied from four to eight square miles for females and eight to fifty-three square miles for males. However, a tiger's territory is not rigid but elastic, with tigers moving in and out to avoid fatal encounters with the dominant male. Male tigers often battle brutally to defend their territory. These fights are vicious and often leave tigers badly mauled, even fatally wounded.

Independent studies undertaken in four different sites—Chitwan in Nepal, Panna in central India, Nagarhole in southern India, and the Primorski Krai region in Siberia—demonstrate that the availability of prey species is the key factor in determining the size of a tiger's territory. In short: The greater the availability of prey, the smaller each individual tiger's territory and the higher the tiger numbers. Unlike lions, tigers do not roam in prides. Except during mating, they roam alone. Nepal's three tiger sanctuaries—Chitwan, Suklaphanta, and Bardia—have high prey density, estimated to be twenty to twenty-five ungulates for every hundred acres, so the number of tigers could easily recover if habitat is protected and poaching is brought under control.

The average life span of wild tigers is twelve to fifteen years, although they survive twenty years or more in captivity. They are polygamous and prolific breeders. They also mate and breed throughout the year. Stephen Mills, a prominent British writer and a famous tiger filmmaker who has studied tigers in both Nepal and India, reports that in order to conceive, female tigers often copulate with more than one male.

One alpha male tiger radio-collared by the Smithsonian project copulated with more than one female. This tiger, designated Tiger 105, sired more than fifty cubs between 1974 when we radio-collared it and 1979 when it died tragically. Tiger 105 could have sired more cubs if it had not drowned under the influence of drugs while we were trying to catch it to retrofit its radio collar. Of the fifty-plus cubs this tiger sired with half a dozen females, we estimated that at least twenty-seven survived in and around Royal Chitwan National Park to produce more tigers. This illustrates that the accidental death of one tiger during field research was not biologically costly.

Hunting records of the early twentieth century indicate that tigers are very resilient animals. The jungles were kept intact and hunting was infrequent, even if excessive kills were made during each hunt—an event exclusively reserved for the rulers of the country. With a good breeding population of tigers and an abundance of prey species, the number of tigers killed was easily replenished. With intact habitat, tigers can also sustain limited culling. For example, in seven years (1933 to 1940), Nepal prime minister Juddha shot 433 tigers in Chitwan and the surrounding areas. However, these hunts were infrequent and did not adversely impact the tiger population. Hunting sites were rotated to preserve a pool of fertile tigers to breed and to enable their offspring to disperse from high-tiger-density sites to low-density sites, including to forests where tigers had been massively culled in previous hunts. The prime minister's hunts averaged about sixty-two tigers per year—a record grossly beaten by Viceroy Lord Linlithgow of India, who killed 120 tigers on his 1939 hunt in Chitwan.

It is paradoxical that such a large-scale massacre occurred in the Indian subcontinent, where the tiger has been an iconic emblem in art, literature, and folklore since the Indus Valley civilization of 2500 B.C.

6

THE TIGER IN ASIAN CULTURE

GREEK MYTHOLOGY CLAIMS THAT THE TIGER EARNED ITS FIRST badge of honor in Asia Minor, today's Turkey. Dionysus—the Greek god of wine—fell in love with a nymph in ancient Babylon, about one hundred miles south of modern day Baghdad. He turned himself into a tiger, carried the nymph on his back, and swam her across a river in Mesopotamia. Dionysus named the river Tigris, the Greek word for tiger.

Rising in the mountains of modern-day Turkey, the Tigris still flows today. With its westerly counterpart, the Euphrates, it is one of the two main rivers of Iraq. The region between these two rivers has been called the Cradle of Civilization.

Not only Greek mythology but also Asian literature demonstrates that no other animal on Earth creates as much awe or matches the tiger in capturing the human imagination. It is the most identifiable and captivating species in the Animal Kingdom and has been displayed on coats of arms and national emblems and employed as a mascot for sports teams in countries all over the world.

The tiger was used as a symbol of civil society as far back as 2600 B.C., when human civilization flourished in the city of Mohenjo Daro in the Indus River Valley. Archaeological finds indicate that the tiger was used to symbolize the glory of the Hindu civilization—the world's oldest living religion. Some scholars claim that the tiger symbolizes the Hindu god Shiva—the destroyer of evil. This Hindu god is also known as the Pasupati Nath, or the Lord of the Animals. Others suggest that the tiger symbolized fertility and prosperity in ancient times, not only in India but throughout Asia as well.

Throughout recorded history, mankind has related its own existence to that of the tiger. Fierce and frightening, beautiful and dignified, brutal and formidable, the tiger has been a symbol of honor, dignity, and righteousness. Five Asian nations—Bangladesh, India, Malaysia, North Korea and South Korea—have honored the tiger with the title of "National Animal." It was also chosen as the mascot for the Seoul Olympics in 1988.

Some minority ethnic groups have used the tiger as an icon to portray the war against injustice and for individual rights. One of these groups is the Liberation Tigers of Tamil Elam (LTTE) in Sri Lanka. This group, which had been fighting for a separate nation of its own, traces its ancestors back to the Chola dynasty. The Cholas ruled southern India from the ninth to the twelfth century and used the tiger as their royal seal.

In contrast to civil wars, the tiger also evokes peace and economic prosperity with names such as the Asian Tigers, designating countries such as Malaysia, Singapore, and Thailand that choose to resolve their ethnic divisions by providing equal economic opportunities for minorities. Yet it is an unfortunate paradox that tigers in the wild rank among the top species persecuted in Asia in this new millennium. This is the greatest irony in the life of the tiger, that an animal so revered is so ill treated, particularly in India, where the country's name, culture, and religions—whether Hindu, Buddhism, Jain, or Islam—have been linked to the life of the tiger.

Ancient Hindu scripture and modern-day folklore are inundated with stories about the tiger. One of my favorites is the story about why God Shiva dons a tiger skin. Portraits of Shiva are common in many Hindu households. One of these portraits, often seen hanging on the walls of the *puja kotha,* or worship room, depicts God Shiva meditating upon a tiger skin. Some pictures show Shiva wrapped up in a tiger skin, while others show Shiva using the tiger skin as a loincloth.

Being the god of gods, Shiva was above any worldly laws, rules, or norms. He was not bound by what he could or could not do. Often he descended from Mount Kailash and wandered around the earth transforming himself into various forms—human or animal.

One legend tells of the time Shiva was roaming naked in a forest on Earth in the form of a handsome young man. He encountered several beautiful women in the jungle. These women were no ordinary women but the wives of sages with supernatural powers. Yet Shiva's well-built physique and handsome face mesmerized them. The women decided to desert their husbands and follow Shiva, their eyes gleaming with hopes of a tryst with him. Their behavior enraged their jealous husbands, who believed Shiva was nothing but a naked vagabond wandering through their domain. The sages decided to destroy Shiva to prevent their wives from leaving them. Using their magical powers, they created the world's mightiest and most ferocious beast—the tiger. The sages set the tiger against Shiva, but it was no match for the god's power. Shiva slew the beast and used its skin to cover his genitals. He also used part of the skin with the attached tiger's head as his meditating mat. Humans continue this tradition today, as indicated by the carpets and rugs for sale in Kathmandu's marketplace. Rather than genuine tiger, Nepalese and Tibetan weavers use the tiger motif in their design.

Shiva's consort is equally revered by Hindus as Goddess Mother Nature—the source of all of the earth's positive energy and the most beautiful and wise of Hindu deities. She inherited the universe in various forms and goes by the various names—Parvati, Devi, and Durga Bhavani. The last name is the most popular form in Nepal, where people worship her stone or metal idols in many of the public temples or her portraits in the privacy of their homes. The most popular representation depicts the goddess riding a tiger to roam the earth. The tiger is her main companion and her means of transportation. Her most powerful form shows her decapitating a water buffalo from the back of a tiger. The water buffalo represents Mahishasura—the demon.

The most compassionate myth that relates the tiger to the South Asian culture comes not from Hinduism but from Buddhism. Seven centuries before Christ was born, King Maharath reigned in Panauti, a picturesque river valley some twenty miles southeast of Kathmandu. He had three sons. Prince Mahasattva, the youngest, was exceptionally kind and full of compassion for animals, birds, and humans alike.

One afternoon the prince hiked to a nearby mountain. On the way to the top, he came across a tigress with five cubs. Having just given birth, the tigress was weak and hungry. Unable to control her hunger, she was about to eat her own cubs. Shocked by the sight, the prince picked up a sharp thorn from a shrub and pierced his own body, allowing his blood to flow. He then moved next to the cubs and allowed them to lick his blood. He then cut up his body and fed the mother tigress his flesh, piece by piece. In a few days the prince died, committing the ultimate act of compassion and sacrifice as the tigers consumed his flesh and blood. The tigress recovered her strength and was able to nurse her cubs.

Prince Mahasattva was reincarnated in the womb of Queen Maya Devi of Kaplilavastu in Western Nepal. In 623 B.C. he was reborn as Prince Siddhartha Gautama to become the Buddha, the prophet of peace. The five cubs were reincarnated as humans. They followed the teachings of the Buddha and became arahats— achieving that perfected stage with powers to overcome the three cardinal sins of humanity: desire, hatred, and ignorance. In short, the reincarnated cubs attained Nirvana and were free from any earthly sufferings.

Legend has it that Siddhartha Gautama came back as a hermit to the site where he had fed the tigers his flesh and blood in his previous life. There he created a stupa—the oldest form of moundlike sacred structure. That stupa still exists today in Panauti, about twenty miles east of Kathmandu. Known as Namo Buddha in Nepali or Tak-mo Lu-jin in Tibetan, it is a sacred place for both Hindus and Buddhists and draws thousands of pilgrims every year to Panauti. One of its major attractions is a stone idol that depicts the deity feeding a tiger.

Another place that draws both Eastern pilgrims and Western tourists is the Tiger's Nest in Bhutan. This monastery, also known as Taktsang, is picturesquely perched overlooking the Paro Valley. It is believed that Guru Rimpoche, revered as the second Buddha, came from Tibet to Bhutan in A.D. 747 riding on the back of a tigress. The animal is believed to have been his consort, who had transformed herself into a ferocious tiger, as Guru Rimpoche's mission in Bhutan was to crush demonic powers that were terrorizing the country.

The Chinese have their own set of mythological tales linking the tiger with a god. One of them is Quan Yin—a deity frequently seen in Chinese temples and on home altars. She was the youngest of the three daughters of King Miao Tohang, who is said to have ruled China in 2587 B.C. Her father tried to force her into a marriage of wealth and fame, but she refused. Instead she went to live a simple and secluded life in a monastery, meditating most of the time.

Quan Yin's father tried to persuade her to return to the palace and take a husband, but the princess was still adamant. The king was enraged and set fire to her monastery, but Quan Yin still refused to abide by her father's command.

Infuriated by his daughter's disobedience, the king ordered her to be decapitated in public. As she was about to be beheaded, a big storm tore the skies and lightning surrounded her in protection. The god of the heavens took the form of a tiger and carried her into the mountains. With the tiger by her side, she continued to meditate and finally reached the Bodhisattva (Wisdom-Being)— the final stages of enlightenment. Later her cruel father repented and converted to Buddhism.

To this day, Quan Yin is venerated as the goddess of mercy and compassion. The Chinese also recognize her as the savior of humankind.

The Ba ethnic minority of China are devotees of the tiger, which they consider a form of god. Consequently they never kill a tiger, even though they hunt other wildlife. During the year of the tiger, they worship wooden sculptures or tiger pictures with animal sacrifice. Like most celestial connections of a god with the tiger, this practice also has a legend behind it.

Long ago, the Nu Valley in China's Yunnan Province was rich with wild animals and plants and sparsely populated by humans. One of the humans was a young orphan woman who had no siblings and thus lived alone.

One day she was collecting firewood on the edge of the forest when a tiger appeared from nowhere. Terrified, she ran and climbed a tree. Looking down from the top of her tree, she saw not a tiger but a handsome young man. She asked him if he had seen the tiger. The young man told her that she might be dreaming and denied that there were any tigers in the area. The girl climbed down the tree, and they talked while the young man helped her collect firewood. He asked her to marry him, and she accepted.

The man loved his wife dearly, and she bore him half a dozen children. Most of the time he left her at home and went to the forest to hunt for deer or collect wild fruits and vegetables. The wife noticed that the deer he brought home did not have any arrow or spear wounds. She was confused about how he hunted them, but she never asked. She was content with having deer to eat.

One day her husband left early to hunt in the forest. A few moments later an old friend walked into her house. Her friend persuaded her to go to the forest to collect mushrooms. Collecting mushrooms, they walked deep into the forest. Suddenly they saw a tiger stalking a barking deer. Concerned that the tiger might see them, the women hid behind the trunk of a big tree. The tiger caught its prey and killed it by snapping its neck. Suddenly, to their surprise, the tiger transformed into a man. The man was her husband.

Her heart pounding with anxiety, she approached her husband. He told her that because his secret had been revealed, he could not return to the village but must disappear forever. Then he threw a magic spell over his wife and her friend. Both women fell fast asleep, and the husband disappeared forever after blessing them and his children.

The couple's children grew up and expanded their family. They became known as the Ba or Tiger People and lived happily and peacefully. To never forget where they came from, they started worshipping the tiger. During festivities they told the story of their origins, singing in their native language. Like China's Ba people, the Warlis—ancient tribes of India who are neither Hindu, Muslim, nor Christian nor follow any modern-day religion—worship the tiger as Baghdeva, or the tiger god. To them the tiger is the god of gods and represents life and rebirth. They offer part of their agricultural harvest to the tiger.

The tiger has become an icon of reverence in Chinese culture representing courage, fear, and magical powers. Ironically, its purported magical power has been a curse to the tiger. Humans kill tigers to feast on their body parts, believing that the bones and meat will transfer the powers from the tiger to the human body.

Chinese folklore is full of stories crediting the tiger with killing evil humans. Tiger motifs decorate children's clothes, shoes, and even rooms to ward off evil spirits. Their image is often carved on tombs and gravestones to protect the souls of the dead from being tormented by demonic ghosts. The pictographic marking on the tiger's forehead is believed to spell out the word *Wang*—a common Chinese name that means "king." Consequently, throughout history it was not the lion but the tiger that was designated as the king of the forests. The tiger also became a popular icon of Chinese opera during the Qing Dynasty (1644–1911).

Recently the People's Republic of China has been promoting several sites as the fabled Shangri-la. One of these sites is a dramatic spot on a narrow neck of the Yangtze River in the Hengduan Mountains of northwest Yunnan Province called the Tiger Leaping Gorge. This site is believed to be the point where tigers leap across the gorge to escape hunters in hot pursuit.

Like Hindu deities, Chinese gods also use the tiger as their transportation animal. One of these gods is the Taoist deity Chang Tao-ling. This holy being is the equivalent of the Hindu deity Laxmi—the goddess of wealth and fortune—except that the Chinese version is male.

The biggest impact that the tiger has had on Chinese culture stems from the fact that it is the twelfth sign of the Chinese calendar. People born in the Year of the Tiger are said to be humanitarian at heart, outspoken, and courageous but obstinate. Some well-known people born under this sign are Marco Polo, one of the first Europeans to travel the Silk Road to China; French president Charles De Gaulle; U.S. president Dwight D. Eisenhower; Queen Elizabeth II of Britain; Ho Chi Minh, president of Vietnam; and Karl Marx, the father of communism.

One of the most prominent and revered persons born in the Year of the Tiger was Prophet Mohammed, regarded by Muslims as the messenger of God. Although tigers do not play as major a role in Islam as they do in the Hindu and Buddhist religions, many Muslims believe that Allah sent tigers to Earth to protect his followers and punish traitors and evil people. In West Bengal and Bangladesh, both Hindus and Muslims venerate the tiger. Paintings from Bangladesh show a Muslim Imam riding a tiger to ward off evil.

Bengalis on both sides of the border between India and Bangladesh are proud that the Indian tiger is called the Royal Bengal tiger, despite its unsavory reputation as a man-eater in the Sunderbans forests of the Bay of Bengal. However, their pride is not restricted only to the animal's name, a vestige of British India. They also view the tiger as an icon of their cultural heritage, regardless of their religion. Images and stories that link the tiger with their culture and religion are common in the Sunderbans.

On the Indian side, images of Dakshin Ray, the tiger god, and Bonobibi, the goddess of the forests, are very common. Hindus pray and sing to the glory of these deities and thank them for endowing the Sunderbans with rich forests, fish, honey, and many other natural resources.

Tiger stories on the Bangladesh side are even more intriguing. Dr. M. Monirul Khan, a Bangladeshi scientist who studied the Sunderbans tigers for his doctoral degree at Cambridge in England, writes that Bengali Muslims believe that a man-eating tiger is Ufari, an evil spirit that descends to Earth from the sky. The spirit lands on treetops and bends the tree. Once the spirit touches the ground, it takes the shape of a tiger and preys on people. As a protection against this evil spirit, people carry threads and beads blessed by spiritual leaders. They also seek the help of professional shamans, who are believed to have the power to jam the jaws of man-eating tigers, preventing them from preying on humans.

Dr. Khan also notes that many Bangladeshis believe that the tiger was born out of the menstrual blood of a saint named Fatema, giving the tiger an overpowering odor. At times people curse the man-eating intruders, reciting verses to the glory of Fatema. One such verse threatens to force the tiger-bodied evil Ufari to tear off its own penis and eat it. As elsewhere, mystical techniques to frighten man-eating tigers rarely worked in the Sunderbans. Yet many Bangladeshis continued to practice the ritual.

In Korea the tiger ranks as the most popular image in folk art. There the animal is viewed as a protective spirit that provides good health, peace and contentment, wealth, and many children. Korean folktales often humanize the tiger to portray its strengths and weaknesses, but rarely do they depict it as a ferocious and cruel beast. In the Tao culture the tiger symbolizes human harmony with nature and is a symbol of eternal life.

"Riding the tiger" is a phrase frequently used by contemporary Western political leaders. This ancient Asian adage portrays this mighty animal used as a horse. One interpretation says that the tiger will soon get hungry and eat the rider. The second interpretation says a rider can never dismount a tiger. As soon as the rider is on the ground, the tiger will devour him. Thus the only safety is to keep riding.

The second interpretation is best illustrated by Winston Churchill's warnings against the rising fascist dictatorship in Hitler's Germany and Stalin's communism in Eastern Europe. In 1938 he aptly remarked, "Dictators ride to and fro upon tigers, which they dare not dismount."

President Harry Truman found himself in a difficult situation affirming America's role in the hostile environment of post–World War II and the emerging Korean War. In a presidential address to the nation he said, "Being a president is like riding a tiger. You have to keep on riding or be swallowed."

Some Western environmentalists interpret "riding the tiger" to mean moving forward and never giving up on efforts to save this magnificent animal. Perhaps no country has evoked the tiger as a symbol of sport more than the United States. Many American sports teams have chosen the tiger as their image, including the Detroit Tigers baseball team and American football's Cincinnati Bengals. Even American educational institutions such as Princeton University and the University of Missouri have named their sports teams, respectively, the Princeton Tigers and the Mizzou Tigers.

Despite fascination with and recognition of the tiger in the West as a symbol of sporting events, the tiger is a wild animal in Asia. Not all Asian religious and cultural beliefs portray the tiger as good. Some Buddhist sects consider the tiger one of the earth's "Three Senseless Creatures." It symbolizes unpredictability and anger. (The other two "senseless creatures" are the monkey, which symbolizes greed, and the deer, which symbolizes lust or the sickness of love.) Yet overall, the tiger continues to be revered in the tiger countries of Asia. For example, an old Indonesian Javan faith believes that the tiger symbolizes Mother Nature's beauty and power. It holds that once the tiger becomes extinct, the idyllic and prosperous island will lose its beauty, peace, and prosperity. But if that belief is true, why was the Javan tiger hunted to extinction? Why is tiger habitat being destroyed? Why are tiger bones and flesh consumed for its purported strengths and sexual powers? It is also a baffling paradox that despite its almost sacred status in religious ritual, the tiger long remained a prized hunting. Is it because the tiger at times displays its supremacy over mankind by eating the occasional unlucky human who crosses its path?

7

THE MAN-EATER OF BHIMLE

"SIR," SIGHED A SOMBER VOICE ON THE TELEPHONE. "WE HAVE a serious situation here." The speaker at the other end of the line was Ram Prit Yadav, warden of Royal Chitwan National Park. Ram was calling from the town of Bharatpur, an hour's drive from the national park headquarters in Kasra.

The phone call on a cool December evening in 1980 was badly timed. I was rushing out the door to join my friend Phillip Trimble, the American Ambassador to the Kingdom of Nepal. He was hosting a dinner party at his residence in Kamaladi in the heart of Kathmandu, more than a mile from my home in Kupondole. I was running late. I had driven for more than six hours on the bumpy highway from Chitwan in my beat-up Indian Mahindra jeep just to attend the dinner. After spending weeks in the wilds of southern Nepal, I was looking forward to fine wine and good food in the American ambassador's plush residence.

"What situation?" I interrupted him irritably.

"A tiger has again eaten a man near the Bhimle guard post," he replied in an equally irritated tone. "We believe it is Tiger 118, one of your radio-collared tigresses! Enraged villagers are mobbing my office. They are demanding that we shoot the man-eater immediately and display its carcass as evidence. Otherwise they have threatened to set fire to our guard posts. We must act immediately to prevent the situation from erupting into violence."

His words shook me. I could visualize the gravity of the situation that Ram was facing. Man-eating is the ultimate expression of conflict between tigers and humans. It also triggers a profound hatred for the tiger. Even if the animal is a fully protected endangered species, the call for revenge is a natural reaction on the part of villagers.

This was not the first human kill that Tiger 118 had made—it was her third. Though there are no written guidelines in Nepal, we normally declared a tiger to be a man-eater only after three confirmed killings. We used this guideline to avoid killing non–man-eaters without properly identifying the real culprit, as has happened a few times across the border in India.

Tiger 118's first kill, three months earlier, had been a middle-aged woman. It took place in the middle of a patch of Impereta grass, a species known as thatch grass. The woman and her husband, from the village of Ghatgai, had sneaked into the patch of grassland along the floodplains inside Royal Chitwan National Park to collect thatch grass, which they needed to repair their hut. Since collecting thatch grass inside the national park was illegal, they were extra cautious not to be caught by the park guards. Husband and wife were both cutting grass in a crouched position, well hidden inside thick grasses and not more than ten feet apart. Suddenly a tiger leaped at the wife and grabbed her with its strong paws. Shocked and horrified, her brave husband attacked the killer. Screaming at the top of his voice, he angrily slashed the tiger's face with his sharp sickle. It was the tiger's turn to be surprised. It dropped its victim and dashed out of sight with a thundering roar. Unfortunately the man's wife was already dead. The tiger had snapped her neck, a classic killing technique.

We got the message about the tiger kill later that day. Instead of acting immediately and going after the tiger, we visited the site and analyzed the situation. We deduced that the kill had been accidental. The site was also a prime habitat of hog deer—a common prey of the tiger. We surmised that as the woman had been crouching while cutting the grass and the tiger, misidentifying her as a hog deer, had pounced upon her as prey. Since the tiger had fled the scene after it encountered the husband, we assumed that the killing was a case of mistaken identity. We believed that the husband's scream and counterattack with his sickle in an erect posture had scared off the tiger. (One scientific theory postulates that unless they have become man-eaters, tigers do not normally attack humans because they visualize a standing person as bigger and taller than themselves, a potent deterrent to attack.)

After making her first kill, Tiger 118 disappeared for a few days. She must have wandered far off, because our radios could not pick up the signals from her collar. She returned a few days later and killed a man near Kasra, the park headquarters. This time the tiger did not flee but devoured virtually the whole body before disappearing.

Again we decided to give the tiger the benefit of the doubt. We assumed that she might have killed the person accidently. But as it was her second kill, she had lost her fear of humans. Having learned that humans were easy prey, she decided to feast on her kill. However, it was very possible that she had killed other humans when she disappeared after making her first kill and had become a true man-eater. Since she was out of signal contact, we could not ascertain this fact. Because the Nepali park boundary merged with the Indian border to the south, Chitwan tigers often crossed the international frontier and spent time in the Indian forests.

We got alarmed when we found that she was back in the Kasra-Ghatgai area where she had made two kills previously. Her pugmarks indicated that she was stalking humans along the public right-of-way, forest roads that were frequented by villagers to travel between villages. We were horrified to discover that she was stalking our guards and had waited patiently outside a guard post at night. This was unusual behavior—tigers rarely come near human habitation—and we decided to capture Tiger 118 as soon as we could locate her.

Ram's phone call sparked a realization that we had made a terrible mistake. Instead of theorizing, we should have gotten rid of Tiger 118 immediately after she had made her first human kill. Guilt coursed through my mind. "When and where did the killing happen?" I asked with a slight tremble in my voice. "Southeast of the Bhimle guard post," answered Ram, "not far from where she had made the first kill. An elephant driver found the remains of the body early today. He was taking his elephant to graze on the banks of the Rapti River when he stumbled on the kill site. I will explain the details when we meet. In the meantime, I need you back in Chitwan immediately to help diffuse the situation."

I sympathized with Ram. He had too much on his plate. Tirtha Man Maskey, his immediate supervisor and the founding superintendent of the national park, was in the United States, earning a PhD at the University of Florida in Gainesville. "Have you consulted Chuck McDougal, Dhan Bahadur, and Sakale Gurung?" I asked. The trio, who had been monitoring tigers at the western end of the national park, knew the habits and habitat of most tigers in Chitwan.

Dr. Chuck McDougal is an American anthropologist who has lived in Nepal for decades. He is also a former tiger hunter who had been studying tigers at the western end of the park since 1970. Sakale Gurung and Dhan Bahadur were his field assistants. They were also the two best tiger trackers at Tiger Tops Jungle Lodge. The three men were Nepal's leading experts on identifying tigers from their facial marks and pugmarks. Chuck was also a senior executive of the jungle lodge. He lived in a bungalow near the lodge and was in charge of all operations at the Tiger Tops concession in Royal Chitwan National Park. We had become good friends over the years and shared common interest in the welfare of tigers.

The park had a symbiotic relationship with Tiger Tops. They were generous in providing us with complimentary accommodations when our work took us to that area. We reciprocated when their staff visited our end of the park, some twenty-four miles to the east. The national park also provided their guests access to visit the Gharial Conservation Project—a research facility where

Ram was trying to breed the endangered fish-eating gharial croco-dile in captivity. In addition, the park authorities assisted Tiger Tops Resort with access to government elephants when they were needed. This included the annual World Elephant Polo Champi-onship, a major event organized by Tiger Tops to lure Hollywood celebrities and the world's rich and famous. We also shared infor-mation on the wildlife of Chitwan.

"Absolutely," responded Ram to my question. "I visited Tiger Tops earlier today and confirmed that the man-eating tigress is Tiger 118. Chuck has ensured that Tiger Tops will refrain from taking their tourists anywhere near the kill site. In addition, he has offered their elephants, vehicles, staff, and any other help we may need. He is also worried about the safety of the staff and supports my suggestion to get rid of Tiger 118. He and his team will join us and help to corner her."

We knew Tiger 118 well. Dave Smith—my counterpart in the Smithsonian Nepal Tiger Ecology Project—had darted the tiger in 1979 and had tattooed number 118 on her ears. After complet-ing his studies, Dave had returned to the United States. I was con-tinuing the project with the help of my Nepalese colleagues. Ram Prit Yadav, the man currently on the other end of the phone, was a key member of the team.

"Ram," I said softly, "I will fly down there first thing in the morning. Pick me up at Megauli Airport. Then we will pick up Chuck and his team at Tiger Tops. In the meantime, go to the Smithsonian Nepal Tiger Ecology Project in Saurah and tell Prem Bahadur Rai to meet us near the kill site tomorrow." I would hesi-tate to track down a man-eater without Prem.

"Ask Prem to mobilize all the shikaris. He must come fully prepared with elephants and all our equipments. Tell him to radio-track and reconfirm that the man-eater is indeed one of our radio-collared tigers," I added. "He should also bait the area with a dozen buffalo. Make sure none of the staff venture into the thick grasslands without being guarded by elephants. Man-eaters are cunning, vicious, and unpredictable."

"Prem and I already visited the site earlier today," interrupted Ram with an air of confidence. "We are fully prepared and waiting for you." I was pleased to note that Prem and Ram had thought through the necessary action. I was fortunate to be working with such a competent team. "I will see you tomorrow," I reiterated. "In the meantime, calm the villagers. Buy us some time. With luck we should be able to bag the man-eater within forty-eight hours." But I was being optimistic in assuming that, like normal tigers, the man-eater would also hang around the kill site for a day or two.

"I will do my best," said Ram. "But do not return to Chitwan without a firm government sanction to kill this tiger. Village leaders and local politicians are pumped up with anger. This man-eating incident is becoming a hot-button issue. We must destroy the beast and publicly parade the body to pacify the villagers. I am afraid that if we do not rectify the situation quickly and prudently, the episode may turn violent," he stressed. Ram's words were harsh but candid.

I had vowed not to kill any tiger unless absolutely necessary to save human lives. My interim plan was to sedate and catch the man-eater live and lock her up in the zoo. Furthermore, the paperwork required to get government sanction to kill a tiger was cumbersome. The tiger was listed as a highly endangered species in the laws of Nepal. Killing the beast required approval from a chain of authorities. Many of them were at least four levels higher than my pay level. But I needed to move fast. Ram's call had shaken me. His plea for the need to destroy the man-eater was deeply embedded in my mind. I trusted his judgment. He had echoed the sentiments of the poor villagers who lived in tiger country. Faced by at least three human kills in a row, the village folk could not care less about the tiger's endangered status. They wanted revenge and protection.

I could not make a decision on my own to kill a tiger. But I did have access to a person who could make that decision on the spot. That person was His Royal Highness Prince Gyanendra Bir Bikram Shah, younger brother of Nepal's monarch. After King Birendra and his wife, Queen Aishwarya, the prince was the most powerful person in Nepal. He was also chairman of the Royal Palace Wildlife Committee, a body that had absolute authority over all matters concerning wildlife. As a member of the committee, I had direct access to the prince and used this access to bypass the maze of Nepalese government bureaucracy.

I called the residence of Prince Gyanendra and relayed Ram's message. The prince, a prudent and pragmatic person, rarely micromanaged his field personnel. He authorized me to make any decision I thought appropriate. This included capturing or killing the man-eating tigress at my discretion.

My next task was to call a host of senior officers who superseded my rank in the pecking order of the Ministry of Forests and the Department of National Parks and Wildlife Conservation. Most of them were also members of the Royal Palace Wildlife Committee. Like most civil servants, they wanted to be kept in the know, particularly on matters sanctioned by Prince Gyanendra. They also hated getting second-hand information, which caused them to lose face among their peers. It was my duty and in my interest to keep them happy and well informed. I needed them on my side, particularly if things went wrong, which is not uncommon when dealing with wild animals.

My last action for the evening was to book a seat on the Royal Nepal Airlines flight to Megauli in Chitwan. As it was off-hours, the airlines office was closed for the day. However, I was not worried. Like some other institutions in Nepal at the time, Royal Nepal Airlines also operated behind closed doors. Airline seats were always available if one knew the right person. Yet I was relieved when a friendly and familiar voice on the phone assured me, "Collect and pay for your tickets at the airport," after I explained the urgency to my friend who worked for the airlines.

"I will be there to make sure you board the aircraft," he said, adding, "Please save me a moustache of the man-eater." Obviously my friend was superstitious. A few Nepalese carried tigers' whiskers for good luck—particularly when gambling.

I was all set to return to Chitwan and capture a wild tiger but hopefully not a man-eating tiger. I prided myself that with a single phone call to Prince Gyanendra, I had gotten a license to kill or catch a man-eater at my discretion. I looked at my watch. Although I would be a bit late, I decided to join the American ambassador's dinner party. After all, I had journeyed all the way from Chitwan for this purpose.

Parties at the American ambassador's house were prized social events—a certification to be listed on Nepal's list of who's who. An invitation was second only to private parties at the royal palace. As I lived most of the time in the jungle, I enjoyed my visits to the city of Kathmandu. I also liked cruising through the cocktail-party circuit of the burgeoning Western community in Kathmandu, lending my ears to current events, rumors, and gossip. However, this evening I was deeply sunk in my thoughts about the man-eating tiger and was not very chatty at the ambassador's dinner party.

"Phillip," I explained as the ambassador's guests flowed out of the dining room to the lounge for coffee and after-dinner drinks, "you will have to excuse me if I sneak out early. I have a small crisis. I have to catch a plane for Chitwan early tomorrow morning." His eyes glowed with excitement as I explained that I had been summoned by the warden of Royal Chitwan National Park to deal with a man-eating tigress. "She is one of yours," I said, referring to the fact that the man-eater was one of the subjects of the U.S.-funded Smithsonian Tiger Ecology Project.

"How exciting," he exclaimed. "I want to join you and watch your operation from afar. I assure you I will not be in your way." I was in a quandary. "I can't take you with me," I blurted out rudely.

Phillip challenged me with a firm "Why?" "Because you are no ordinary human," I countered jokingly. "You are the American ambassador—the most powerful, the most prominent, and the most watched diplomat in the Kingdom of Nepal. Hundreds of prying eyes watch your movements. I need clearance from the Ministry of Foreign Affairs to invite you to join me in the jungle. I will be crucified if we have any accident. My mission does not concern any ordinary tiger but a man-eater. I can take no chances. I am sorry but not this time. Maybe next time."

"What if," he replied coolly, "I tag along on the same plane tomorrow on my own and go to Tiger Tops Jungle Lodge as a normal tourist, assuming I get a seat on the flight at the last minute? If you feel in any way that my presence will get you into trouble with the government, I will stay in Tiger Tops and join you later in your camp after your operation is over."

His suggestions were logical. I could not stop him from going to Tiger Tops. Furthermore, his predecessor has been to our camp and even participated in our operation to catch and radio-collar tigers. Our project was funded by the Smithsonian Institution, a U.S. entity, and we were obliged to give the American ambassador unhindered access to visit our camp and observe our field operations. It would also be a good public relation exercise for us to keep the American ambassador well informed and involved with our field operation. A few good words from him to the Smithsonian Institution in Washington could help keep those funds flowing to continue our research. Phillip was also a decent and humble person. He had traveled through remote parts of Nepal—living, eating, and sleeping in the rough. He was more interested in the people and culture of Nepal than diplomatic niceties at cocktail parties in the capital city of Kathmandu.

"What the heck," I agreed. "Okay, come along. But I did not invite you. And I never knew you were going to be on the same plane on a private visit to Tiger Tops. Once in Chitwan we can do whatever we like. With no electricity and no telephone, the hot and humid jungles of Chitwan are more isolated from Kathmandu than Chicago. If there is an accident, or if I am questioned, I will lie through my teeth and swear that you forced us to let you join our party."

I did not tell Phillip that when I got home, I thought it would be prudent to protect myself from any unforeseen bureaucratic pestering from the Ministry of Foreign Affairs, which often looked for a crisis even when there was none. My strategy in these situations was "Don't ask—but inform." I called Narendra Raj Pandey, a high-powered aide to the King of Nepal and liaison with the Ministry of Foreign Affairs.

Pandey, a graduate of Claremont College in California, was a practical and pragmatic man. He also did not like to beat around the bush. "Use your own judgment," he advised. "The American ambassador is no fool. He can take care of himself without interfering with your works. I know that you took his predecessor, Ambassador Doug Heck, to one of your tiger-catching and radio-collaring operations. Why not him? Nevertheless, if questioned, I will inform the Foreign Ministry that you had reported to me." Clearly he seemed to have no qualms about Phillip Trimble joining me in Chitwan.

Early next morning, Phillip met me at the crowded and chaotic domestic terminal in Kathmandu's Tribhuvan International Airport. Fortunately the flight to Megauli was on time. The British management of Tiger Tops Jungle Lodge had curried favor with virtually all the Royal Nepal Airline staff, from top management to the porters that loaded the designer bags of their rich clients. Occasional complimentary invitations to the airline's top brass to one of Asia's premier jungle lodges and gifts of Scotch whisky to the lower echelons ensured that their flights took off and landed on time, a rarity for this Nepalese airline, which had a monopoly on all internal flights. This flight, also known as the Tiger Tops flight, catered exclusively to wealthy tourists who could afford a stay at one of the most expensive wildlife resorts in South Asia. I was the only Nepali on the flight.

The plane shot off the runway and vaulted upward to the clear blue sky. It circled the broad green valley of Kathmandu and headed southwest. The tourists on the plane gazed out the windows, muttering a cocktail of several Western languages. Taking out their cameras, they rushed to catch a view of the dazzling snowcapped mountains of the mighty Himalayas that border Nepal in the north. Though I had taken this flight many times, the beauty of my motherland never ceased to mesmerize me. It also forced me to ponder the harsh realities on the ground 12,000 feet below. My country—a land of exceptional natural beauty—is also a land of harsh and cruel reality to its denizens.

"God gave us a beautiful country," I muttered. "But we Nepalese screwed it up." Phillip was too busy enjoying the view. He either did not hear me or chose to ignore me. Yet I was right. The social and economic disparity fueled by poverty and population growth often rattled me. Nepal ranked as one of the world's poorest countries. Infant mortality and illiteracy were among the highest on Earth; life span and gross national income were among the lowest. Fate of birth had cheated more than three-quarters of my unfortunate fellow citizens. Preoccupied with their search for food and fuel, they lived hand to mouth. Food hunger and wood hunger were rampant in Nepal—food to fuel their bodies and wood to fuel their hearths and cook their food.

"Your effort to save tigers in Nepal is like farting against the monsoon thunder," said a friend of mine from the GTZ, Germany's equivalent of the U.S. Agency for International Development (USAID), who never minced his words. "Focus on saving humans and not bloody tigers and rhinos." It was not the first time that the futility of my endeavors to save wildlife in an economically impoverished country like Nepal was bluntly pointed out. Nevertheless, my German friend's remark often made me question my choice and love for my profession. How could I think about saving wild mammals in a country that was sinking in poverty and population growth?

While I was deep in thought, the plane turned south to rise above the rugged river valleys of midland Nepal with its picturesque but poverty-stricken villages crowning the hilltops. Soon the plane lost altitude to fly over the flatlands of the Terai. The rolling sal and riverine forests were sprinkled over stretches of grassland. Braided with fertile farmlands, a few rivers and streams glowed in the morning sun. We were flying over the land of the tiger. The ground below was home to an estimated hundred of the biggest, most ferocious, and most beautiful of all the world's wild cats. One of them was a tigress that I intended to punish for developing the habit of eating humans.

The plane dipped as it flew over the Narayani, a river that demarcated the western boundary of Royal Chitwan National Park. The pilot throttled the engine and turned east. The plane bumped up and down as it finally screeched over the dusty runway of the Megauli airstrip. Starry-eyed tourists applauded spontaneously as the plane taxied over the dirt runway. I was not sure if the applause was a sign of relief from fear of flying over rugged terrain or a display of joy for reaching their destination for a once-in-a-lifetime adventure in the subtropical jungles of the sequestered Himalayan Kingdom of Nepal. The aircraft jerked over the uneven surface of the runway and came to a halt next to a mud-and-thatch shed—the airport terminal.

A dozen elephants strode toward the aircraft. Their drivers were elegantly perched on the neck of the elephants—all of them smartly dressed in green khaki uniform. Similarly dressed *pachuwas* stood elegantly on the elephant's rump. (A *pachuwa* is a back rider whose job is to spot game.) They were holding tightly to a rope that stemmed from the howdah—a wooden pillion specially designed to carry tourists. The elephants lined up in a single row near the aircraft as the tourists disembarked the airplane. Four open-topped Land Rovers parked behind the elephants. The sight of elephants stirred the tourists. The air was filled with their exclamations and the sound of clicking cameras. I was not surprised by the curiosity of Western tourists. After all, Megauli airport is the only airport in the world where passengers are directly transferred from an aircraft to the back of an elephant.

"Welcome to Tiger Tops," greeted a European redhead with a big smile on her young, sun-tanned face. I knew her by her nickname: "Major Major." A cynical journalist had given her the name for her flair for military-like precision, particularly when ordering the elephant drivers and other Nepalese staff of Tiger Tops. Apparently the woman reminded him of a character in the novel *Catch-22* by Joseph Heller. Heller's character exemplified the absurdities of command and control in any hierarchical bureaucracy.

Tiger Tops' Major Major was a lanky Englishwoman in her late twenties. She was dressed smartly in khaki shirt and shorts similar to those of the elephant drivers. Efficiently she herded the tourists to the mud-and-thatch airport terminal. A few raggedly dressed village urchins milled around the tourists, staring at them with curious eyes. A *gainey*—a traditional village or street singer—was playing his *sarangi* and singing a melody. (The *sarangi* is a traditional string instrument often called the "Nepalese violin.") His lyrics portrayed the prime minister of Nepal as the biggest crook in the kingdom. The tune was soft and soothing but satiric in meaning. It accused the prime minister of deforesting the Nepalese Terai and selling the timber to Indian lumber smugglers.

The gaineys are a sect of Nepal's Hindu hierarchy. They are poor, and their standing ranks among the lowest in the Nepalese caste system. But they had the right of free speech as long as it was in musical form. Traditionally the gaineys were the political pulse of the society. The public and the rulers of Nepal relied on the gaineys as their ears and eyes to expose the social and political shortcomings. The gaineys also spread prevalent rumors and gossip in the community through their songs.

"Ladies and gentlemen," barked Major Major in a commanding tone, "may I have your attention please. You have two ways to go to the lodge: by Land Rover or by elephant. Once you have settled down at the lodge, we will brief you about your program." Her upper-class accent was flawless.

It was just over forty-five minutes since we had left Kathmandu. I scanned the airport looking for Ram, our esteemed national park warden, who was supposed to pick us up at the airport. However, I was not surprised that he was late. It took him longer to drive the fifteen-mile journey from park headquarters in Kasra than for me to fly from Kathmandu. In the jungle you are either early or late—never on time.

I watched Major Major serve beverages to her clients. Then she calmly herded them into two groups. One rode the elephants. The others hopped into the Land Rovers on their way to Tiger Tops Jungle Lodge. Once the tourists took their chosen rides, Major Major waved them off and melted into the background. The tourists would cross two rivers, patches of grasslands, and riverine forests before they reached their destination. Those on elephants would meander through the jungle looking for rhinos and other wildlife and birds. They would have to be extremely lucky to see a tiger at that time of day.

"Managing tourists is like managing livestock," I muttered to Philip. "Like cattle and sheep, you have to herd them, feed them, water them, shelter them for the night, move them to the next grazing ground, and lastly clean up their shit and wait for the next herd to move in." To me, the way Tiger Tops processed tourists reminded me of sheep and cattle herders, and Major Major was their shepherd.

As the American ambassador and I were watching the tourists, Ram Prit's grayish Toyota truck roared toward us, leaving a trail of dust. It stopped in front of the airport shed, where we were sitting on a wooden bench. Ram greeted us with a "Nameste," a big smile on his handsome face.

"Phillip, please take the front seat next to the driver," I suggested to the American ambassador after a brief introduction. "I will share the back with Ram. I need to talk with him and get a grip on the situation. I apologize, as we will be conversing in Nepali." Ram was more comfortable talking in Nepali, even though he was also conversant in English. We piled into his Toyota.

"There were more than one hundred angry villagers gathered in Kasra," Ram began as we drove south to the Rapti River. "I have persuaded them to return to their villages. But I promised that we would get rid of the man-eater by sunset tomorrow, at the latest."

I listened to him and asked, "Did the tiger take a buffalo bait?"

"No," replied Ram, "but that is unnecessary. We can locate the tiger from its radio-collar signals. Prem is waiting by the roadside along the Bhimle–Sukhibar road. We are fully prepared to shoot the tiger." I was glad to hear his words, but I was not yet certain whether I should destroy the tiger or try to capture it live. I decided to probe further. "Shoot the tiger?" I questioned, raising my eyebrows. "I have no rifle, nor can I shoot."

"The army has rifles," he snapped back giving me a dirty look. "They should know how to shoot. All they need is orders. I am sure you are equipped with that." The Royal Nepalese Army had a contingent that was assigned in Chitwan to combat poaching.

"Too much paperwork," I uttered casually. "They probably need clearance from their headquarters in Kathmandu. God only knows how long that will take. Furthermore, I hate to see a tiger gun downed by a bullet. Thus, I did not pursue this option in Kathmandu."

"Sir," said Ram irritably, "yesterday over the phone, I pleaded that you return to Chitwan with a sanction to kill the tiger. I thought you realized the gravity of the situation and came here fully equipped."

I knew Ram was right. But I wanted to keep my options open and see how far I could push him. "I did," I said mildly, "but we do not need a bullet to kill a tiger. Drugs are better. We can certainly use our dart gun to overdose the man-eater. That would be the least-painful way. Furthermore, we would not have to deal with a wounded man-eater if the bullet does not kill the beast instantly. Using drugs is a much safer bet."

Ram stared at me quizzically. He seemed to be confused. He did not seem to know where I was going with my argument. "Ram," I added, "M99, the drug we use for rhinos, is not safe for most other animals, including tigers. Let us use it. If at any time you feel that the tiger will survive the drug, you can stone or ax the tiger or have it trampled to death by elephants."

Ram glared at me. He thought I was joking and did not like it. "You are the boss," he replied sarcastically. "My task is to find the tiger. You decide how to kill the man-eater. After all, it is one of your radio-collared tigers. The villagers will not care how you kill the man-eater as long as they see the tiger dead. Neither do I. I am happy as long as the job gets done today."

We crossed the Rapti and Reu Rivers and reached Tiger Tops. There we collected Chuck and his team of tiger trackers. We tracked back south to the Bhimle guard post and turned sharply to the east. Prem and his team were waiting for us. He was standing on the top of an Isuzu truck, flanked by fifteen elephants and two other trucks. Two elephants carried a mountain of white vhit cloth that we use to corral tigers. Another elephant carried a black box that contained all our drugs and capture equipment.

Badai, our chief elephant driver, was perched on his elephant's back. He was holding a dart gun that was casually balanced on the pachyderm's neck. Gyan Bahadur, his deputy, was carrying the other dart gun on top of his elephant. Man Bahadur, one of our ace shikaris, was parked in a treetop with a second set of our radio receivers dangling from his neck. Both Prem and Man Bahadur were scanning the forest with their antennas. They did not have to speak. Their behavior indicated that they were monitoring radio signals from the collar on the man-eater's neck.

"Where is the tiger?" I asked Prem after briefly introducing him to the American ambassador. Chuck and his team needed no introductions. "Southeast from here," Prem replied. "We will be able to pinpoint the exact location when we get closer."

I got off the truck and picked up the radio receiver from Prem. Phillip followed me along with Ram and the others. I could hear the *beep-beep* at a distance. Slowly the sound became louder and louder, indicating that the tiger was moving closer to us. But we did not yet have visual contact.

"Jump into the truck now!" yelled Man Bahadur from his treetop. "I can see the tiger." We scrambled into the back of our Toyota truck as Man Bahadur pointed down the road behind us. Some fifteen yards away, standing by the roadside, a tiger was calmly watching us. The beautiful beast kept staring at us with a majestic posture; yet we knew it was a vicious killer. We were very edgy. Our nervous elephants rumbled their bellies. Our driver started the truck and moved forward. The tiger raised its head and quietly melted into the grassland. Our elephants moved up to the back end of our truck, and Prem mounted one of them.

"Do you think," I asked uneasily, "we can round it up today?" He looked at me as if I had asked a stupid question.

"Absolutely," he replied. "Since it is a man-eater, we will have to be more cautious using the radio signals. We will have to flush out the tiger from a distance quietly and steadily."

Two men I had never seen before were mounted on one of the elephants. "Who are they?" I signaled Ram quietly, pointing at them by protruding my lips and jerking my head. "They are the victim's relatives," answered Ram solemnly. "They are anxious to pick up any remains of the victim and perform the final death rite by cremating whatever little pieces of bones and hair they can find scattered on the ground."

I looked back at the victim's relatives. Their dresses were unkempt and ragged. Their faces were distressed. They gave me a heart-wrenching look that echoed the deep wound in their hearts. I could not make eye contact. At that instant I decided not to make any attempt to capture the man-eating tigress alive. She deserved to die for causing death, pain, and agony to innocent, impoverished villagers who were only trying to survive. "What about them?" I asked Prem with a heavy heart. "Will they agree that we try to round up the tiger before they can pick up the remains of their dead?"

"I have talked with them," answered Ram. "They have agreed to let us finish our operation. However, if we are not successful today, they will pick up the remains of the dead later. I have promised them elephants and safe transportation to their cremation site. I have also assured them that, one way or another, we will punish the killer." Prem looked around toward Chuck, Sakale, and Dhan and asked, "Where is the shooter? I thought you were bringing sharpshooters from the Royal Palace Hunting Department."

"We will use our equipment and drugs," I answered, "and we will overdose the tiger to death." I explained to Prem my plans to overdose the tiger in a quiet and humane way. He liked the idea. We huddled on the ground. I loaded the dart gun with five milliliters of M99—a drug prescribed only for rhinos. I did not know how the drug would work on tigers, but I was confident that the drug would totally immobilize the 350-pound beast, even if it did not euthanize the man-eater within a short time. The dose I was using was two and half times what I would use to sedate a two-thousand-pound rhino.

We mounted our elephants and traversed quietly through the tall grasslands. We rode southwards, with Prem and Man Bahadur on the lead elephants. The rest of us followed them in a single file. Prem stopped occasionally to scan his antennas and confer with Man Bahadur, who was also tracking the tiger with his own radio equipment. After nearly half an hour, Prem signaled us to halt. He scanned his antenna in the air, occasionally looking at Man Bahadur, who was doing the same a few yards to his left. Both antennas were pointed toward the same direction. I knew that they had triangulated and pinpointed the location of the man-eater. Thanks to our elephants, the tiger has moved away from us.

It was time for me to give some attention to my guest. "Phillip," I asked, "what do you want to do? Go back to the car? Climb up a tree? Or join Chuck and the shikaris on the drive and help flush out the man-eater to my tree? If you wish, you can go back and wait for us in the car. We can fetch you once I immobilize the tiger."

I explained to him how we normally catch tigers using vhit cloth and elephants. "If I may, I would like to be part of the drive," replied Phillip.

"Fine," I agreed. "You are a brave man. But hold tightly on the rope of the *lampat*. You also need to keep your ears and eyes open at all times, watching for overhanging branches." A *lampat* is a kind of jute bag packed with straw and covered with a cotton cushion and functions as a saddle on top of elephants.

I admired Phillip's courage, especially for a first-timer. The drive could be risky. I had seen tigers track back and attack elephants. At times elephants even bolted in panic. And there was always a risk of falling off an elephant or being smashed into low-hanging branches. I eyed Chuck and signaled him to stay close to the American ambassador.

Prem conferred with Man Bahadur in a hushed voice. He escorted me to a sturdy tree. I climbed high and from the treetop watched him group the elephants into two fleets, one on the left side of my tree and the other on the right. He led the elephant on the right side of my tree and started laying down the vhit cloth.

His assistant, Man Bahadur, copied him on the left side. Since we were dealing with a man-eater, Prem was extra cautious. Four elephants flanked two shikaris who were tying the vhit cloth on the ground as they moved south toward the Rapti River, setting up the V-shaped enclosure. The laying of the vhit cloth took longer than I had expected. But from my tree I could see the vhit forming a perfect funnel on the ground.

I watched the elephants line up across the wide mouth of the V-shaped funnel. Soon they moved forward, noisily flushing the grassland with a slow and steady pace. I did not have to wait long before I saw the man-eater zigzagging from one side of the vhit to the other, steadily creeping toward my tree. I cocked the dart gun. I followed the tigress's movement, sighting the beast with the barrel of my dart gun. Its behavior was no different from the other twenty-five tigers we had darted and radio-collared under the Smithsonian Nepal Tiger Ecology Project. I was sad that the tiger was a healthy female and I was going to take out a potential breeder from the gene pool of Chitwan's tigers.

As the tiger approached, myriad what-ifs crossed my mind. What if I missed my shot? What if the tiger jumped up the tree and snatched me? What if the tiger saw me? What if it attacked the line of elephants? What if it attacked the elephant carrying the American ambassador?

The tiger suddenly stopped momentarily on the edge of a small opening. Each piece of hair on my body stood upright. Acutely aware of my fear, I froze sixteen feet up in my tree. Composing myself, I took a deep breath and squeezed the trigger of my dart gun. *Phut*, the dart sounded as it hit the right shoulder of the man-eater. Despite my anxiety, my shot was perfect. The tiger thundered the grassland with a nerve-wrecking growl. I watched it jump about six feet high over the opening in the grassland and sprint into cover behind my tree. It was an awesome but scary sight. A short distance away, the elephants trumpeted in response to the tiger's growl. The elephants' call made me feel better. I felt that they were warning the tiger, saying, "Watch out. We are behind you." I was relieved, but I prayed to the deities of the jungle that the drug would work.

Soon the elephants reached my tree. Since the tigress wore a radio collar, she was not difficult to locate. We found her lying on her left shoulder, stretched flat in a patch of grassland. We gave the tiger another ten minutes before approaching, keeping in mind that she was a man-eater. We threw sticks at her. There was no flickering of the ears and no sign of breathing. Stretched flat across the ground, she appeared to be in a deep coma.

Prem and I dismounted from our elephants. I poked her belly with a long stick; the tiger did not react at all. Prem moved in the front and gently poked at her face; he too got no response. Unlike other tigers we had darted, there was no movement or sign of the animal breathing.

"She is dead," announced Prem in a jubilant tone. We examined the tiger thoroughly. She looked normal. There were no wounds on her body. Her teeth and powerful paws appeared in good condition. She did not seem to be handicapped in any way.

Inability to hunt their natural prey seems to be a key factor that drives large cats to prey on humans. Driven by hunger, they sometimes become man-eaters. I stared at the tigress's dead eyes and pondered how such a beautiful creature could be a man-killer. Sadness rushed through me. I had killed my first tiger. Deliberately. I pondered if it would have been better to catch it, cage it, and take it to the zoo in Kathmandu.

"Sir," I heard Prem call, forcing me back to reality. "Let's go to the kill site. It is very close." The kill site was in the middle of a big patch of thatch grass, similar to where the tigress had claimed her first victim. It was in the middle of the hog deer's prime habitat, one of the tiger's prime prey species. Except for the skull and a part of the victim's lower leg, the tigress had eaten almost all of the man.

An iron sickle glowed in the bright sun next to the victim's toes. A Nepali *topi*—a kind of cap—and some bloody rags of clothing were scattered all over the kill site. With a wrenching heart, I watched the two villagers collect the remains of their relative and put them in a jute sac. I did not ask them their names or the name of the victim. Neither did they talk with me. Talk was unnecessary and even untimely. I shared their pain as I pondered what I would do if our positions were reversed. It was also a moment when the stark and brutal economic and social disparities in my country jolted me. There was no way I could converse, even to express my heartfelt condolences to the two solemn relatives of the victim of a man-eater, which we had radio-collared and unceremoniously named Tiger 118.

We returned to the site where I had darted the man-eating tiger. The shikaris had taken the tiger to the roadside and loaded it on a truck. They were taking the body to the national park headquarters in Kasra. Ram dispatched a truck to carry the villagers to Kasra, where we would exhibit the tiger's carcass to the public as evidence. This was a gruesome thought to us conservationists. Yet it was essential for us to appease the angry villagers, whose support we needed to maintain the national park.

Preoccupied by the tiger hunt, I had ignored the American ambassador. Without any fuss or complaint, he had joined the shikaris and helped flush the tiger to my tree. "Good job," he said, congratulating me with a firm handshake. "I am very impressed with the professionalism of your staff and your prompt actions." Phillip was a good sport. He saw that I was content in doing my job as we returned to Kasra, the headquarters of Royal Chitwan National Park.

Later that afternoon, villagers from across the Rapti River streamed in and out of the park headquarters. Some touched the tiger with their hand. Some kicked it angrily with their feet. Some spit on its head. I was told that some even tried to urinate on it. In contrast, they thanked me and patted me on the back and treated me like a hero. I was relieved that I had done my duty and fulfilled Ram's promise to the villagers that we would punish the killer. Any guilt I felt for overdosing Tiger 118 slowly evaporated from my mind, at least for the moment.

The villagers left Kasra at nightfall. We had a small party at the park headquarters. Over bottles of beer and a good Nepali *dal-bhat* (rice-and-lentil soup) with goat-meat curry, we talked late into the night about the world of the tiger. As I wiggled into my sleeping bag, I could not forget the first tiger that I had killed. That sad memory and my vow not to harm but to protect tigers haunted me. This vow was easy to make but hard to keep. I was continually challenged by surprises throughout my career in conservation. One such challenge emerged unexpectedly while I was escorting a senior American official on a sightseeing tour in Chitwan National Park.

It is either feast or famine for tigers in the wild. *Masahiro Iijima*

A couple in the Madi Valley point out the pugmarks of a man-eating tiger that prowled around their home in the dark of night. *Masahiro Iijima*

Angry villagers mob the author and his colleagues in their jeep as they reach the edge of a village terrorized by a man-eating tiger. *Masahiro Iijima*

A radio collar is fixed on a sedated tiger to monitor and study its behavior in Nepal's Chitwan National Park. *Masahiro Iijima*

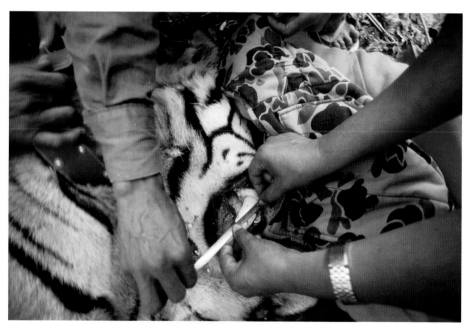

The canines and the jaws of a sedated tiger are examined for deformities before they are measured. *Masahiro Iijima*

The author cautiously measures the exact dosage of the drug to be loaded into a dart gun under the watchful eye of one of the members of his tiger-catching team. *Masahiro Iijima*

Nepal's Rana prime minister Juddha Shamsheer poses with his clan and two of the 433 tigers he shot between 1933 and 1940. *Masahiro Iijima/Kaiser Library*

In the bygone days before 1947, the rulers of Nepal often invited the viceroy and senior officials of British India for tiger hunts in Chitwan. This is a photo of one day's kill.
Masahiro Iijima/Kaiser Library

A family of tigers. The average litter size in Chitwan is two to three cubs per birth.
Masahiro Iijima

A tiger quenches its thirst after a hearty meal. Tigers are also excellent swimmers.
Masahiro Iijima

The face of the tiger. Markings on the tiger's forehead symbolize "wang" (or "king") to the Chinese people, thus earning the tiger the title "The King of the Jungle." *Masahiro Iijima*

Chitwan National Park's Megauli is the only airport in the world that transfers international travelers from an aircraft to the back of an elephant. *Lisa Choegyal/Tiger Tops*

Sedated tigers are measured and fitted with radio collars. *Chris Wemmer*

An elephant in Nepal is driven by two drivers. The main elephant driver sits on the neck and uses his feet to drive the elephant. A spotter stands on the back of the elephant to spot wildlife. *Dave Smith*

The author (standing center) with his crew and elephants in front of the Nepali Tiger Ecology Project camp. Prem Bahadur Rai, the veteran tiger tracker, stands on the far right wearing a white shirt. *Chris Wemmer*

8

DR. BRZEZINSKI'S TIGER

THE MORNING OF DECEMBER 31, 1984, WAS NO DIFFERENT FROM any wintry morning in Royal Chitwan National Park. The sun had emerged out of the thick fog to warm the damp and dewy riverine forests in the western sector of the park. The jungle was alive with a choir of birds flitting from tree to tree. Sixty miles north as the crow flies, the mighty Himalayas glittered in the midmorning light.

Near Dhakre Nala, a stream west of Tiger Tops Jungle Lodge, a man-eater was silently prowling for prey beneath the tranquil, clear-blue sky. The killer was Bange Bhale, a male resident tiger of the Tiger Tops jungle. Although it did not have a radio collar, it did have a calling card in the form of its pugmark. One of its toes was slightly out of shape and left a prominent bended imprint on the ground. Hence the name Bange Bhale, meaning "bent-foot male." Bange was a man-eating tiger with at least three known human kills, which meant that we were supposed to kill or capture it. It had dodged us for the past three months, often crossing the border into India.

That same morning, unaware that a killer tiger was lurking in the vicinity, Tiger Tops employee Khadga Bahadur, an elephant driver, was performing his daily tasks. His younger deputy was assisting him. The elephant caretakers were deep in the forest collecting fodder for the elephants. His assistant was up on a tree cutting leafy branches and dropping them to the ground, where Khadga was methodically bundling them. Khadga's young male elephant, Shamsheer Gaz, was quietly foraging only a few feet away, partially hidden in the tall grass. The delicate branches that Khadga was collecting would be the elephant's evening meal back at Tiger Tops' elephant stable.

A soft breeze carried their human voices across the jungle and lured the tiger. Using its highly sensitive powers of sight, hearing, and smell, the tiger cautiously crept toward them. At first, it did not see Khadga but spotted his assistant twelve feet up a tree. The tiger stopped and crouched inside a thick bush about twenty yards from the tree. While patiently waiting for the man to climb down the tree, the tiger spotted Khadga on the ground. It became alert and transformed its body into attack posture.

Raising its tail erect, the tiger charged at Khadga, who had bent down to pick up a tree branch. The tiger was targeting Khadga's neck but missed its mark. By lucky coincidence, Khadga stood erect just as the tiger charged him. This motion saved Khadga from instant death—the tiger was unable to break the man's cervical vertebrae on the spot. The tiger's strike also pushed Khadga against a tree, giving him enough support to fight back with his sharp sickle. But the tiger did not release its grip on the man's shoulder. During the tussle, the man and the beast rolled several feet on the ground.

Khadga continued to strike desperately at the beast with his sickle as the tiger dragged him into a patch of grassland. Suddenly the tiger released Khadga and melted into the thick grass. It is inexplicable why the tiger abandoned its kill. It could have been scared off by the shrieking of Khadga's assistant up in the tree, the sight and sound of Khadga's elephant, or both.

Khadga's assistant climbed down from the tree, placed his still conscious boss on top of the elephant, and rushed him back to the lodge. Khadga was extremely fortunate that his young elephant had not bolted at the sight of the tiger. He was also lucky that he reached Tiger Tops in time to catch their flight from Megauli to Kathmandu. Within three hours of the tiger attack, Khadga was in the intensive care unit in Shanta Bhawan, Nepal's best hospital. In a month's time, Khadga had recovered from the tiger attack. However, the tiger mauling left him with an unwelcome memento. His sight and hearing abilities were impaired on the left side, the area where the tiger's canines had punctured his face. Nevertheless, he returned to his job at Tiger Tops, where he worked for more than ten years and lived to tell the story of his close encounter with a wild tiger.

I was in Kathmandu on the day that the tiger attacked Khadga. Two days earlier I had been summoned by the Ministry of Foreign Affairs for a briefing on the visit of Dr. Zbigniew Kazimierz Brzezinski, the National Security Advisor of the United States under President Jimmy Carter. Mr. and Mrs. Brzezinski were visiting Nepal on the special invitation of King Birendra, who was encamped in Pokhara. My job was to escort the Brzezinskis to Tiger Tops Jungle Lodge for a tour of Royal Chitwan National Park before their meeting with the king in two days' time. It was normal practice in Nepal to allow the monarch's guests to relax for a few days at this five-star jungle resort before plunging them into officialdom. The ambience of Tiger Tops and Royal Chitwan National Park was a perfect venue for such relaxation.

Following my marching orders, I met Dr. Brzezinski at Kathmandu's Tribhuvan International Airport on December 31, 1984. My first impression was not inspiring. Dr. Brzezinski's attention was focused on a small transistor radio glued to his ears as he paced back and forth on the airport tarmac. Dr. Brzezinski's interest in his radio was a blessing in disguise. We had to wait a long time at the airport before our plane would be ready for takeoff to Chitwan. I did not want to go through the motions of explaining the causes for the delay to the king's guest. In those days in Nepal, Americans had a reputation for being impatient and often jittery when men and machines did not move on time, which was a regular occurrence in the Himalayan Kingdom of Nepal.

As bad weather started closing in over the airport, I knew I needed a backup plan. I walked up to Brinda Malla, joint secretary of the Ministry of Foreign Affairs, who was in charge of the Brzezinskis' visit. "Let's drive," I proposed. "With the weather closing in, I am sure the flight will be canceled." Sure enough, it was. Brinda was not keen on subjecting His Majesty's American guests to a grueling six-hour drive on a rough and winding mountain road to Chitwan. She believed that the ride would be too torturous for the Brzezinskis.

"What will you do with them in Kathmandu," I teased, "wear them out before their audience with Their Majesties the King and the Queen? I have no problem if you cancel his Chitwan trip. It is your call. But I have no orders to be a bloody tourist guide in Kathmandu. I am driving to Chitwan on my own today."

Brinda and I knew each other well and could converse candidly. "Since you are in charge of his visit to Chitwan," she growled, "why don't you ask Dr. and Mrs. Brzezinski yourself what they would like to do? Stay back in Kathmandu or drive to Chitwan?" With these words, she headed for the airport's VIP room. I knew she had gone to get a telephone and update her superiors in the Foreign Ministry—and cover her ass.

I walked over to Prabhakar Rana, a trustee of the King Mahendra Trust for Nature Conservation—my employer and a member of Dr and Mrs. Brzezinski's entourage. He agreed with my proposal to drive. Dr. Brzezinski and his wife concurred with our suggestion to make an overland trip to Chitwan. In fact, they seem pleased that we would be traveling by road rather than by air. Despite my description of the bad condition of the road, they believed this would allow them to see the real Nepal better— mountains, river valleys, jungle farms. Above all, they would see how people in the rural areas lived. Clearly the Brzezinskis were not softies but adventurous Americans. I liked them instantly.

Brinda was enthused by their decision. I had a feeling that she had clearance from the Royal Palace to take them to Chitwan by any means, as originally scheduled. She promptly organized two vehicles. She also made arrangements to send messages about our travel plans through the Royal Nepal Army wireless system to Chitwan, including to the park superintendent.

Brinda rode with the Brzezinskis in one vehicle. Prabhakar; his wife, Amar; and I rode in the other. In those days we did not have to worry about security for American dignitaries in Nepal, so our entourage did not include any gun-toting security officers.

We drove through the heart of Nepal, meandering through scenic river valleys and rural landscapes. Prabhakar, an anglophile who had spent a long time in Great Britain, was a treasure trove of English jokes. He kept me amused with his Winston Churchill jokes, adopting an English accent most of the way to Chitwan. We passed the Megauli airport and reached the *ghat,* the crossing point of the Rapti River. It was about 8:00 p.m., pitch dark and chilly. A group of Botes, fishermen who ferried tourists across the river, were waiting anxiously for us. They were huddled around a small fire of burning logs. Their duty that evening was to help us ford the river and ensure that our vehicles did not get stuck in either the Rapti or Reu River on our way to Tiger Tops Jungle Lodge.

"We are grateful you arrived as expected," said one guide with a dark face and deeply sunken eyes. "It has been a nightmare waiting for you in the dark with a man-eating tiger on the prowl." His voice soft and serious, he recounted the mauling of Khadga Bahadur that had occurred that day by the tiger that was now lurking around Tiger Tops.

When we pulled into Tiger Tops, I was mobbed by a terrified and weary Tiger Tops staff, led by my friend Ram Prit Yadav. Ram repeated the story of Khadga's near-death encounter.

"It's glamorous of you to come down here to sip expensive Scotch and hobnob with American statesmen," Ram grumbled accusingly, "but what about the people who have to work in the jungle with a hungry, man-eating tiger on the prowl?" He waved his hands toward a group of solemn-faced Tiger Tops' staff and added, "These people must work alone in the jungle in the dark.

Likewise, the Botes that guided you here have to walk home and often sleep in open sheds on the banks of the river." He was clearly angry and concerned about his Tiger Tops colleagues, with whom he had worked for more than a decade.

Ram was then and remains to this day a wildlife conservationist, dedicated to the preservation of animals and their habitat, but his work was not easy. He lived and dealt with a range of people problems—tourists, fishermen, staff of tourist lodges like Tiger Tops, and above all, the sea of poverty-stricken humanity that circled Chitwan National Park. He was no different from any other national park warden in the world when it came to ensuring the safety of humans from wild animals. Humans came first. Killing or mauling of humans by tigers in areas under his command infuriated him. Furthermore, that evening his tone indicated that he had imbibed a drink or two.

I did not want to provoke him further. "Is it one of our radio-collared tigers?" I probed. Instead of responding, Ram signaled Dhan Bahadur and Sakale Gurung—Tiger Tops' seasoned tiger trackers—to speak out.

"Pugmarks confirm that the tiger is Bange Bhale," Dhan asserted. We followed its pugmarks today and believe we know its location." My good friend Chuck McDougal, Dhan and Sakale's boss, had first sighted the tiger in 1982 when it was about four years old. Since then the trio had been monitoring its movements.

Bange Bhale became the dominant resident tiger of Dhakre Nala, an area west of Tiger Tops, for two years from 1982 to 1984. In 1984 the tiger got into a fight with a new male intruder that was named Lucky Bhale. Bange was severely wounded but survived this fight with only a slight limp. Nevertheless, Lucky took over his territory and Bange's two mates that roamed in the area. Bange was marginalized and became a man-eater.

His first kill was a villager who was cutting grass inside the national park southwest of Tiger Tops. His second kill was a man collecting firewood in a small patch of forest on the western bank of the Narayani River. He ate them both. After the kills, the tiger disappeared for a few weeks. We had presumed that Bange Bhale had crossed the border into India and gone into the Valmiki Forests, where he could prey on more humans. But he seemed to have returned home to Nepal with the daring and cunning of a seasoned man-eater.

His third kill was a Bote. After a hard day's work, the fisherman was sleeping in a small hamlet on the bank of the Narayani River. Under the cover of night, Bange broke into his mud-and-thatch hut and killed the fisherman by snapping his neck with one strike. Then he quietly carted his quarry deep into the forest and feasted on the man's body before disappearing again. Since the tiger did not have a radio collar, we were unable to track him unless we chanced upon his unique pugmark. We assumed he had gone back to India.

I am not certain why Bange sneaked into the heart of his old territory near Tiger Tops and attacked an elephant driver on December 31, 1984—New Year's Eve. I presume that he was either looking for his two females or was prowling for an easy kill among the elephant drivers and staff of Tiger Tops, who often walked alone in the heart of the jungle doing their daily chores. Except for his slight limp, Bange was a young, healthy male. I cannot be sure what caused him to become a man-eater, but I think his losing fight with Lucky Bhale and the loss of his territory were contributing factors.

The thought of catching Bange and attaching a radio collar on the tiger crossed my mind a few times over the years. But now it was pointless—we had to kill or remove the tiger from the national park.

"We may be able to bait the tiger and catch it or even kill it," added Sakale. Ram shifted his glance from Dhan and Sakale and gave me a penetrating look. "We are fully prepared to catch Bange Bhale," he said firmly. "All your staff from the Nepal Tiger Ecology

Project is here. They are fully equipped with a dart gun, drugs, and all your tiger-capture paraphernalia. We even have a sturdy sal-timber cage to imprison the man-eater if you wish only to capture the beast and decide what to do with it later. But we must act now."

The Brzezinskis and members of his entourage were watching us from a distance, with a Tiger Tops staff member interpreting our conversation. Except for nodding their heads and stealing a few curious glances at us, they remained silent.

"Ram," I responded softly, "my duty for the next two days is to take care of the king's guest. Can we wait a day or two before we go after the tiger?"

"No," he blurted. "Saving our own people should be your priority. Bange has already eaten three people in the last three months, and we have not been able to catch or kill him. We do not know how many more he will kill. We believe he is around here, and we must not miss this opportunity. At the least let's set bait around here and see how it goes."

I was among the few who were sanctioned by the Royal Palace to capture man-eating tigers. Yet I was in a quandary. I was torn between my official duty of guiding the Brzezinskis on their holiday and Ram's immediate concerns that we first hunt the man-eating tiger. I quickly realized that Ram was right. It was not only absurd but also inhumane and cowardly to debate appropriate duties at a time when an elusive killer was running amok in our own backyard. I realized that I must take the action Ram had insisted upon and that we must, at the very least, try to bring the man-eater Bange Bhale to justice—dead or alive.

It is not difficult to understand why my friend Ram and our Nepalese shikaris were anxious to see the man-eater punished. However, they were also committed to saving tigers. Their jobs depended on the existence of tigers, rhinos, and other endangered species; but they also knew that the harsh realities in Chitwan dictated that some individual tigers must be killed for the good of the species. The management of Tiger Tops also shared this view. They too were keen to see Bange Bhale punished, particularly as he had recently attacked one of their own elephant drivers without provocation.

After observing our discussion from a distance, Jim Edwards, managing director of Tiger Tops, quietly approached me. "We are fully behind you," he said in a soft and encouraging voice. "Any help you need—just ask. We will mobilize all our elephants and staff to help you."

I had known Jim since 1964 when he came to Nepal to work for U.S. Agency for International Development (USAID). He was a tall, handsome, and flamboyant Briton well known for hosting lavish cocktail parties both in his quaint bungalow in the city of Kathmandu and in the jungles of Chitwan. He was in Chitwan that evening with a fleet of special guests who had converged on Tiger Tops to celebrate the New Year in the heart of tiger and rhino country.

I thanked Jim. Indeed, I needed his elephants, his staff, and above all, his buffalo to use as tiger bait. I explained my plans to him. The shikaris had examined pugmarks earlier in that day of the incidence. Flanked by four elephants, they had surveyed the kill site and found a trail of Bange Bhale's pawmarks leading into the forests all the way from the banks of the Narayani River. They reckoned that the tiger was in a patch of forest not far from where it had attacked Khadga. That night, carrying kerosene lamps on elephant back, we hastily tethered a dozen live buffalo to a few selected trees along the tiger's trail in the area. Normally this procedure would have to be done before sunset, but it was too late for that. I doubted that Bange Bhale would take any of the baits this late at night, even if he were in the area. In fact, as the tiger was now a man-eater, I believed that it had crossed the Narayani River to prowl near the densely populated villages in the district of Nawalpur.

It was nearing midnight when we returned to the lodge. The midnight gong of the New Year was approaching, and a party was in full swing in the main dining hall of Tiger Tops. It was dominated by a group of Western tourists of mixed nationalities and genders who worked in Saudi Arabia and were on holiday in Nepal. Some of them donned dresses to imitate tigers and rhinos. Drinks were tall, stiff, and flowed freely. Dresses were expensive, short, and cut low. The music enticed a few couples to dance on the cement floor. Everyone was having a good time.

Unlike the tourists, I still had serious matters to handle. I grabbed a beer from the bar and approached Brinda Malla, my friend from the Ministry of Foreign Affairs. I explained the situation to her in Nepali and asked to be excused from the Brzezinski program the following morning. She agreed that we all would look like cold-hearted bureaucratic pencil-pushers if we did not attempt to resolve the problem of the man-eating tiger. "Do what you have to do," she said "but you must let the Brzezinskis know."

The Brzezinskis were only a few feet away. I told them the story, seeking their consent to be excused from their entourage. "Can we join you and watch your operations from a distance?" asked Dr. Brzezinski, his eyes shining with excitement.

I did not know how to respond to his request. I thought that for a first-time visitor to Chitwan, this American certainly had guts. But I did not want to take responsibility for his safety by saying yes. However, like so many of my fellow Nepalese, I often suffered from my inability to say no, particularly to foreigners.

Furthermore, Dr. Brzezinski was the guest of the king, and I did not want to take any chances with the king's guests. I stared at Brinda for a moment and said softly in Nepali, "Bail me out of this. Tell him no."

Brinda surprised me. For a city slicker, she proved to be gutsier than I was. "That is your problem," she said. She paused and added, "But I think it would be a good idea. They may find it more exciting than the usual routine of Tiger Tops. I would also like to join in."

Brinda probably had been on a few tiger shoots in her past. Her father was a famous doctor who rubbed shoulders with royalty. She was also married to a doctor who came from an ancient Nepalese noble family. Yet I was still unsure. I stared at my friend Prabhakar Rana and gestured a plea to come to my defense.

I should not have been surprised when he ignored me and agreed with Brinda. When he was barely ten years old, Prabhakar had shot his first tiger with his great-grandfather Juddha, then the prime minister of Nepal. He knew that the elephants of Tiger Tops were well trained and safe. He and his wife, Amar, also wanted to be a part of the operation. He did not see any danger if one was high up in a tree or at a distance on the back of well-trained elephant.

I thought all of them had had too much to drink and that the alcohol had raised their courage. Obviously I was the only one in the Brzezinski entourage who wasn't a big game hunter. I also learned not to underestimate the quest for thrill and adventure of the denizens of Kathmandu, who I often used to brush off as city slickers. Yet I knew that it would not be Brinda or Prabhakar who would have to face the wrath from the king's palace if we had an accident during our tiger-capture operation. Furthermore, I was dealing not with a normal tiger but a sly man-eater.

"We will see," I responded. "First the tiger has to take the bait, and that we will know only early tomorrow morning when we go and check the sites." After a late-night New Year Eve's party, I doubted if any of them would be up early in the morning. With luck, I would have done my job before they were out of bed—if the tiger took the bait. I hung around the party for some time, sharing drinks with Ram and the shikaris and revisiting our plans to capture Bange Bhale. The dining hall erupted with "Happy New Year" as the clock struck the midnight hour. I extended my best wishes to my guests and quietly sneaked out of the party that was still going full swing. In the past I would have been there until the wee hours of the morning.

Next morning, just after the crack of dawn, I joined Ram and the shikaris to rush to the bait sites on the back of two elephants. I had doubts if the tiger would have taken any of the baits that were laid out late the previous night. But to Ram's delight, I was in for a surprise. The tiger had killed one of the buffalo, proving that he had not crossed the Narayani River to lurk near the villages of Nawalpur. The kill site was located along a jeep track, indicating that the tiger was using the trail used by humans. It had snapped the buffalo's tether and dragged its kill a few yards into cover.

With the help of the shikaris, and with two male tuskers protecting us, we surveyed the area and determined the orientation of Bange Bhale by the drag mark the tiger had made as it pulled its kill from the open roadside into the thick forests. All signs indicated that the man-eater was positioned in an ideal location for our operation. An open, motorable forest road was on the east side. The west was demarcated by a small rivulet, a short distance for the tiger to quench its thirst after its meal. The north and south were bounded by thick jungle that provided ample cover for the tiger to hide and for us to organize our capture operation.

I returned to Tiger Tops to load the dart gun with anesthetic drugs and mobilize all Tiger Tops' dozen elephants before they were dispatched to take their clients on a game-viewing jungle safari. I was surprised to see the Brzezinskis up and ready in the yard in front of the dining hall. So were Prabhakar and his wife, Amar; Brinda; Jim Edwards; and Lisa Van Gruissen—Tiger Tops' director of public relations. The last two had also thought ahead. They had already mobilized all their elephants, anticipating that I might need them in a hurry. How on Earth could everyone except me have foreseen that Bange Bhale would be lured by our late-night bait?

The first day of 1985 seemed to be a lucky day for me. But I still had to catch the man-eater. We also had two minor problems that morning: First, in their rush, Ram and the shikaris had forgotten to bring a second dart gun, which was in our store in Saurah, some twenty-four miles and a two-hour trip east of Tiger Tops. As a backup, I often took a second dart gun during my field operations, particularly when catching badly behaving tigers. Our dart gun fired only one dart at a time. Loading and reloading drugs into the dart is also a cumbersome and slow process in the field. I was pondering whether some kind of a safety backup was needed, when Jim Edwards, managing director of Tiger Tops, came up with a suggestion. "We have a shotgun in the Lodge," he said. "I will be glad to provide you with a backup." I had never carried a gun in any of my field operations. I felt safe in the jungle without a gun. Plus they're prone to accidents. Furthermore, a shotgun may not be powerful enough to kill a tiger. Wounding a tiger can create a dangerous situation. Yet, given the circumstances, I took up Jim's courageous offer. I had no other choice.

"Jim," I proposed, "you stay up in a tree, a few yards behind me with the shotgun. But make sure you do not shoot the tiger or me. Or for that matter, the king's guests or your elephants." Jim burst into laughter. But, as an old hunter, he knew that I wanted him to fire into the air to scare the tiger from mauling any people or elephants.

The second problem was mostly psychological. For reasons that I cannot explain, I had had an uncomfortable feeling that morning. I do not know if it was due to the fact that Bange Bhale had attempted to eat Khadga Bahadur in broad daylight—this beast seemed fearless of humans. Or because everything was going so perfectly—too perfectly. Perhaps, being superstitious, I was uneasy about not having performed the worship of Ban Devi—the goddess of the forest—a ritual that preceded all our capture operations. With a cunning man-eating tiger lurking nearby, time was too precious to prepare a goat, a red rooster, and two pigeons for sacrifices to appease the goddess, or to fetch our shaman from camp, twenty-four miles away in Saurah Village.

We decided to flush the tiger by beating the jungle south to north. Using elephants, we laid the vhit cloth to form our standard funnel configuration, with the tiger roughly positioned in the center of the V. More than a dozen elephants dispersed across the wide end of the funnel. Armed with a loaded dart gun, I stepped up from my elephant into a tree at the narrow end of the V. Armed with his double-barreled shotgun, Jim Edwards took his position up in a tree some five yards behind me. Atop their elephants, the men and women at the other end of the funnel advanced, shouting "haat" and thrashing the vegetation to flush the tiger toward me.

I soon saw Bange Bhale and watched as he cautiously zig-zagged toward me. He stood alert to look back and scan the row of noisy elephants. No matter how many times I had darted tigers, the effect on me was the same. I was particularly frightened and nervous this time. I had an American dignitary chasing a tiger toward me. And that tiger was a violent, cunning man-eater not easily intimidated by humans.

The tiger stopped about thirty feet from my tree. I must have moved or rustled the branches of my tree. The man-eater raised its head and looked at me. Since it did not roar to challenge me, I was not sure if the tiger had spotted me high in the tree. But to my horror, I saw the tiger turn back and stride toward the row of elephants. It was heading directly toward Dr. and Mrs. Brzezinski's elephants.

Enclosed by the vhit cloth, the tiger would have to charge the elephants to break out of the funnel. Anything could happen in this kind of situation. The tiger could attack the elephants head-on or pull a passenger off an elephant's back. The elephants could bolt in terror and smash their passengers into low-hanging tree branches. My blood boiled with fear. I was in panic as I thought that the king's American guests and my dear Nepali friends would soon be facing a cornered tiger. It was okay to take risks when it was just I, but it was utter stupidity on my part to have invited inexperienced guests on a hastily planned mission.

Suddenly the jungle was filled with a loud huffing and puffing sound. Two huge rhinos emerged from a patch of tall grassland. These two-ton pachyderms were about twenty feet away from the tiger inside the ring of the vhit cloth. The rhinos and the tiger had an eye-to-eye encounter. Then the tiger turned back and started walking steadily toward my tree.

I thanked the rhinos from the bottom of my heart. They had rescued the situation. Moments like these strengthened my belief that rhinos are magical and supernatural animals. The tiger stopped in an opening directly under my tree. It sniffed the ground and slowly raised its head as if trying to catch me in its line of sight. Although I was shaking with fear, I thought, *It is now or never,* and fired the dart gun. The tiger made one loud call and raced past me to melt into thick cover behind my tree. All the apprehensions that I had harbored since the morning evaporated. My mind and my body suddenly felt light. However, the time for elation was a long way off. The drug had to work, and we still had to cage the man-eater.

My next actions were routine—the step-by-step tasks we did with military precision in any of our tiger-capture operations. The first task was to signal the elephants to stop moving and let the tiger settle down in the quiet. We also had to cut the two rhinos off from the pathway of the tiger. That task was not difficult. The well-trained elephant drivers of Tiger Tops knew that with a show of force, the rhinos would shy away from their elephants. They lined up their elephants on one side of the funnel, and three of them hurried to be positioned between my tree and the rhinos. Then they slowly moved forward, forcing the rhinos to turn around and stride toward the big, open end of the vhit funnel.

After ten minutes I descended onto the back of an elephant to look for Bange Bhale. We found him fast asleep only thirty yards behind my tree. The tiger had a prominent scar across its face, indicating that Khadga Bahadur's sickle had hit its mark. I did not see any other wounds. The teeth were also in good condition. We weighed the tiger and found it was about 450 pounds.

It was time for us to load the tiger into the cage. At these juncture, we were comfortable with our task. Except for the occasional jerking of head or limbs, we never had a tiger wake up in the middle of our operation. The drug would keep the tiger sedated for at least two and a half hour. Even after waking up, the tiger would still be wobbly and too weak to attack.

My colleagues and I got our usual commendations from our American guests for the success of our operations. Since the Brzezinskis were among the highest-ranking Americans ever to visit Nepal, everyone wanted to have their picture taken with them and the tiger. I was no exception.

After the photo session was over, we hauled the tiger inside the cage that Ram had carted all the way from park headquarters. We then loaded the caged tiger on one of Tiger Tops' Land Rovers and headed back to the lodge.

We were welcomed at Tiger Tops Jungle Lodge by a group of excited tourists. They did not seem to be upset that we had taken their elephants and cheated them of their morning ride to watch wild rhinos and other big game in the grasslands. We let them peek though the slats of the wooden cage to quench their curiosity. Once the novelty died, we covered the cage with a dark cloth and stored it in a garage.

I had no clue about what to do next. How long should I keep the tiger in the cage? What would a wild tiger do once the drug wore off in the next three hours? With its sharp teeth, could it chew its way out of the wooden cage?

To get answers to my questions, I did what any good Nepalese bureaucrat does in that situation: I reported to headquarters in Kathmandu to ask for instructions. I wrote a lengthy message and asked Ram to send it using the Nepalese Army radio. My message described the situation and specifically asked permission to bring the tiger to Kathmandu to hand it over to the zoo.

Since I did not know how long I would have to wait for a response, I also needed a backup plan. That plan was to keep the tiger sedated by darting it inside its cage every four to five hours. This was a risky option—the tiger could die from an overdose. I bore a small hole on the top of the cage to fit the nozzle of my dart gun. I would later use this hole to shoot drug-loaded syringes to keep the tiger tranquilized.

While the tiger slept peacefully inside the cage under the influence of the drugs, I spent the rest of the day performing my duty as guide to the Brzezinskis. We had a great time watching my favorite animal, the rhino, from the back of our elephants. We also did some birding and watched other game.

I did not get any response from Kathmandu. I thought my orders might come in the form of an air-document on the Tiger Tops flight the next morning. There was nothing of the kind. All I got was a large envelope from my wife, Sushma, containing two of the largest circulating newspapers: the *Gorkhapatra*, a Nepali daily, and its sister publication, *Rising Nepal*, an English-language daily. Both splashed my picture with the Brzezinskis and the man-eating tiger on the front page. Apparently someone who had been present during our capture operation had dispatched the film to their contacts at *Rising Nepal* immediately after the event.

My wife's envelope also contained a note in Nepali, which in short translated to "Have you gone mad?" The media reports had triggered all kinds of rumors around Kathmandu. A few accused me of being reckless and stupid for daring to take His Majesty's distinguished guests on a rash operation in the jungle. Others said that it was a preplanned operation and questioned whether we would do the same when Dr. Henry Kissinger, former U.S. president Nixon's secretary of state, visited Nepal a few months later.

Sushma believed that I would be fired from my job, but there was nothing I could do to reverse the situation.

I bid good-bye to the Brzezinskis as the king's helicopter picked them up in Chitwan. They flew to Pokhara, a town in western Nepal, for their meeting with King Birendra.

I returned to check on Bange Bhale. He was lying flat on the floor of the cage. Suddenly he leapt to his feet and growled, shaking the cage and scaring the daylights out of me. I backed away from the cage in a flash. I felt a bit silly when I realized that the tiger was a caged animal, presumably trying to recover from the effects of the drug. Nevertheless, I loaded my dart gun and gave him another shot, ignoring his snarls from inside the cage.

At this point my mind raced through alternating cycles of utter dislike and high esteem for Bange Bhale. He was a man-eater. Yet no free-ranging tiger, even a man-eater, should be packed in a narrow cage and kept constantly drugged and immobilized.

I had nothing to do but wait for instructions from Kathmandu, which arrived late in the afternoon the next day. To my surprise, I was neither fired nor reprimanded for my actions. On the contrary, I was highly applauded for making the right decision at the right time. The message also instructed me to bring the tiger to Kathmandu and hand it over to the zoo.

It is rare to get a complimentary note from the Nepalese bureaucracy. A few days later, I found out why. Dr. Brzezinski had played a vital role in the complimentary tone of the message, perhaps unknowingly. During his meeting with King Birendra, the capture of Bange Bhale was a topic of conversation. Besides relating an exciting and memorable experience that he and his wife had had in Nepal, Dr. Brzezinski also lavishly praised me and my team for our professionalism. His conversation with the Nepalese monarch filtered down the chain of bureaucracy. In no time, my decision to capture Bange Bhale had made me a hero and not a reckless villain.

I transported Bange Bhale to Kathmandu. It was a sad fate for a magnificent creature. He would live out his days imprisoned within the narrow confines of a cold, cement-floored iron cage in Jwalakhel Zoo. Sadly, his notoriety as a man-eater would attract bigger crowds than his beauty and grace.

When I look back on this experience, I often wonder if I should have euthanized Bange Bhale. To this day, I am unaware of any successful attempts to rehabilitate man-eating tigers and return them to the wild. I believe that such programs are too risky in terms of human lives. Furthermore, they would likely generate fear, public outcry, and hatred toward the tiger, pitting local communities against the ideals of a national park. The only solution, at least for now, remains either death or imprisonment for the tiger. At least at the zoo, the tiger remains alive and there's a chance it may breed more tigers. Such is the case when we are unable to stop human encroachment on tiger habitat, which seems to be the main factor that transforms tigers into man-eaters in the first place.

9
THE MAKING OF A MAN-EATER

"A MAN IS EASY MEAT" IS A COMMON CLICHÉ AMONG NOVICE tiger-watchers, who are enthralled by stories of man-eating tigers but who do not realize that humans are not the natural prey of tigers, In reality, preying on humans is an aberration in tiger behavior and a rare event.

Throughout history, the rare instances in which tigers have devoured humans have captivated humanity all over the world. As early as the thirteenth century, Venetian explorer Marco Polo described the tiger as a deadly menace to the lives of wayfarers in China. However, Marco Polo had no descriptions or paintings that clearly described a tiger, so he mistook the animal's taxonomy by calling it a lion.

Marco Polo's story seems to be entirely hearsay. He had never seen a tiger or a lion in China. Scholars such as Frances Wood, the head of the Chinese department of the British Library at St. Pancras in London, believe Marco Polo's travel tales are mostly fabrication. In her book *Did Marco Polo Go to China?* she claims that he never traveled beyond Persia.

Nevertheless, unlike Marco Polo, a fourteenth-century Asian sculpture was right on target when it came to portraying the tiger. The anonymous Indian artist who created the sculpture lived in the city of Hampi on the banks of the Tungabhadra River of southern India. He created one of the oldest stone murals that correctly depict a wild tiger. The mural depicted a tiger towering over a man that it had trapped in its claws. The artist lived at a time when the Vijayanagara Empire flourished in India, from 1336 to 1646. The kingdom was infested with tigers. Descendants of these tigers still survive in the nearby national parks and wildlife reserves of southern India.

The British were most consistent at recording statistics on humans killed by tigers throughout their Asian empire and particularly in India. Renowned naturalist and writer Michael Bright, development director for the British Broadcasting Corporation (BBC), is one of these chroniclers. In his aptly titled book *Man-Eaters,* he estimates that during the past four hundred years, more than a million people have been killed by tigers in southern Asia. He describes inscriptions reading DIED OF INJURIES RECEIVED FROM A TIGER on gravestones of Britons killed by tigers during their service in British India. He has also noted that in a district near the modern-day city of Nagpur in central India, several tigers killed four hundred people in 1769. Humans killed by tigers per year ranged from 880 to nearly 1,050 between 1902 and 1910 and peaked to more than 1,600 in 1922 in the British Empire in Asia.

Besides killing humans, tigers also found it easy to prey on domestic cattle. In the early half of the twentieth century, human agriculture and livestock development in British India steadily expanded into tiger territory. This expansion triggered direct conflicts between tiger and man.

My good friend Dr. Chuck McDougal has studied incidents of tigers killing humans from both a historical and a regional perspective throughout the tiger's range. He points out that Sir Thomas Stamford Bingley Raffles, founder of Singapore, discovered the whole area teeming with tigers when he visited in 1819. Except for one tiny Malay hamlet, the island was totally covered with tall trees of the tropical jungle, with a mosaic of steaming swamplands. Tigers easily swam back and forth across the Straits of Johor from mainland Malaya to establish their territory in the prey-rich enclaves of Singapore.

The British cleared the forests and reclaimed the land. They also expanded settlements and plantations too rapidly. With a large influx of settlers, close encounters with tigers resulting in violent confrontation were inevitable. By 1840, humans killed by tigers ranged between two hundred and three hundred per year; most of those killed were imported Chinese laborers.

The availability of domestic prey dwindled. Rubber and palm oil plantations supplanted raising livestock, and the hungry tigers took an unprecedented toll on humans. Tiger attacks rose to an average of six hundred to eight hundred humans, mostly in areas near mainland Malaya.

Considering the animal to be a form of vermin, the British rulers instituted a bounty on tigers in Malaya. Within two decades, they reduced the incidents of man-eating by indiscriminately slaughtering tigers with guns and booby-traps. As a result, the tiger had become extinct in Singapore by the 1930s.

Compared to Singapore and Malaya, the incidents of man-eating tigers were sporadic in British Burma, largely because human population was sparse and isolated in the tiger country. Yet it was epidemic in neighboring British India. The number of people killed by tigers averaged 860 humans per year in the nineteenth century and the early part of the twentieth century. Reports estimated that five hundred people were killed by tigers in 1822 near the metropolis of modern-day Mumbai.

Farther to the east, the province of Bengal and the United Province gained unsavory reputations as havens for man-eating tigers. In 1887, Reginold George Burton, a British Army officer, noted that more than 40 percent of the eight hundred people killed in India were lost in Bengal. In the first half of the twentieth century, the United Province replaced Bengal as the epicenter for man-eating tigers. It also produced several famous tiger hunters in the British India service, but no one can match the fame of Colonel Edward James Corbett for his passion for hunting man-eating tigers. Corbett was born in the rugged mountainous district of Naini Tal in northern India in 1875. He became a living legend as a tiger hunter. Even after his death in Kenya in 1955, his exploits were still glamorized in India by the true tales of man-eating tigers that he shot in the Kumaon-Garhwal region of northern India. Corbett was a passionate hunter, an avid photographer, and a devoted naturalist. He was also among the few colonial masters of British India who was able to win the hearts and minds of the Indian people. In 1957, twelve years after his death and ten years after the British were driven out of India, the Indian government designated a tiger reserve in northern India as Corbett National Park in honor of their beloved Briton.

Corbett was known for his zealous efforts to minimize conflicts between humans and tigers. Armed with a high-powered rifle, he stalked problem tigers alone and on foot. To Corbett, a passionate hunter, any tiger that killed or ate humans—even a single person—was a problem tiger. He slew a dozen man-eaters between 1907 and 1938. Among them, these man-eaters had killed more than fifteen hundred people in northern India.

Corbett vividly narrated his life of hunting man-eating tigers in many of his books. One of them was the *Man-Eaters of Kumaon*. This classic, first published in 1944, has been translated into twenty-seven languages. The book describes eight notorious man-eaters that Corbett bagged in the rolling hills and river valleys of Uttar Pradesh, a mountainous state in northern India. One of them was a sly killer called the Champawat Man-eater, for the district it terrorized for half a decade. This infamous tiger holds the record (436) for the total number of humans attacked and eaten by a single tiger.

Corbett reports that this female man-eater was born in neighboring Nepal, presumably in the Kanchanpur District of western Nepal. After she had eaten more than two hundred Nepalese peasants in the early 1900s, a battalion of armed Nepalese soldiers chased the killer across the border into the northwest Indian territory of Kumaon in 1905. Compared with Kanchanpur, the Champawat tiger's new home in Kumaon was densely populated. The opportunities for the tiger to prey on humans were widely expanded. The tiger settled in India, never to return to Nepal, and wreaked unprecedented havoc by preying on men, women, and children around the village of Champawat.

In 1907 Jim Corbett was commissioned to destroy this vicious killer. He searched for the tiger tenaciously for four years. Yet every time he got close, the tiger outwitted him. Finally he changed his tactics. In 1911 he deployed a fleet of villagers to bang drums, pots, and pans and force the tiger out into the open from a crevice in a cliff. They were supported by a team of screaming villagers armed with spears, axes, swords, and shotguns.

Corbett's strategy worked. They drove the angrily roaring tiger out of its den. The man-eater saw Corbett and charged at him with full fury. Keeping his cool, Corbett raised his cordite rifle and felled the vicious beast with three rapid shots.

After killing the tiger, Corbett examined its body. He found that the tiger's jaws were malformed, a consequence of a sloppy shot of an amateur hunter that had hit the tiger's canine teeth. Instead of tracking and destroying a wounded tiger, the reckless hunter had left the tiger to fend for itself. Unable to hunt its natural prey, the tiger had become a man-eater.

Before its life was terminated, the Champawat Man-eater had preyed on 436 innocent humans—a record unmatched and unchallenged until 1972, eighty-six years later. That year, another savage tiger challenged the Champawat tiger's infamous record. This tiger was known as the Baitadi Man-eater after the district the tiger terrorized in Nepal.

Interestingly, both tigers were born in the same area along the Nepal-India border—highly populated districts relative to human density in adjoining areas. But unlike their actions with the Champawat tiger, the Nepalese authorities did not forcefully chase this man-eater across the Indian border into Kumaon. Instead they deployed a dozen sharpshooters and killed the man-eater within Nepal—but only after the beast had killed more than one hundred people (mostly children) within a period of ten months. The local villagers called the Baitadi tiger a *gahite bagh,* meaning "wounded tiger," suggesting that man had a hand in injuring the tiger and eventually turning it into a man-eater.

The man-eaters of Champawat and Baitadi clearly demonstrate that bodily damage caused by hunter's guns or traps laid out by humans can be a factor in compelling tigers to feed on human flesh.

Valmik Thapar, a leading global tiger expert who has studied tigers in Ranthambore, India, for more than thirty years corroborates this theory. His research shows that tiger aggression against humans; including man-eating incidents, have decreased dramatically since tiger hunting was banned on the Indian subcontinent in the 1970s. However, it is not only humans who impair wild tigers and catalyze the making of a man-eater. Severe injuries are also inflicted on tigers by other tigers and by the tiger's wild prey, particularly when the tiger fails to make an instantaneous kill with its first strike.

In *The Man-Eaters of Kumaon,* Jim Corbett described two tigers that were unable to hunt wild prey after being injured by porcupines. One of them was a young female tiger.

During their battle, the porcupine punctured one of the tiger's eyes. The porcupine also sank more than fifty sharp quills deep into the predator's legs. The wounds soon became infected, impairing the tiger's ability to catch its natural prey. It lay hidden for days in a thick bush, slowly starving to death. By sheer coincidence an unfortunate grass cutter edged close to the tiger, which was quietly licking its wounds. The tiger attacked the woman, whose death was instantaneous. The tiger did not feed on the woman, indicating that its first human kill was an accident, presumably as a means of reflexive or defensive reaction, and not driven by hunger. Leaving its victim behind, the tiger staggered deep into the woods. Two days later, a woodcutter stumbled upon the starving beast. The tiger killed the man and this time partially feasted on his flesh. This killing induced her to become a man-eater.

Despite these incidents, the belief that once a tiger eats humans, it acquires a strong taste for human flesh and stops eating any other meat is a myth. In fact, it is the loss of its fear of humans that induces a tiger to become a man-eater incrementally. Humans are easier to catch than wild animals, but that does not stop the man-eating tiger from preying on wild or domestic animals when the opportunity arises.

Presumably, her second kill taught the porcupine-scarred tigress that humans were easy prey. Consequently the tiger developed a cunning habit of stalking and killing humans. Jim Corbett eventually shot this tiger, but only after it earned notoriety as the Muktesar Man-eating Tigress after having consumed twenty-four people.

Besides bodily harm caused by humans or other animals, there are other causes that spur tigers to eat humans. During the Vietnam War, for example, dead bodies of American and Vietnamese troops were widely scattered on the forest floor; a consequence of brutal jungle warfare. They provided easy meals for tigers in the dense tropical rain forest of Indochina, where catching prey is often arduous work. Soon these tigers learned to scavenge dead soldiers. It is believed that feeding on human corpses changed the tigers' innate behavior, making them man-eaters.

This behavior was also described in the Burmese forests during World War II. There the forests were littered with corpses of Japanese and British soldiers. Soon the ease of scavenging dead humans prodded tigers to snatch a few live soldiers from their trenches or while on jungle patrol. When the war was over and the soldiers left, tigers continued to prey on villagers.

A similar theory has evolved from the Sunderbans forests of Bengal, which straddle Bangladesh and India. Bangladesh occupies 60 percent of the Sunderbans; India owns 40 percent of the contiguous patch of swampy mangrove forests along the shorelines of the Bay of Bengal. In Bengali. *Sunder* means "beautiful," and *ban* translates as "forest." The forests are prized by the Bengalis on both sides of the border as the "Beautiful Forest" of their *Sunnar Bengal,* or "Golden Bengal," despite the fact that the forests have earned a perverse reputation for being home to the highest number of man-eating tigers on Earth.

The area spreads over four thousand square miles at a junction where three great rivers of the Indian subcontinent drain into the Bay of Bengal. At the mouth of the bay, these rivers—the Ganges, the Brahmaputra, and the Meghna—have created the largest tidal mangrove forests on Earth. Throughout history, the Bay of Bengal has been famous for its high-powered hurricanes, monsoon rains, and sea storms that kill thousands of people in Bangladesh and West Bengal (India). As the storms simmer down, a large number of corpses are washed all over the forests, swamps, and mangroves in the deltoid bay. Tigers feed on these corpses. Over time, they lose their fear of humans, and a large number of them become man-eaters. As predators, tigers mostly eat freshly killed meat. However, they are known to scavenge when presented with the opportunity, particularly when they find dead bodies along their trail.

The physical characteristics of the Sunderbans are dynamic. They change daily with the changing tide. Most of the land is submerged at least twice a day, with tidal water rising up to fifteen feet. Landmarks appear and disappear constantly.

Dominated by this ever-changing coastal environment, the ecology and behavior of the area's tigers are extraordinarily different from the drier tiger domains elsewhere on the Indian subcontinent. The habitat is crisscrossed by a network of islands, creeks, and estuaries and interspersed with a mosaic of wetlands and forests in a sea of saline water. Tigers constantly swim across these waterways in search of prey. Rich in fish, honey, wildlife, and plants much needed for their livelihood, thousands of villagers also venture into the Sunderbans to harvest these products and are vulnerable to tiger attack.

The tigers of Sunderbans remain as unpredictable now as they were four hundred years ago, when the epidemic of man-eating tigers was first reported in the seventeenth century by François Bernier, a French physician in the court of Mughal Emperor Aurangzeb. The first European to report on the menace of Sunderbans tigers, he described tigers ambushing fishing boats and feeding on humans in the territories of Bangladesh.

Little seems to have changed today, despite the fact that most of the forests of the Sunderbans have been destroyed over the past three hundred years. Compared to tigers in other areas, most man-eaters in the Sunderbans are young and healthy. This finding undermines the theory that man-eaters are old or injured. However, the biogeographically environment of the Sunderbans is much different from most other tropical jungles or dry forestland areas. Furthermore, low visibility mixed with large numbers of fishermen, honey collectors, and other people harvesting forest resources multiply opportunities for tigers to encounter humans.

Unlike tigers elsewhere that stalk on foot, the tigers in the Sunderbans frequently swim in search of prey, traversing along many of the hidden water channels in the delta. As fresh water is scarce, they have also adapted to drinking the saline water of the mangrove estuaries.

In the early 1970s Dr. Hubert Hendrichs, a German researcher, studied tigers in the Bangladesh Sunderbans. His findings suggested that drinking salt water damaged the tigers' liver and kidneys, causing them to become aggressive and consequently lose their fear of humans.

Another intriguing observation was made by two Indian scientists, M. K. Chowdhury and P. Sanyal, who studied Sunderbans tigers for a decade in the 1970s and 1980s. Their studies indicated that most fatal tiger attacks came from behind the victim and from the right side.

These studies triggered a series of programs to protect humans from being snatched by tigers, creating a cottage industry in how to survive the man-eaters of the Sunderbans. Humans venturing into the Sunderbans carried a heavy stick on the right side of their neck. Masks were designed to baffle the tiger. They were worn on the back of the head when traveling by boat or on foot inside the Sunderbans, with the assumption that tigers attacked only from behind. Other creative ideas included wearing helmets that also extended to encircle the neck. These helmets were embedded with sharp spikes as prevention against tiger bites.

Authorities designed human-size mannequins that were dressed as fishermen, honey collectors standing adjacent to a colony of bees, and woodcutters squatting on the ground. The mannequins, strategically placed at sites where tiger attacks had taken place, were wired to give electric shocks in an attempt to program tigers to stop attacking humans.

These programs had limited success. The helmets did not work—the tigers quickly figured them out. Tigers attacked a few dummies and were jolted by electric shocks, but it was a major challenge to keep the batteries charged for any length of time in the swamps of the Sunderbans.

The influx of humans into the Sunderbans shot up in the mid 1980s. So did the number of tiger attacks. The anti-attack experiments had demonstrated that the tigers of Sunderbans were more cunning and resilient. They were also more daring than tigers elsewhere on the Indian subcontinent. Efforts to protect humans called for patience and innovations that were costly. The poverty-stricken people of the Sunderbans had neither time nor money. Nevertheless, the studies and lessons learned proved that the conditions that help create man-eating tigers in Sunderbans are unique. The pervasive wet environment, including the lack of fresh water that forces tigers to consume salt water, could be a major factor. Elsewhere, diseases such as arthritis, old age, and the wear and tear on tigers' paws by thorns and other sharp objects have also been blamed for turning tigers into man-eaters.

There are many theories about what makes a normal tiger become a man-eater. These include old age, injuries caused from fights with other tigers, and wounds inflicted by human bullets or snares. All these indicate that the primary cause of man-eating behavior is that the tiger has become incapacitated and unable to hunt its natural prey.

The skinny Mad Tiger of Madi I describe in Chapter 11 is an example of an aging man-killing tiger. Bange Bhale, the man-eater described in Chapter 8, exemplifies behavioral changes after a tiger has been injured in a fight with another tiger. The Champawat tiger described in this chapter typifies the making of a man-eater as a direct result of wounds inflicted by humans.

But I am in a quandary about how to explain the case of the Bhimle tiger described in Chapter 7. This man-eater was healthy. It had no wounds inflicted by humans or another tiger. The only hypothesis that I can come up with is that this tiger may have learned to kill humans from its mother. But many tiger experts would dispute this theory. Kailash Shankala, founding Director of India's Project Tiger, has noted that tigers do not normally attack standing humans. However, people who are crouched or bent over to cut grass or harvest crops are susceptible to tiger attacks. His theory is that these postures cause the tiger to mistake two-legged humans for its four-legged prey. Once they make their first kill, tigers loose their inherent fear of humans and become man-eaters.

Stephen Mills, a British naturalist and talented filmmaker who studied tigers in Nepal and India for more than twenty years, appears to second Shankala's theory, although with a new nuance. In the 1980s Stephen worked with us in Chitwan, where he made an outstanding tiger documentary for the BBC's *Living Dangerously* series. He postulated that tigers do not eat humans because they are two-footed and not four-footed animals. In contrast to its natural prey—an ungulate—a person standing erect looks towering and formidable to a tiger.

Citing himself as an example, Stephen said that to a tiger his height of six feet could make him appear to resemble a gigantic eighteen-foot-long beast. He would appear to be a menacing and formidable foe in the eyes of a three-foot-tall, nine-foot-long tiger. Mystified by the sight, the best recourse for the tiger would be to shy away from a standing or walking human.

Mills, a frequent visitor to Royal Chitwan National Park, has also lampooned his own hypothesis. He warned us of the perils of using the squatting position to relieve our bowels. The tiger could mistake us for a small deer and have us for lunch. I often remembered Stephen's words nervously each time I did just that in the heart of tiger country. Although amusing, Stephen's warning was based on a spine-tingling personal experience. He was once followed by two wild Asiatic lions while he was squatting and filming in the Gir Sanctuary of Gujarat, India.

The best and the most comprehensive data on tiger behavior was provided by an old colleague of mine, Dr. Bhim Gurung, a Nepalese scientist who has been studying tigers in Chitwan for more than twenty years. Bhim painstakingly studied decades of anecdotal reports on the man-killing tigers of Chitwan. He undertook this monumental task as a part of his doctoral program at the University of Minnesota in Nepal.

Gurung's 2008 dissertation provides the most thorough investigation of ecological and sociological characteristics of the victims of man-killing tigers in Chitwan National Park and its surroundings. He documented eighty-eight people who had been killed by thirty-seven tigers in the past thirty years. This included forty-six men and thirty-five women, indicating that more men ventured in or around the tigers' territory than women. (Gender of the remaining seven could not be determined as nothing but patches of blood and a few pieces of bone were found near the kill sites.) The ages of the tigers' victims varied but averaged thirty-six years. The youngest was a seven-year-old girl, who was killed by an old, impaired tiger while she was sleeping on the verandah of her hut. The oldest victim was a man of seventy, who was killed while collecting fodder for his goats in a patch of forest that buffered the national park from human settlements. He had been warned that a known killer tiger had been seen in the vicinity of his village. He ignored the warning and was devoured by the man-eater.

Of the thirty-seven killer tigers that Bhim studied, thirty-one were classified as man-eaters or potential man-eaters after signs that they ate their quarry, even partially. Six of them were given the benefit of the doubt and classified as accidental killers. Three of these were captured and relocated to the eastern corner of the park. One of them disappeared. The other two killed again and were eventually destroyed. Eleven of the man-killers were sentenced to death. One of them, the Bhimle man-eater, I darted and euthanized in 1980 with a fast-acting drug (described in Chapter 7). Five of the man-killing tigers were captured alive and were shipped to Kathmandu to be incarcerated in the cold and narrow confines of the national zoo. These include the three killer-tigers described in this book, namely the schoolteacher killer of Madanpur (Chapter 4); Bange Bhale, Dr. Brzezinski's Tiger (Chapter 8); and the Jogi Pothi Tiger of Madi Valley (Chapter 11).

Eighteen of the killer tigers accounted by Bhim Gurung were physically examined after they were killed or captured. Ten were impaired with wounds on their paws, jaws, or other parts of their body. Three were impaired by old age. Five had no abnormalities, indicating that wounds or old age were not always the criteria for tigers attacking humans. The physical condition of eighteen man-killers was unknown. They could not be examined because they were neither killed nor captured. They may still be at large or may have died a natural death. Or they could have crossed the border to take refuge in the Indian forests.

Gurung also classified the gender of the thirty-seven man-killers. There were hardly any differences in the gender ratio of killers over the past thirty years in Chitwan. Fifteen were male and sixteen were female. The gender of six could not be determined, as their tracks were masked before they could be examined. Five of the sixteen females were with cubs. Two subadults were with their mother when the first killing occurred. Both of them were males. Bhim has named them the Ayodhyapuri Bhale and Khumrose Bhale, after the villages they terrorized. Both became notorious man-eaters. Bhim reports that they killed at least five humans altogether.

The number of people killed inside the park boundary equaled those killed outside the boundary, mostly in the forests that buffered the park from human settlement. However, the killing rates increased dramatically—from one or two per year from 1979 to 1997 to seven to eight kills after 1998. Bhim Gurung attributed this disparity to the increase in the number of tigers moving into the buffer zones. Of the eighty-eight humans killed, 66 percent were killed less than half a mile from the edge of their village. This indicates that tigers kill people most often where encounters between man and beast are relatively frequent.

Bhim Gurung's research provides a comprehensive view of the habits and habitat of man-eating tigers. Consistent with Jim Corbett's theories and my own assumptions, noted above, Gurung's empirical data confirms three main factors in the making of man-eating tigers: First, bodily injury and/or old age retard the tiger's ability to hunt natural prey, forcing it to kill or feed on humans as easier prey. Second, the reductions of the number of natural prey available, coupled with the scarcity of domestic cattle to feed on, may force tigers to eat humans for survival. Third, initial killings may be merely defensive or accidental. Yet these first killings may liberate the tiger from its fear of humans and subsequently energize its impulse to prey on its prime enemy—man.

Despite these statistics, the killing of humans by tigers is a rarity. More people are gored by rhinos in Nepal than are killed by tigers. In India, more people die from snakebites than are killed by tigers. In fact, more people are killed by Kathmandu taxicabs than by tigers in the whole of the southern Nepalese Terai. Torturous deaths from rabies inflicted by dog bites in India, Nepal, and Bangladesh far exceed deaths from tiger attacks. Yet nothing matches the passion and uproar aroused by the killing of a human by a tiger.

In the Haldwani district of northern India, a free permit was issued to hunt one man-killing tiger in 1944. The result: Six innocent tigers were shot by professional hunters, each claiming that he had bagged the man-eater. Yet none produced any concrete evidence to prove that his trophy was the right tiger. Even if one of the tiger's shot was the man-eater, the emotionally charged human uproar caused the massacre of five innocent tigers.

In 1986 a tiger allegedly killed three people in Dudhwa National Park in northwest India. Billy Arjan Singh, a former tiger hunter turned leading tiger conservationist in India, reported on the retaliation by humans. He counted twenty-three tigers brutally butchered by booby-traps, guns, and snares in an attempt to punish one tiger suspected to be a man-eater. He also reported that a large sugarcane field adjacent to his homestead was burned down in a futile attempt to drive out a suspected man-eater hiding on a privately owned farm. The tiger was not even there.

The hysteria created by man-eating tigers led to abuses in the 1970s, when tiger hunting was banned in India. Corrupt government officials devised shady schemes when news of the presence of man-eating tigers spread like wildfire in various districts of India. For a lucrative price, negotiated privately, these corrupt civil servants permitted hunters with deep pockets to shoot the alleged man-eaters.

These plans to bypass the national ban had a two-pronged strategy: First, by sanctioning an operation to shoot man-eaters, these corrupt bureaucrats established their credibility in the local community. In the eyes of innocent villagers, they became saviors by demonstrating that saving human lives was more important than saving tigers. The second strategy was more important and more lucrative. The officials made money from extremely wealthy hunters driven by dreams of hunting wild tigers. Shooting a tiger—often for the first time—enhanced the hunter's standing, with unrivaled bragging rights among his peers. He earned the right to tell tales over cocktails or dinner in his opulent home, decorated with his tiger trophy. The recurring theme of these tall tales always revolved around singlehandedly hunting vicious man-eaters and saving the lives of Indian peasants.

These self-glorifying tales caught the attention of India's central government. Officials apprehended the corrupt civil servants who masterminded this cunning scheme. They also plugged the loophole that allowed private parties to kill problem tigers. Consequently, false rumors of harrowing attacks by man-eating tigers reduced drastically in most provinces of India. However, discreet pressures to allow foreign hunters to shoot man-killing tigers for very high fees still exist, particularly in neighboring Nepal. Large hunting clubs and fraternities, particularly those based in Europe and the United States, continue to wave hundreds of thousands of dollars under the noses of bureaucrats in wildlife departments throughout Asia.

"The tiger must pay for its own survival" has remained the mantra of wealthy Western hunters. As the tiger is a profitable commodity, sacrificing one or two to high-paying sportsman can benefit the species and its habitats. A few of these wealthy trophy seekers continue to make subtle attempts to lure top civil servants to participate in their conventions in tourist cities like Las Vegas, with purported plans to raise funds for tiger conservation. One such scheme is to auction tigers to super-rich American hunters. These specious fund-raising auctions, held under the glittering lights of ballrooms of five-star hotels, are run to raise funds in the six figures for a single tiger prize.

"Why waste a tiger for free when you can raise so much money for conservation?" is the core message. The idea that people are willing to pay big money to shoot a problem tiger that has already been earmarked for eradication sounds tempting at times when wildlife departments throughout Asia and the Russian Far East are starving for government funds to save the tiger. Because of lack of political patronage, these departments are short of cash and equipment to provide to the frontline field staff entrusted to protect tiger habitat from the saw, the plow, and the poacher. Population growth has propelled demands for conversion of tiger land to farmland for the poor peasants who live near tiger sanctuaries.

Lucrative Asian markets for wild tiger bones, meat, and skins remain open avenues for corrupt officials and dealers. Pressures for economic and infrastructure development at any cost continue to destroy prime tiger habitat throughout its range. The diminishing political and economic support to save the tiger and its habitat is exacerbated by the fact that the tiger is the largest predator in Asia. At times tigers do kill and eat humans, turning the votes of politicians and decision makers against the beast.

With battles to wage on all these fronts, it is hard to predict how long government departments entrusted to save the tiger and its habitat can resist the temptation of selling out the occasional problem tiger to wealthy hunters for big dollars. After all, such a transaction could fund the budget of a tiger reserve for a year, help save dozens of tigers, and keep their habitat intact.

Soon it may seem a logical and an economic necessity to sell one "dead tiger walking" to a wealthy hunter, even if it is not morally right. However, experience indicates that human greed can convert the most well-intended programs into fraudulent practices. As noted earlier in this chapter, many tigers that are innocent of man-eating have been killed in the hunt for man-eaters just to promote the perverse thrill of a blood sport. Very few people are guilt-free or spotless when it comes to protecting the tiger from the lusts of the marketplace or the sadistically entertaining pleasures of blood sports.

10

BLOOD SPORT

HUMAN FASCINATION WITH TIGERS HAS NEVER WANED throughout history. The tiger became an icon that challenged human courage—a ferocious wild beast prized for blood sport either in captivity or in the wild.

Since the days of ancient Greece and Rome, capturing, killing, or harnessing the predator has remained a fascination for the rich and powerful. Seleucus Nicator, a Macedonian warrior, presented a tiger to the city of Athens in 300 B.C. He had earned his laurels during the victorious campaign of Alexander the Great in India in 326 B.C. However, it is unclear whether the beast was a tiger he had brought from India or a Caspian tiger he had captured in the wilds of the Macedonian province of Mesopotamia.

The Romans saw their first tiger in 11 B.C. Emperor Augustus paraded a caged tiger during the inaugural ceremony for his landmark theater—Teatro di Marcello in the Sant'Angelo district of Rome. Gaius Plinius Secundus, a Roman scholar, who later wrote the *Naturalis Historia* in A.D. 77, described one of the earliest forms of tiger hunting. He says hunters in the kingdom of Hyrcania—currently parts of today's Iran, Turkey, and Turkmenistan—south of the Caspian Sea stole cubs by sneaking up to tigers' dens and then galloping away on horseback with their prize. These animals were Caspian tigers, a species that survived hunts for nearly two thousand years. They are thought to have become extinct in 1959.

The greatest example of pure blood sport did not occur in the wilds of the far-flung Roman Empire but in the metropolis of ancient Rome in the majestic amphitheater now known as the Coliseum. Completed in A.D. 80, this gigantic arena seated more than fifty thousand spectators. Roman rulers paraded hundreds of exotic animals, including tigers, to demonstrate the grandeur of their empire and their rule. Yet the artistic brilliance and the beauty of the Coliseum was no match for the cruel and gruesome events that took place within the stadium. Roman rulers set criminals, prisoners of war, and other undesirable humans, such as early Christians, loose in the arena to defend themselves against vicious predators. Bloodthirsty crowds roared for the glory of Rome as lions and tigers savaged helpless humans.

Emperor Marcus Aurelius tested the ferocity of tigers and lions by forcing them to fight one another to the death. During his rule (A.D. 161–180) he often publicly displayed his passion for animal fights. Once he forced an elephant to battle a group of tigers—the elephant lost.

Asian potentates were not far behind European rulers in using tigers for blood sport. One of them was Kublai Khan, grandson of the great Genghis Khan. Ruler of the Mongolian Empire from 1260 to 1294, Kublai Khan kept thousands of wild animals in his palace and often feasted on their organs. The tiger, which he mistakenly referred to as a lion, was his prized animal. He hunted tigers using dogs as bait. Presumably he dined on tiger penises to maintain sexual virility, a belief prevalent in his time and still practiced in some parts of the world to this day.

The *bagh shikar* (tiger hunt) was introduced to the Indian subcontinent as a regal sport not by the British but by the Moguls. Babar, a descendent of Genghis Khan who ruled India from 1526 to 1557, developed the shikar into its finest art form. He hunted tigers from horseback using bows and spears. His grandson Akbar used thousands of horses and humans to ring the tiger as he speared his trophy with a long lance. He also played war games during his hunts, largely to display his military might in the lands he had conquered.

Akbar's son, Emperor Jahangir, was the first Indian ruler to use firearms for hunting. He shot tigers with muzzle-loaded muskets.

Jahangir also made one of the biggest blunders in the history of India. In 1617 he gave the British East India Company exclusive rights to trade in India. The crafty Britons did more than trade. They took over the country and ruled India from 1858 to 1947 as the primary jewel in their colonial crown.

The British rulers did not want to fall behind their Indian predecessors in demonstrating their courage and ability to hunt tigers. Unprecedented slaughter of tigers, disguised as sporting events, increased during the British Raj. Sadly for the tiger, the British were better equipped. They shot tigers mercilessly with high-powered rifles, using trained elephants to corner their kill. By the nineteenth century, any Briton worth his salt had shot a tiger to prove his standing in colonial society.

"Bed a native wench in private and shoot a tiger in public," became a motto of many male Britons. India's British masters often organized extravagant shikar parties where civil and military officers competed aggressively to tally the highest number of tigers killed. Shooting tigers topped the agenda of any British gentleman of the Empire visiting India. All were expected to return home with at least one tiger skin as a trophy to display in their living rooms.

There are amusing stories about how the Indian Forest Service organized tiger hunts for visiting London dignitaries. One such story is set during the era of the first Marquess of Willingdon— Freeman Freeman-Thomas, thirty-second Viceroy of India (1931– 1936). He was fond of inviting influential Londoners to visit India. One was a Lord in the Upper House of the British Parliament with whom the viceroy needed to curry for favors. His guest was a pompous and demanding Englishman who was long on wants but short on time.

Shooting a tiger topped his wish list. The Englishman did not realize that compared with England, India is a vast country. Travel arrangements took time and organization. Shooting tigers in India was not the same as shooting grouse in Scotland.

The viceroy summoned a group of officers of the Indian Forest Service to his durbar (palace) in Delhi. He ordered the foresters to organize his guest's tiger hunt—promptly. The forest officers were used to the viceroy's tall orders. They were also well prepared for dealing with arrogant visitors from England, sometimes using unorthodox methods. They selected the princely hunting preserves of Keoladeo, about 100 miles from Delhi, as the venue for the viceroy's guest tiger hunt.

Early the next morning, the foresters escorted the VIP to the Delhi railway station, where he boarded the luxurious first-class compartment in the front of the train. Unbeknownst to him, the foresters loaded a big wooden crate in the freight compartment at the rear of the train. A thick black cotton sheet covered the crate. No one knew or questioned what the crate contained. On reaching Keoladeo, the foresters escorted the viceroy's guest to a forest bungalow to rest for the night. They then returned to the railway station and carted the crate to the middle of the jungle in the nearby hunting preserve.

Next day at the crack of dawn, about an hour before the VIP was ready for his hunt, the foresters unlocked the crate and a huge striped cat calmly walked out. He was a tame tiger from the Delhi Zoo. The tiger was one of a few animals that the Indian Forest Service kept in reserve to feed the egos of eccentric British VIPs obsessed with shooting tigers in the easiest and quickest way. The forest officers fed the tiger goat meat and kept it at bay, surrounded by three dozen elephants.

Just before the first rays of sunlight penetrated the jungle, the foresters escorted the viceroy's guest to a *machan* (tree stand) on the other side of the jungle. On the way they pumped up the viceroy's guest with tales of the dangers of tiger hunting in the dark forests of India.

The Londoner was already electrified with excitement when he perched on his machan. His excitement grew as the elephants started to beat the jungle and slowly drive the tiger toward him.

He fired his rifle and shot the tiger dead on the spot—a few yards beneath the machan. Gloating in triumph, he asked the foresters to take his picture with the tiger from several different angles. One was a shot of him proudly balancing his rifle on the tiger's head while three dozen elephants flanked him from behind.

No one dared tell the fool that he had just shot a tame tiger. It was a sad end to a splendid and innocent animal—just to satisfy a man's ego. Shooting sparrows in Delhi would not have been easier. Regardless, the viceroy's guest had earned the right to brag about his successful tiger hunt to his peers at his London club.

Valmik Thapar, one of the world's leading tiger experts, has outlined the carnage that took place in India in his famous book *Tiger: Portrait of a Predator*. In 1877 a record 1,579 tigers were killed in India. A Briton named George Yul shot more than four hundred tigers in the middle of the nineteenth century in northeastern India. Britons who shot record numbers of tigers during the second half of the nineteenth century include Gordon Cummings, who killed seventy-three tigers in 1872 along the Narmada River Valley in western India. William Rice shot 158 tigers during his four-year assignment in Rajasthan in northwestern India. The bloody orgy did not decline in the beginning of the twentieth century. Montague Gerard bagged 227 tigers in the state of Hyderabad in 1903.

By the first half of the twentieth century, the Indian maharajas whose ancestors had valiantly fought against the Mogul began to behave like the British. This Anglophile lot had gone to school in England and earned the derogatory title of "WOG" (Westernized Oriental Gentleman) from their British peers. These Indian aristocrats competed with the British gentry in shooting tigers. After all, "shikar" was an Indian word. The tiger was an Indian beast, and India and not Britain had perfected the art of the *bagh shikar*.

The greatest mayhem took place in the first half of the twentieth century. The Maharaja of Jaipur created his own lavish hunting lodge in Ranthambore in northwestern India during his reign

(1922–1949). In addition to the British aristocracy, he invited Greek and Russian royalty to hunt tigers. In early 1961 Great Britain's Queen Elizabeth shot two tigers in the maharaja's facilities in Ranthambore. The queen was the guest of his celebrity wife, Maharani Gyatri Devi. But the queen's feat pales in comparison to the maharajah's counterparts in other parts of India.

The Maharaja of Udaipur, a city 250 miles south of Jaipur, shot more than a thousand tigers during his reign (1930–1955). Likewise, in the first five decades of the twentieth century, the Maharaja of Vijayanagaram killed 325 tigers in southern India. The Maharajas of Rewa (central India) and of Gauripur in Assam (northeastern India) each have five hundred tigers in his tally. But the highest record goes to the Maharaja of Surguja in central India. He shot more than 1,710 tigers in a twenty-five-year period ending in 1956.

Nepal was not behind India when it came to tiger hunts. As Briton, E. A. Smythies described it in his book *Big Game Shooting in Nepal,* tiger hunting in India was a mundane affair compared with the gala events within its neighbor's boundaries.

In December 1911 King George V went big-game hunting in Bikhna Thori Forest on the southern side of Chitwan's Churia Hills. The British monarch was the guest of Maharaja Chandra Shamsheer. On this particular hunt, the Rana prime minister, who ruled Nepal from 1901 to 1929 with an iron fist, mobilized six hundred elephants, twelve thousand porters, and two thousand palace attendants to entertain King George and his eighteen-member entourage. During a ten-day hunt, the king shot thirty-nine tigers, eighteen rhinos, and large numbers of leopards, sloth bears, and deer.

King George's tiger tally was surmounted in 1939 by Victor Alexander John Hope, the second Marquess of Linlithgow and Viceroy of India. But no one could match the carnage of Nepal's own son—Maharaja Juddha Shamsheer. He shot 433 tigers in a period of seven years, between 1933 and 1940, averaging sixty-three tigers per hunt.

Unlike the Chinese, the maharajas of Nepal of the early twentieth century did not believe that tiger meat or bones or any of the animal's body parts had medicinal or restorative properties. Except for keeping the skin as a hunting trophy, they discarded the rest of the tiger's body.

History has recognized the Chitwan Valley as one of the best shikar sites since the first Rana ruler of Nepal, Jang Bahadur, shot thirty-one tigers in a single hunt in 1850. Even in modern times, state guests ranging from the deposed King Zahir Shah of Afghanistan to Queen Elizabeth II, the reigning sovereign of Great Britain, have hunted tigers in Chitwan.

In 1961 the queen made a state visit to Nepal. Like her grandfather fifty years before her, she too went tiger hunting in Chitwan. But her hunt was different from her grandfather's 1911 shikar. Her host was not a Rana prime minister but her Nepalese counterpart King Mahendra, the all-powerful Shah King of Nepal.

Mahendra's father, King Tribhuvan, had sided with the commoners to overthrow the Ranas in 1951 and introduce a multiparty democracy. Ten years later, Mahendra seized power in a bloodless coup in March 1961 to become absolute ruler of Nepal. Queen Elizabeth was his first state guest. A tiger-hunting safari in Chitwan topped the events of her visit.

At the time, the queen's hunt was the biggest spectacle on Earth. The French writer Michel Peissel describes this lavish display in his book *Tiger for Breakfast: The Story of Boris of Kathmandu.*

Nowhere else, even in Great Britain or the British colonies in Africa, had the queen's subjects matched such grandeur of pomp and pageantry. King Mahendra mobilized the Royal Nepal Army, the Nepal Police Force, and the Nepal Civil Service for the queen's visit. Thousands of laborers cleared a patch of dense forest in Megauli in western Chitwan to establish a royal hunting camp. A road was bulldozed through thick subtropical forests to connect Megauli with Bharatpur, the district capital of Chitwan. The

Nepalese Army constructed a four-thousand-foot airstrip in the heart of the jungle to land the royal aircraft. Working from sunrise to sunset, laborers removed a layer of soil one foot deep and then carpeted the dug-out ground with turfs of evergreen *dubo* or Bermuda grass to create a lawn in the middle of the forests. They also killed millions of insects, scorpions, and a few snakes. The military liberally sprayed insecticides to eradicate mosquitoes and other lesser creatures from the royal camp, and the Kathmandu Fire Brigade dispatched three engines to water the lawn to keep it green and well manicured.

Within a month, the hardworking Nepalese created a tented city covering two square miles of forest on the banks of the Rapti River. A big sand-and-mortar replica of Mount Everest stood in the center of the royal camp. A wide avenue stemming from the replica divided the tented city in two parts. One side was reserved for the Nepalese and the other for their distinguished British guests. Arches constructed from moss, bamboo, banana plants, and red cloth lined the avenues leading to Queen Elizabeth's tented suite. Huge brass vessels decorated with red vermilion, flowers, and yogurt in large oval pottery decorated the royal walkways. A huge board displaying the colorful insignia of both the British and Nepalese monarchs stood at the opposite ends of the Mount Everest model.

Queen Elizabeth had an eleven-room tented suite. Two of the rooms were bedrooms—one for the queen and one for her husband, Prince Philip. Consequently, the Nepalese knew long before her subjects did that the British queen and her husband slept separately. This information spread like wildfire and raised eyebrows among the Nepalese courtiers, but no one dared say a word. Tongues could be cut out for talking about the bedding habits of the royals.

The queen's suite also included a huge tent in front of her bedroom. This functioned as her living room, where Her Majesty could have her afternoon tea or evening cocktails. The queen and her consort's bedroom tents had attached European-style bathrooms with flush toilets and hot and cold running water. In addition to tents for dressing rooms, meetings, and storerooms, the royal suite included two more huge tents, connected to the royal bedroom tents by a canvas corridor. One of the tents was reserved for Queen Elizabeth's lady-in-waiting. The other was for Prince Philip's aide-de-camp. Colorful woolen rugs and upscale furniture from the Nepalese royal palace lavishly furnished the regal suites.

The quarters of the king and queen of Nepal were similar but decorated less extravagantly. Tents of the entourage were lined up outside the monarchs' tents. Their size and furnishings varied according to the pecking-order protocol of the royal household: The higher the rank, the bigger the tent.

Meals were gastronomical events unprecedented anywhere for a two-day hunting event. They included more than twenty-five delicacies of Nepalese game animals and birds, including the Bengal florican—a rare and endangered species in Chitwan. The choicest aperitifs, wine, champagne, and after dinner liqueurs were served. Smokers had a choice of English cigarettes, Cuban cigars, or Burmese cheroots. But smoking was permitted only after Her Britannic Majesty announced, "Gentlemen, you may smoke." There were two feasting areas. Lunch was served outdoors on the scenic banks of the Rapti River. Dinner was served in a large tent that was superbly decorated to match any of the regal banquet halls in the Narayanhiti Royal Palace in Kathmandu.

A fleet of four hundred elephants assembled for Queen Elizabeth's shikar, providing the biggest show on Earth. The pachyderms were colorfully decorated with traditional Nepalese painted designs and the British royal coat of arms. The elephants had been trained to raise their trunks and trumpet a salute to the British queen.

The setting, the site, and the sounds of the jungle, synchronized with the chorus of four hundred elephants, enthralled the Britons, who had never had such an experience. During a safari deep into the tall grasslands and riverine forests, the royals and their entourage relaxed languidly on their howdahs, cushioned wooden platforms fixed on top of their elephants. Some elephants served as a mobile jungle bar, their howdahs fully stocked with the choicest drinks— chilled champagne, beer, and gin and tonic water, the favorite of the English. Sequestered from the glaring eyes and ears of the media, the British royals were totally relaxed in the enchanting jungles of Chitwan—and they had the greatest adventure of their lives.

The British media claimed that their queen shot not with her gun but with her movie camera. Apparently Her Majesty filmed the birds and animals of Chitwan from atop her elephant, while the members of her entourage did the hunting. Her husband, Prince Philip, was offered a choice but also declined the opportunity to shoot a tiger. He wanted to be seen as a preserver, not a killer, of wildlife.

Prince Philip had a strong incentive not to hunt on this trip. The prince, who had shot tigers with his wife in India, was detested by the British press. A story in *Time* magazine reported that the English media called him the "Grim Reaper" after he shot hundreds of birds and a tiger during a visit to India and Pakistan in the late 1950s. This time the London tabloids were anxiously waiting for opportunities to prove that their queen's consort was the biggest hypocrite in Britain.

Earlier in 1961 Prince Philip and Prince Bernhard, the consort of Queen Juliana of the Netherlands, had vowed to give up hunting to help preserve the world's diminishing wildlife. In collaboration with several European intellectuals such as Sir Peter Scott, Julian Huxley, Edward Max Nicholson, Victor Stolan, and Guy Mountfort, the princes had just created the World Wildlife Fund (WWF). The mission of the WWF was not to shoot but to save the world's wildlife. As a founding father of the newly born WWF, Prince Philip could not afford to be seen shooting rhinos and tigers in Nepal.

But the prince faced another dilemma. As a guest of honor, it would not be diplomatic for him to change his program at the last minute and refuse King Mahendra's invitation to have the honor of shooting a tiger. He needed a solid pretext to decline the king's offer.

Philip was a canny man. During the morning of his scheduled tiger hunt, he walked out of his tent with a huge dressing on his trigger finger. He showed his bandaged finger to King Mahendra and explained his inability to use his badly infected finger to shoot his rifle. The king, who had attended the opening meetings of the World Wildlife Fund in Switzerland, was not a fool. With a mischievous twinkle in his eyes, he graciously accepted Prince Philip's alleged wound. The king knew that Philip would have had no qualms about shooting a tiger had it not been for the presence of British media representatives in Kathmandu. Even if Chitwan was kept out of bounds for news hounds by the Nepalese police, some members of the hunting party could leak the news to an English reporter.

King Mahendra offered Philip's wild tiger to Lord Home—the British Foreign Secretary. Lord Home was delighted by the offer, but he was a terrible shot. With the vhit cloth keeping the tiger at bay, four hundred elephants encircled the tiger and drove it to Lord Hume. The jungle thundered as he fired his rifle. In his edginess, he missed his shot. The tiger dashed into the bush roaring in anger. The sight and sound of the tiger heightened Lord Home's anxiety. The tiger could easily jump at him. He previously had seen tigers only in zoos in England. The sight of a roaring wild tiger unnerved him.

The elephants again rounded up the tiger and drove it toward Lord Hume. He fired—and missed again. The tiger roared and dashed to cover, crouching in a thick bush. But the ring of elephants and the wall of vhit cloth kept the tiger from escaping. Missing his second shot, Lord Home became even more nervous. The elephant drivers reorganized their elephants and again drove the tiger to Lord Home. He fired his rifle when the beast was about twenty yards from his elephant—and missed for the third time. Lord Home was embarrassed. He was losing face. He gave up on the tiger and moved his elephant to Rear Admiral Christopher Bonham-Carter and Sir Michael Adeane—two members of Queen Elizabeth's entourage. The trio consulted and decided that Lord Home needed additional guns.

The elephant drivers rounded up the tiger again, driving the beast toward the three Britons perched atop their elephants. The jungle again thundered as Admiral Bonham-Carter and Sir Michael fired simultaneously and on target. The big male tiger dropped dead about fifteen yards from the hunters. Lord Home, who did not fire his gun, sighed with relief. But he could not claim the tiger as his trophy. The prize would be shared with the admiral and Sir Michael.

King Mahendra felt sorry for Lord Home. He did not want the British Foreign Secretary to leave Nepal without a trophy. He offered him the biggest beast of Chitwan—the rare and endangered greater one-horned rhinoceros, the pride of Nepal. Lord Home's rhino was a two-ton female. (A female was chosen because they have bigger and shapelier horns.) Even a child should not be able to miss a target as huge as a rhino. But Lord Home had never before hunted from the back of an elephant; for that matter, he had never even ridden an elephant. His reputation would be ruined if he missed a two-ton rhino. He would be a laughing stock.

Again he asked Admiral Bonham-Carter and Sir Michael for their backup, even though his target was humongous and barely fifteen yards from his high-powered rifle. The trio fired simultaneously. The poor rhino had no chance. She collapsed and died in a pool of blood that oozed from her chest. Lord Home claimed the head and horn as his trophy. The admiral and Sir Michael chose the legs and the thick, armored shoulder skins to be made into wastepaper baskets back home in England. None of the Britons, not even Prince Philip, one of the founders of the WWF, said anything about wasting a breeding-age female of a species that the International Union for Conservation of Nature (IUCN), the scientific wing of the WWF, had listed as one of the world's most threatened.

Queen Elizabeth's shikar in Chitwan was controversial. The wildlife-adoring British were appalled to learn from the media about their royals' participation in a blood sport in one of the world's poorest countries. The queen's shikar was a big, expensive, and glamorous event of unsurpassed pomp and pageantry, doubt-ful to be repeated. For years, the lavish tiger hunt of the British monarch remained the talk of the town in Nepal.

Even as late as 1988, many Nepalese knew and talked a lot about the 1961 hunt of Her Britannic Majesty. They also took the liberty of spicing their stories with juicy rumors about what happened behind the scenes during the royal hunt. They gossiped about the sex and size of the tiger shot by the queen's Foreign Secretary. Yet only a handful knew or cared about the plight of Chitwan's remaining tigers. Jogi Pothi, prowling hungrily in the Madi Valley, less than ten miles southeast as the crow flies from the British queen's 1961 playground, was no exception.

11

THE JOGI POTHI TIGER
OF MADI VALLEY

IN JANUARY 1988 FEW UNKNOWN SITES REMAINED IN ROYAL
Chitwan National Park. The Madi Valley was a notable exception.
Undiscovered by tourists, avoided by scientists, and totally ignored
by the government, it was a pathetically poor prefecture in both its
lack of wildlife and the economic condition of its human inhabitants. Few people visited Madi either for business or for pleasure. Sequestered in the southwest corner of the park, Madi was
no match to the Rapti and Narayani River valleys of the north in
terms of accessibility or attraction. Being adjacent to an isolated
international frontier, the Madi Valley also had a reputation for
being a haven for armed thugs, mostly involved in robbery along
the border with India.

Surrounded on all sides by the rugged slopes of the Churia
Mountains and the ravine-slashed slopes of the Someshor Hills,
Madi saddled Chitwan's southwestern flank. Lying about five hundred feet above sea level, the valley was one of the most isolated
parts of the national park. Paradoxically, it was one of the most
ecologically significant sites in the park as far as the wild tiger's
range was concerned. The few remaining plots of forest and grasslands formed a vital travel corridor for three groups of tiger population in the region: the northern group in the Rapti River Valley;
the eastern group in Parsa Wildlife Reserve; and the western
group that occupies the forests and grasslands south of Reu River,
including tigers across the border in India's Valmiki National Park.

The Madi Valley had also earned the reputation of having the
most man-eating tigers in Chitwan National Park. One of them

was a female that I named Jogi Pothi. *Jogi,* or yogi, means a hermit or a sage; *pothi* translates to "female" in the local vernacular. However, the name was not a correct description of this man-eater. Unlike most hermits or sages I have met in Chitwan, Jogi Pothi was neither docile nor calm.

Having given up family life and the earthly sins of lust, greed, and envy, jogis often lived at the edges of forests, subsisting on alms from nearby villagers. They spent most of their time in deep meditation at a *dhuni* (campfire) with ashes all over their bodies, living a life of saintly celibacy in the serenity of the forests. However, the tiger I had named Jogi Pothi was no saint. She was a vicious killer that had devoured at least four humans. I gave her the name after she tried to eat her fifth victim, a real-life jogi, who dwelled inside the forests of Bankatta on the northern edge of the Madi Valley.

Jogi Pothi was an unusual man-eater. She prowled along the edges of the villages not at night but during broad daylight, terrorizing the people of Madi. Her daytime prowls through farmlands led many villagers to believe that the tiger was mad or, at the least, rabid. I have never known tigers to have rabies or suffer from insanity. However, I also knew that no sensible tiger, not even a man-eater, would venture out in the open near human settlements in daylight.

Like any other serial killer, man-eating tigers usually hunt under cover of darkness. But Jogi Pothi had developed an odd but deadly strategy. Instead of waiting for or stalking her victims along a roadside, she often dragged them right out of their houses into a nearby ravine, where she would feast on her kills. These homes were simple mud, wood, and thatch huts with easy access. After each kill in the Madi Valley, she would disappear, sometimes for months. Consequently, she had eluded our efforts to capture her.

One wintery morning in January 1988, the man-eating tigress prowled along the edges of the village of Bankatta. She saw an isolated hut, some hundred feet deep in the forest from the edge of the village. The hut belonged to a well-respected jogi who pre-ferred to live in isolation without much contact with the local vil-lagers. As dawn was breaking across the horizon, the tiger strolled across a small farm field and reached the jogi's hut at the edge of the forest. The tiger pushed the door of the hut, but the door was firmly bolted from the inside. The tiger's attempts at entry created a sound as though some human was knocking on the wooden door. The sound enticed a human inside the hut to walk up to the door. That human was not the jogi but a female companion, who saved his life but destroyed his reputation as a celibate.

Upon hearing the knocking sound, the jogi's lady friend peeked through a hole in the wooden door. Shocked to see a huge tiger, she shrieked *"Bagh! Bagh!"* ("Tiger! Tiger!") in terror at the top of her lungs. Her jogi consort jumped out of his bed and joined her, banging pots and pans in the hut and yelling for help. Their cries rang across the forest to the village. Equipped with axes and *khukuris,* Nepalese machetes, villagers rushed toward the jogi's hut, causing the tiger to flee into a nearby ravine.

His mistress's sharp sense saved the jogi's life but not his pious standing in the eyes of his fellow villagers. Until the man-eating tiger exposed his nocturnal habits, they had revered the jogi as a holy man who practiced celibacy. They had also revered him for giving up all the earthly sins. However, losing his reputation was a small price to pay. He was glad to be alive and not eaten by a tiger. He married the woman who saved him and continued to live in the same village as a normal "sinful" man.

I was not in Madi but at Tiger Tops Jungle Lodge when this incident occurred. Biswa Nath Upreti, director general of the Department of National Parks and Wildlife Conservation was on an official visit, and I had to accompany him on his inspection tour of the western end of the park.

"Tiger eating man Madi" babbled my good friend Masa-hiro Iijima in his trademark pidgin English as he barged into the dining hall of Tiger Tops and delivered the message. Upreti and I were having tea with my friend Chuck McDougal, a leading tiger expert and the resort's operational manager. Although he was an outstanding Japanese wildlife photographer, Iijima's English was horrendous, only faintly better than his Nepali. He could read and understand English well, but speaking or writing it was another story. He did not seem to care, as long as his messages were understood.

"But no success kill" added Iijima, rolling his eyes in excitement. Iijima was working with Chuck and me to write a book about tigers for a Japanese publication. We did the writing, and he took the photographs.

"Tiger run gully. Village Bankatta. Man wife alive," added Iijima. Despite his garbled English, we got his telegraph-like message. We always did. We hurriedly finished our lunch and rushed to Bankatta in one of Tiger Tops' Land Rovers. Chuck and his two best tiger trackers, Sakale Gurung and Dhan Bahadur, also joined us. Using pugmark tracks and face marks to identify tigers, Chuck and his trackers had been studying tigers at the western end of the park for more than a decade. On our way to the village, we stopped at park headquarters in Kasra to send a runner to my camp in Saurah, asking my team of shikaris to meet us at Bankatta with elephants and our tiger-immobilization drugs and equipment.

We were mobbed by hundreds of villagers when we reached the edge of the village of Bankatta at noon. Fact blended with rumor had reached them before we did, and they were expecting us. The villagers knew that no less than Mr. Upreti, director general of the Department of National Parks and Wildlife Conservation was coming himself to kill the tiger. Some in the crowd made angry and snide remarks, something we had become accustomed to over time. Others politely demanded that the tiger be killed.

Mr. Upreti, who was trained as a lawyer, was also a good speaker. As Chuck, Iijima, and I sat quietly in the car, Mr. Upreti stood on the hood of the Land Rover and pacified the villagers with promises that our team would encamp in Bankatta until the tiger was captured and imprisoned in a cage in Kathmandu. That was easier said than done. Catching man-eating tigers is not straightforward. Since the man-eater was not one of our radio-collared tigers, it would be difficult for us to locate.

After appeasing the villagers, Mr. Upreti and Chuck left to attend to other business. However, Chuck left his ace tiger trackers behind to assist my own team from the Smithsonian Nepal Tiger Ecology Project.

We visited the jogi's hut to scout for telltale signs of the tiger. The man-eater had left its pugmarks on the dirt path leading to and from the jogi's hut. We noted that the tiger had circled the hut a few times before trying to push the door open. After failing to get the door open, the tiger had sprinted across a field into a ravine about half a mile from the jogi's hut. The screeching sound of the jogi's girlfriend, coupled with the rattling of pots and pans, seemed to have caused the tiger to give up its quarry.

We followed the tiger's pugmarks about a hundred yards into a narrow ravine. They indicated that the tiger was hiding deep inside the gulch. The width of the ravine was too narrow for an elephant and too risky for us to venture on foot. We had to lure the tiger into the open, so we decided to bait the wide mouth of the gulch with live buffalo.

It was almost mid-afternoon when Man Bahadur Tamang, our head shikari, arrived with our capture equipment. Three government elephants based at park headquarters at Kasra arrived an hour later. (Our elephants at Saurah were too far away to make it to Bankatta for the night.) We tethered two young buffalo on sturdy poles sunk deep into the ground about twenty feet inside the ravine.

It had been almost five hours since we had arrived in Bankatta at noon. I parked on one side of the ravine, and Man Bahadur took up position on the opposite side. Both of us were equipped with drug-loaded dart guns. One elephant stood about twenty feet behind each of us on the flat top of the ravine. The third elephant was stationed at the mouth of the ravine. They were there for our safety, just in case the tiger ignored the bait and decided to come after us.

Our buffalo bait failed to draw the tiger into the open so that we could shoot it with our dart gun. Jogi Pothi remained deep in the ravine, forcing us to give up as darkness fell.

Hoping the tiger would come and make its kill under cover of darkness, we left the bait in the same position. We wanted to lure the tiger out to eat the bait and then stay put near the bait site. Before going back to the village to sleep for the night, we tied three elephants in the open about hundred feet from the bait. We hoped that these elephants would keep the tiger at bay, even if the tiger ignored the buffalo bait and decided to hunt humans inside the village. We were not sure if the lure of human flesh would prove stronger than the lure of buffalo meat for the man-eating tiger. The placement of guard elephants was also aimed at providing a sense of security to the frightened villagers, but it was probably a futile action. We had stretched our imagination beyond our knowledge. Any determined man-eating tiger could easily circumvent the elephants and sneak into the village in the hours of darkness.

Next morning, an hour after daylight, we went to check on our bait buffalo. They were alive and calmly resting on their sternums. They mooed as we approached them, and guilt rushed through my body. The sight of two docile young buffalo anchored to poles as sacrificial animals is neither a tasteful nor compassionate scene. Yet I often had to make similarly distasteful choices as a wildlife biologist in one of the world's most impoverished countries. I had learned to control my compassion.

We fed and watered the buffalo but left them there at the mercy of the man-eater. Bishnu and Harkha Man, two of our shikaris, replaced Man Bahadur and me to take their turns in waiting to dart the tiger. They spent the whole day waiting, but the man-eater did not come out of the ravine. They too withdrew from their positions as darkness fell over the Madi Valley. As on the evening before, we left the bait in the dark, with our elephants at a distance. Next morning, the result was the same. There were no signs of the tiger. The man-eater was determined to remain deep inside her hideout.

"Perhaps the elephants are keeping the tiger tucked inside the ravine," said Man Bahadur. I was not sure he was right. The elephants were a long distance from our bait. Furthermore, the wind was blowing away from the ravine, so the tiger could not smell the elephants. Nevertheless, we decided to move the elephants inside the village. As I had guessed, that effort had no impact.

The man-eating tiger proved to be an obstinate beast. For reasons we could not understand, it kept hidden inside the deep ravine. Perhaps she possessed some kind of sixth sense and knew we were waiting to get her. There were no pugmarks leading out of the ravine indicating that the tiger had bypassed our bait. We also did not find any evidence that she had crawled up the steep walls of the gorge. We could not analyze why the tiger stayed firmly inside the deep ravine, without food or water.

Again we fed and watered the buffalo and left them tethered for the third day. Assuming that the tiger had become aware of human presence, we also withdrew the dart shooters from waiting over the live bait. We thought the best tactic now would be to let the tiger make a kill and only then decide on how to deal with it. The buffalo were tied firmly by strong nylon ropes to stop the tiger from breaking the rope and dragging the beast deep into the gully. We wanted to force the tiger to feast on its kill at the bait site.

The third day and night of our attempted capture proved to be another abortive drill. As on the previous days, we found our bait alive and kicking. There was no sign of the tiger.

That morning we had a visit from an Indian ironsmith. He was equipped with several vicious snares in a variety of sizes and makes and claimed that he had trapped many man-eaters in India.

My shikaris and I were cynical. We knew the ironsmith would disappear across the border after selling me his wares, leaving us alone to deal with the tiger. We also believed that no sensible tiger would be caught in that kind of crude trap, particularly one that was laid out in plain sight on the barren and open ground. However, after the failures of the last three days, we were desperate to try anything.

We ventured a little deeper into the gorge and laid the snares along a narrow animal trail that penetrated the ravine. But I hadn't given up on the bait. In addition to the snares, we left our buffalo in the same position.

Neither the iron snares nor the buffalo bait worked. The man-eater was still at large. The tiger had either found food and water inside the ravine or decided to remain in the safety of the narrow gorge. Or it had somehow vanished from the gorge. I was losing my patience.

"It is a matter of time," advised Dhan Bahadur, one of Chuck McDougal's tiger trackers. "Although it can go without food for a week or more, I can not see how it can go without water for long." I looked at our shikaris, who nodded their heads in agreement. "I believe it will venture out of the gorge either today or tomorrow," added Sakale, his partner from Tiger Tops. I was not convinced. I thought the tiger—an agile animal—must have found an alternate path and moved out of the gorge into the nearby forests.

"I have tons of work to do with some of the village elders in Saurah," I said. "You guys stay and deal with the man-eater. I will go to Saurah and be back in a day or two." They bobbed their heads in agreement. "Dhan Bahadur and Sakale," I added, "you do the honors and dart the tiger. You have never darted a tiger before—maybe you will enjoy beginner's luck."

Despite my encouraging words, I did not believe that the man-eater could be bagged in the next two days. I was convinced that we had lost the tiger.

Our shikaris gave Dhan and Sakale a crash course in shooting straight, using a straw-filled jute sack as a target. It was not necessary; both men were sharpshooters. Leaving behind a trail of dust, I thundered out of Madi in my jeep. My business at Saurah proved to be a simple affair that did not require much time. I do not know if it was a sense of duty, the quest for camaraderie with my shikaris, the excitement of chasing man-eating tigers, or all three that stirred me to return to Madi Valley the next morning.

One mile before the village of Bankatta, I was surprised to see Bishnu, one of our shikaris, emerge on a bend along the trail. He was perched in front of a bullock cart that was crawling toward my jeep. The cart was driven by a villager who had kindly provided us with space to sleep in his house when I was in Bankatta. Three elephants quietly marched behind the bullock cart.

"Where on Earth are you going?" I yelled as my driver slowed the jeep.

"We nailed the man-eater," he said proudly, pointing to the back of the cart. The cart's load, hidden beneath a black blanket, resembled household goods the villagers often moved along the Bankatta trail. But I knew that the cargo was more precious than any human possessions. It was the mad man-eater of Madi. I was elated.

"When?" I asked gleefully.

"A few hours after you left," answered Bishnu.

"Dead or alive?" I blurted without thinking.

A smirk on his face, Bishnu answered, "Alive, of course." He waved the thumb of his right fist to the back of the cart. His tone of voice indicated, "What a stupid question!" I also thought his gestures held a subtle message. His body language clearly signaled that the shikaris were capable of catching man-eating tigers without having me micromanaging them.

"I must have been the bad luck," I remarked, trying to disguise my embarrassment at opening my mouth without thinking. Of course the tiger caught by my shikaris could be nothing but a live beast. "Can I peep in the cage?" I asked sheepishly.

Bishnu nodded his head. He jumped down from the bullock cart and walked me to the rear of the cart. I lifted the black cover and peeked inside. Through the gaps of a wooden cage, I saw the man-eating tiger. My first impression was that it looked awfully thin. Its coat was disheveled. I estimated that the tiger weighed less than two hundred pounds and measured seven to eight feet from nose to tip of the tail. Still under the influence of the drug, the man-eater was fast asleep. I looked at the mangy tiger for some time before putting the cover back.

"When did you catch it?" I asked Bishnu, lighting a cigarette.

"I didn't," he replied with a smug smile. He was being cheeky. He knew that I wanted to hear the whole story, and he was playing a game with me to build up my anxiety. My lips remained sealed. I accepted that he had a right to gloat. After all, he was a lead member of a team that had successfully captured a notorious man-eater, a team that had made the right decision without waiting for my orders. My silence seemed to have conveyed my message.

"After you left," he began, "we decided to place two shooters on both sides of the ravine, as we had done on the first day. As there were no pugmarks leading out of the ravine, we were certain the tiger was hiding inside the narrow gorge. It was only a matter of time before thirst and hunger would compel the tiger to leave the ravine. Our assumption proved to be right."

I was excited by his story. "What happened next?" I asked with curiosity.

"It was dusk when Sakale spotted the tiger," continued Bishnu. "It was creeping toward the mouth of the ravine. Soon the tiger spotted the bait. The buffalo were mooing in distress, noisily moving around the bait poles in a futile attempt to break the ropes that tethered them. They seem to have sighted or smelled the tiger before the tiger saw them. The panicky sounds of the buffalo caused the tiger to pause. It took a crouching position. It was at this instant that Sakale nailed the man-eater with his drug-laden dart.

The tiger did not appear to know what had hit her. It stood erect, looking around 360 degrees. Unsure of what lay ahead, the tiger began to track back into its hiding place. However, the drug was taking effect. The tiger took a resting position after moving a few yards."

Bishnu paused and stared at the back of the bullock cart. I waited patiently for him to continue. "I was the backup shooter, positioned on the opposite side of the ravine, lying on the ground on the top of the gully wall," continued Bishnu. "I was worried that the tiger would see me, as I was in its line of sight. However, the sight and sounds of the buffalo bait distracted the tiger. Nevertheless, I was very scared and watched the tiger nervously. As soon as I saw it collapse, I went back to camp and returned with the rest of our capture team.

Bishnu told me that they had loaded the tiger on a make-do stretcher improvised out of jute bags and moved it to the edge of the village. A few angry villagers tried to stone the tiger. Some tried to express their anger by kicking the unconscious animal. But overall, the villagers were peaceful and even helped transfer the tiger into a sturdy cage and load it on the back of a bullock cart.

Since nightfall was approaching, the shikaris decided to spend the night in the village. They got very little sleep. The cause of their sleeplessness had little to do with the man-eater and a lot to do with the free flow of alcohol and food at a party organized by the villagers for our team in honor of their capturing and incarcerating the man-eater.

Early the next morning, they found the tiger awake but still groggy from the effects of the drug. It might have been overdosed for its body weight. However, it gave an angry growl as Bishnu, Sakale, and the other shikaris peeked inside the cage. They decided that it was best to keep the tiger totally sedated during its transfer to the park headquarters in Kasra, a journey that could take three hours. Using the dart gun, they gave her another shot of the drug. Consequently, the tiger was totally immobilized when I met Bishnu on the roadside and peeked into its cage.

While I was talking with Bishnu, the rest of the shikaris caught up with us, with our third elephant carrying all our capture paraphernalia. I patted the shikaris on the back and congratulated them for their successful and timely operation. I rushed back to Kasra, returning to meet them with a small truck. We transferred the tiger from the bullock cart to the truck to be transported to the zoo in Kathmandu.

"Did the tiger have any wounds on its body, jaws, or paws?" I asked the shikaris over dinner later that evening.

"I examined the body and the paws thoroughly," answered Man Bahadur, our head shikari, "Its jaws were a bit eroded. We could find no other abnormalities."

"But" added Bishnu, interrupting Man Bahadur, "I think the tigress had seen better days. The body was too boney and its coat too scruffy. I reckon she is more than ten years old—an old and weak tiger."

We drove the tiger to Chitwan National Park headquarters in Kasra. There we decided to truck the deeply sedated man-eater to Kathmandu Zoo immediately. I did not drive with the tiger, as I had other commitments in Chitwan. I assigned the task to transport to Bishnu and Kuber—the best among the best of the drivers in the national park.

Perched on the banks of the Rapti River, I watched Kuber maneuver the truck across the quiet and low-flowing river until it disappeared behind noisy villages across the river to the north. Similar to the other four killer tigers I had captured in the past ten years, Jogi Pothi would spend the rest of her life behind bars in a dark, narrow, and cold cage.

Two decades later, as I was writing this book, my mind teemed with thoughts about man-eaters I had captured during my days in

Chitwan. My brain seesawed with conflicting questions: Should I have euthanized killer tigers like the Bhimle Tiger, Bange Bhale, and the Madi Pothi? Is it inhumane to confine man-killing tigers—or any wild tiger, for that matter—in narrow cages in a zoo? Or is it more compassionate simply to shoot badly behaving tigers on the spot?

A common practice among zookeepers in the West is to destroy tigers at their zoo that are potentially dangerous. No attempts are made to rehabilitate the beasts. A well-published example is the story of Tatiana, a magnificent Siberian tigress. She escaped from her enclosure at the San Francisco Zoo and attacked three young men—killing one of them and severely wounding the other two. Even though she was most likely provoked, she was shot dead on the spot.

Zoo records document a dozen incidents of tigers behaving badly in captivity in Europe and America, but this behavior is not restricted to captive animals. The stories in this book show that this abnormal behavior occurs even in the wild. But in either case, the killing of humans by tigers is rare. Humans are neither the tiger's natural prey nor its natural enemy. Yet the killings reflect an ultimate expression of conflict between man and tiger—a root cause that breeds contempt toward the beast. When an outburst of emotional and psychological anger against the killer tiger occurs, all tigers lose their standing as a respected and valued animal.

In part it is these unusual attacks that have caused humans to treat the majestic tiger as nothing but a wild animal to be hunted and killed, captured for a zoo, farmed, traded, or even eaten.

12

FARMERS, POACHERS, AND PROFITEERS

"USE IT OR LOSE IT" IS A SERMON FREQUENTLY PREACHED BY modern-day resource economists to save forests and wildlife resources in developing countries. They argue that wild mammals such as the tiger are products of the land. Consequently, they claim, the best way to ensure their survival is to mainstream the tiger's inherent economic value into a consumer-based market mechanism —complete with price tags and cost-benefit analyses. One of their clarion calls is to apply free-market principles to preserve tigers in the wild through sustainable use of captive-bred tigers to meet the cultural demand for tiger body parts.

The People's Republic of China (PRC) has taken this economic mantra to the ultimate form of freewheeling capitalism. In the 1980s they began to farm tigers to satisfy the lucrative market for tiger body parts, which included meat for human consumption, bones for beverages, and skins for rugs and robes. Other body parts are used as ingredients for traditional Chinese medicine. As a result, by the beginning of the twenty-first century, China became the largest consumer of tigers. It not only consumed body parts from captive-bred tigers in China, but it also became the largest illicit market for bones, skins, and other parts of wild tigers from neighboring countries.

Beginning in the early 1990s, several international organizations studied the trade in tigers for more than a decade with a missionary zeal. They included the Trade Record Analysis of Fauna and Flora in Commerce (TRAFFIC), an international body that monitors trafficking of endangered species; the International Fund for Animal Welfare (IFAW), a global organization that rescues animals from cruelty, abuse, and extinction; and the Environmental

Investigation Agency (EIA), an undercover watchdog that exposes illegal trade in wildlife.

These studies found that to hard-core believers in traditional Chinese medicine, the tiger is a carnivorous pharmacopeia. Virtually all parts of the beast's body have supposed medicinal properties. However, the belief that the tiger's body is a powerful panacea for all kinds of illnesses is not restricted to China but exists throughout Asia, including Japan, Korea, India, Malaysia, Indonesia, and Chinese communities in Europe and America.

Investigative studies both inside and outside China indicate that all the tiger's body parts, from its tail to its nose, are used to treat a wide range of ailments from malaria to meningitis and even alcoholism. The tiger's tail is used to treat skin infection. Its eyeballs are supposed to cure epilepsy and malaria. Powdered claw is used to cure insomnia. The pointed and curved nail of the claw is also worn around the neck as a charm that provides protection from evil spirits. People often carry tiger whiskers as a good-luck charm, particularly when visiting gambling establishments. They are also used to cure toothaches.

Beyond China, tiger fat is widely used in Nepal and India as an ointment for treating rheumatism. Tiger bile is used to treat meningitis and spasm. Even the tiger's feces and urine are used to treat boils, hemorrhoids, and alcoholism. The tiger's penis is prized as an aphrodisiac and is used to make love potions. This belief seems to have stemmed from the tiger's ability to mate frequently when in heat. Some even claim that Pfizer, the pharmaceutical company, subtly named its anti-impotency drug Viagra after *vyaghara,* the Sanskrit word for tiger. Unfortunately, the introduction of Viagra and other anti-impotency drugs has not reduced the demand for tiger parts as an aphrodisiac across the globe.

The use of tiger body parts for medicinal purpose and the consumption of tiger meat was once restricted to the upper crust of Chinese society—largely because they were rare and expensive.

However, the economic boom has made these parts affordable to a larger segment of the Chinese population. Consequently, consumption of tiger body parts has spiraled upward at an unprecedented rate, giving rise to captive breeding of tigers to satisfy market demand. These facilities are commonly known as tiger farms, even if the commercial names of the establishments are disguised as animal or amusement parks.

Although the use of tiger and other animal body parts for medicinal purpose is an ancient practice, farming tigers for human consumption is not a Chinese tradition. Tiger farming evolved in the 1980s after China made a major transformation in its economic paradigm. Instead of relying on Marxist models, the Chinese shifted to free-market instruments to boost economic growth. Hence, tiger farming is nothing but a by-product of Communist China's great leap forward toward Western-style capitalism. The growth of tiger farms was largely driven by the Chinese government policy that prescribed captive breeding as an integral part of saving wildlife. China's Wildlife Protection Law (1998) explicitly states that the State shall encourage the domestication and breeding of wildlife, including private sector participation.

International trade in tiger parts was banned in 1975 under the Convention on Trade in Endangered Species of Wild Flora and Fauna (CITES). Tigers were listed in appendix 1 of this United Nations–administered covenant banning trade and trafficking of wildlife as being among the world's most endangered species threatened by extinction. Export or import of any tiger body parts was forbidden. However, in-country trading of tiger bones and other body parts continued openly within the national boundaries of Asian countries such as Korea, China, and Taiwan as well as Hong Kong. Sale of tiger bones, skins, and other parts flourished in the open market.

In response to international pressure, in 1993 the Chinese government issued a ban on all trade in tiger bones or by-products only. This ban was not effective largely because of legal loopholes, weak enforcement, and differences between national and local priorities and procedures. Furthermore, the bourgeoning demand for tiger bones, skins, and other body parts made the market even more lucrative. The ban forced tiger market prices up and traders to innovate. They found ways to circumvent the ban. Tiger farms—often disguised as conservation or educational centers or public exhibits—sustained the Chinese trade in tiger bones and body parts. The number of tigers in these farms grew rapidly.

The International Fund for Animal Welfare (IFAW), an international nonprofit organization, reports that there are at least five tiger farms in China, four of them licensed by China's State Council. The most recent farm was created in 2002 with partial government financing in Hainan Province and given the catchy name "Extinct Wildlife Breeding Center."

Currently the exact number of tigers in captivity in China is unknown. IFAW estimates that there are more than five thousand captive tigers in China. Most of them are concentrated in the five main tiger farms in Hengdaohezi (Heilongjiang Province), Guilin (Gunangxi Zhuang Autonomous Region), Shenyang and Dalian (Liaoning Province), and Tiandu (Hainan Province). It is estimated that annual reproduction is more than eight hundred tigers. These tiger farms often double as tiger-themed parks with exotic names. For example, the tiger farm in Hainan is called the Greatest World of Love, even if the love and care provided to the tigers and other animals in captivity are minimal.

In December 2003, a tiger farm in the Hainan province of China created scandalous headlines in Bangkok newspapers. To their embarrassment, Thai authorities discovered that one hundred Royal Bengal tigers had been clandestinely shipped to China from Bangkok's Don Maung International Airport on a chartered jumbo jet. These live tigers belonged to the Sriracha Tiger Zoo, a private theme park outside Bangkok, and were exported in violation of both Thai law and CITES. The scandal was badly timed. The story broke when Thailand was preparing to host the thirteenth meeting of the Conference of the Parties to CITES and was expecting thousands of delegates from 166 countries to arrive in Bangkok. Curbing illicit trade in tiger parts was a key item on the agenda of this global gathering. The news reinforced Thailand's unsavory reputation as an illicit megamall for the US $12 billion illicit global trade in wildlife because media reports indicated that these tigers from Thailand were to be butchered to feed burgeoning markets for their meat, skin, bones, and other body parts in China. The Chinese are not alone in recommending a market-driven model to save the tiger. A number of Westerners have also ardently promulgated this credo. They claim that captive breeding of tigers to satisfy market demands for their body parts would reduce both the price and illicit trafficking and thus help save tigers still in the wild.

Yet records on poaching and quantities of wild tiger bones and skins seized in transit to China indicate that the "use it or loose it" mantra remains largely hypothetical at best. Nevertheless, the debate between proponents and opponents of the hypothesis has become a spirited topic at many global congregations of tiger experts. The International Tiger Symposium, held in Kathmandu in April 2007, was no exception. Representatives from twelve tiger-range countries participated in this gathering, which was hosted by Nepal's Department of National Parks and Wildlife Conservation (DNPWC). Participants included delegates from both governmental and nongovernmental organizations (NGOs), including the International Tiger Coalition, a global alliance of more than one hundred organizations whose membership are mostly dominated by the "Tiger-Wallahs."

Tiger-Wallah is an Indian term that means a "tiger-person," connoting people who are devoted to or professionally engaged in saving the tiger. *Wallah* is a Hindi word used to designate a person's profession or trade. Geoffrey Ward, an American historian and screenwriter, coined the term in his book *Tiger-Wallahs*. The book, which he wrote with Diane Raines Ward, described iconic conservationists who have been stalwartly waging war to save tigers from extinction for decades.

Geoff, an old friend, is an encyclopedia of who's who in tiger conservation. A New Yorker and himself a Tiger-Wallah, he spent a lot of time in the jungles of India and Nepal studying and writing about tigers. Geoff is also pragmatic. He remains unchallenged as one of the earliest realists who warned that past efforts to save the tiger had not been as successful as claimed by governments or international NGOs. Launched with loud sound bites and extravagant fanfare and spearheaded by European royalty such as Britain's Prince Philip and the late Prince Bernhard of the Netherlands, these efforts only delayed the tiger's demise. Tigers remain on the threshold of extinction in 2009 as they did in 1972, when the World Wildlife Fund (WWF) launched "Operation Tiger" to bring the tiger back from the brink of extinction.

Public criticism, largely from NGOs, is that three decades of national and international efforts to save the tiger have failed in China and provided an impetus to the International Tiger Symposium in Nepal, where the contentious issue of tiger farming was on the agenda.

The key objective of the international gathering in Kathmandu was to promote regional collaboration and cooperation and find common ground on how to curb illicit trade in wild tigers. However, to the embarrassment of its Nepalese hosts, the meeting was neither civil nor collaborative. Instead it culminated in an all-out brawl.

Scuffles broke out between Westerners and the Chinese delegation on the issue of tiger farming. Some western NGOs, equipped with a video camera, confronted the Chinese delegation on the legality of selling tiger body parts. These NGOs were armed with DNA evidence obtained by Britain's Independent Television

News (ITN) proving that tiger meat was on the menu at such restaurants as the Xionsen Bear and Tiger Mountain Village, a government licensed center near the city of Guilin. They argued that serving tiger meat was illegal because China had ratified CITES in 1981 and had banned the sale of tiger meat, tiger bone, or any part of the tiger's body since 1993.

The aggressive questioning by Western NGOs on camera triggered tempers. The Chinese were angered by the implication that tiger farms were deliberately subverting CITES and Chinese laws. One of the members of the Chinese delegation became enraged, and the dialogue ended in a fight. The Nepalese hosts were forced to summon the police to cool down the highly charged atmosphere.

The Chinese delegation took the incident to be yet another case of "China bashing" by the West. They claimed that the agenda to review China's domestic use of tiger parts had been included in the International Tiger Symposium agenda not at the behest of Western NGOs but at the request of the Chinese delegation. They also accused Western NGOs of deliberately provoking and then recording the brawl on camera to create anti-Chinese sentiment in the media. The Chinese delegation accused the Western NGOs of being self-righteous and complained that they were oblivious to the efforts of China's State Forest Administration to seek guidance from experts attending the symposium on a proposal to lift the 1993 ban on the sale of products from captive-bred tigers in China's domestic markets.

The Chinese delegation included owners of tiger breeding centers, who did not believe their activities were illegal under Chinese laws. Their operations were licensed by the government, and they paid taxes like any other business in China. Furthermore, state or provincial governments subsidized some farms with monetary credits and loans. The Chinese "tiger farmers" argued that they were business executives trying to protect legitimate assets. They demanded compensation for their investments from the international tiger community if their critics wanted them to close their operations.

Some of the NGO participants believed that the owners of business entities like the Xionsen Bear and Tiger Mountain Village ran illicit operations and then cajoled and corrupted government officials to ensure that they could continue to make huge profits from the selling of tiger parts. The participation of these business owners was unacceptable to the NGOs, who accused the Chinese tiger farmers of being merchants of greed and perpetrators of dishonest practices.

Yet to the Chinese officials, these business owners had a major stake in the captive breeding of tigers because they had invested heavily in their government-sanctioned facilities. They claimed that provincial governments were under immense pressure to lift the ban or pay compensation from the owners of the captive-breeding facilities that had been lawfully created. Thus it was only right that the voices of these key stakeholders should also be heard at the symposium. They also argued that CITES had neither prescribed nor prohibited how dead tigers bred in captivity are disposed of internally.

The major criticism focused on China's wildlife protection laws, which encourage captive breeding and domestication of wildlife as a tool for conservation. Although China has successfully demonstrated breeding and reintroduction schemes for endangered species such as the giant panda and Père David's deer, the captive breeding of the tiger has remained purely a commercial venture. The reintroduction of tigers into the wild is a key policy of China's State Forestry Administration! Yet facilities such as the Xionsen Bear and Tiger Mountain Village are nothing more than breeding factories, where the tigers are raised in tightly packed cages. Consequently, China is no different from most developing countries, where there is often a total discord between written policies, their factual interpretation, and their actual implementation.

Feasting on tiger is an expensive culinary taste and thus a highly profitable business for tiger farm owners. For example, a meal of tiger soup followed by stir-fried or curried tiger meat could easily cost between US $100 and $150. Discerning diners who wish to follow this exotic dinner with tiger bone wine pay another $30 to $125, depending on the vintage of the liquor and the freshness of the tiger bone. Aficionados order the penis of a freshly killed tiger at a cost of up to US $5,700, making it one of the most expensive of gastronomic experiences.

China is not the only country in Asia with restaurants that serve tiger meat or body parts of other wild animals, including endangered species. Eateries that serve tiger are also found in Thailand, Malaysia, and Indonesia, where they operate more covertly than in China.

Recent adverse publicity generated by an international campaign against serving tiger meat has forced even eateries in China to be more discreet. Consequently, many restaurants in China have stopped serving tiger meat openly to foreign visitors. Tiger farms in China attract hordes of visitors, who pay high entry fees to see or even feed tigers. However, the entry fees are not the only source of revenue for the tiger farms. Dead tigers are equally profitable. In addition to being sold for meat and other body parts, virtually all the tigers at these facilities end up in huge vats of rice wine. There they are left for a few years to decompose and ferment into an alcoholic beverage that is marketed as "tiger wine."

The most sought-after tiger wine is made with tiger bones, making the bones the most lucrative part of the tiger's body. The demand for tiger bones by China's wine industry is a primary factor in driving wild tigers toward extinction. Because the trade is illegal, there is no exact data on the illicit trade in tiger bones. However, it is believed that China's tiger wine industry consumes between five thousand and seven thousand pounds of tiger bones annually. Depending on the size and subspecies of tiger, this is equivalent to the killing of two hundred to three hundred tigers per year.

Those who have drunk tiger wine describe it as an overpoweringly foul smelling cocktail of methylated spirits and rotten meat; seemingly unfit for human consumption. Yet the tradition of using tiger and animal products as an ingredient in distilling liquor dates back to the Han Dynasty, which ruled China for four centuries (202 B.C. to A.D. 220).

Even today, tiger bone wine is prized by well-heeled connoisseurs. Brands and prices range widely (from US $20 to $125 per bottle). Some of the wines are even sold in bottles that resemble the shape of a tiger. Most of the purveyors claim that their wines are made from tigers raised in captivity. However, online wine auctions often offer wine they claim is made from wild not captive-bred tigers. These wines carry higher price tags on their opening bid.

Tiger bones are also marketed in two other forms: powder and gel. The former is extensively used in traditional Chinese medicine to treat rheumatism. The prescribed daily dose is 0.2 to 0.4 ounce per person per day. It is estimated that more than sixteen million people in China use tiger bone medicine annually as a cure for rheumatism.

The rising demand in China for bones and other tiger body parts has spurred the illegal trading of tigers in Nepal and other neighbors of the People's Republic of China. Prominent Tiger-Wallahs believe that tiger farming has not reduced but actually increased poaching and the illicit cross-border smuggling of tiger bone. The arrests of smugglers became more frequent as the price and the quantity of tiger bones illicitly exported into China increased.

Until the late 1980s, little was known in the Indian subcontinent about the use of tiger bones in winemaking or in traditional Chinese medicine. Nepal's Department of National Park and Wildlife Conservation (DNPWC) was no exception. The DNPWC were also unaware that Nepal was a major transit point for smuggling tiger bones and tiger skins from South Asia to mainland China via the Tibetan Autonomous Region (TAR), People's Republic of China. In 1989 we were astounded when the chief district officer of the Darchula District in western Nepal reported that he had intercepted more than six hundred pounds of tiger bones bound for Tibet. Darchula, near Nepal's northern border with Tibet, is one of the country's most remote districts. That same year, a post office in Jumla, another remote district in northwestern Nepal that borders Tibet, reported the seizure of 550 pounds of tiger bones that had been mailed in twenty-pound parcels from Nepalgunj, a bustling trade town on the Nepal-India border. Investigation by my colleagues in the DNPWC revealed that these bones had been purchased in Rupaidya, an Indian town on the other side of the Nepal-India border. Before these two interceptions, the Nepalese authorities had not been aware of the illicit trans-border trade in tiger bones.

During the next ten years, almost 2,200 pounds of tiger bones were intercepted on their way to Tibet. This may be only the tip of the illicit iceberg, as law enforcement in Nepal was ineffective due to the insurgency led by the Nepal Communist Party (Maoist), which peaked by the year 2000. Nevertheless, the interception of tiger bones revealed two important facts: First, Nepal was a major transit point for the illicit trade in tiger parts. Second, the demand for tiger bones had increased dramatically due to a major paradigm shift in China from state-controlled economy to free-market economy.

Under the communist state-regulated economy, the trade in tiger bones and other body parts was rigidly controlled. Consequently, tons of tiger bones were being hoarded in warehouses throughout China. These stockpiles presumably included bones of tigers poached or confiscated within China, the Russian Far East, and elsewhere. The price of tiger bones went up as China opened its markets to private enterprises. The hoarded stock quickly dwindled and was exhausted by 1990.

However, the demand for tiger bone wine, gel, and powder did not wane. It surged as the Chinese became wealthier and the private sector became a key player in the demand and supply of tiger parts. Wealth also heightened demands for traditional Chinese medicines. Consequently, market forces induced the smuggling of tiger bones from neighboring countries.

Like contraband drugs such as heroin and cocaine, the price of tiger bones to the consumer market in China varied widely from source countries such as Nepal, Bangladesh, and India. Given the black market nature of the trade, the retail price of tiger bones was very speculative. Nevertheless, interrogation of smugglers indicated that raw tiger bones retailed for US $100 per pound in Nepal in the 1990s. By the time smuggled bones crossed the border into Tibet, the price had soared to as much as US $1,000 per pound. The price of the bones when they reached markets in mainland China is not known. However, according to the Environmental Investigation Agency—a Britain-based international wildlife trade watchdog—the 2009 price for tiger bone ranged from US $1,400 to $3,000 per pound.

Tiger bone gel is sold for much less, as it can easily be adulterated. Currently it is believed to retail for about US $1,000 to $1,500 per pound, indicating that it is not derived from 100 percent pure tiger bones. However, the practice of using tiger gel for medicinal purposes is not as common in China as it is in the countries of Indochina, particularly Vietnam, and in Hong Kong and Macau.

Tiger bones and other internal body parts are not the only parts used by humans. By late 1980s, the TAR emerged as the biggest market for tiger skin. In the 1960s tiger-skin coats were in vogue for the wealthy in Europe and America. However, Western conservation organizations and animal rights group were successful in stopping that trade by running aggressive campaigns that demonstrated that it was not fashionable but cruel to sport a tiger-skin coat. One of their successful strategies was to use the media to harangue sixties sex symbol Gina Lollobrigida for wearing a US $200,000 tiger-skin coat made from ten wild tigers. By the 1980s garments made of tiger skin had disappeared in the West but emerged in Tibet. Isolated from the outside world, Tibetans were unaware that wearing tiger-skin garments was unacceptable to the global community.

With economic growth propelled by a free-market economy, Tibetans became fashion conscious in their daily life. In the 1980s Western conservation organizations were unaware that new lucrative markets for tiger-skin *chubas* were emerging in the bazaars of the Tibetan Plateau. The *chuba,* a traditional Tibetan garment, is a long cloak tied around the waist with a long sash. This ankle-length robe is often worn over thick woolen trousers.

By the year 2000, Lhasa's Barkhor Street, a vibrant market in the Tibetan capital, was saturated with tiger skins, mostly used to trim or skirt parts of the chuba or the entire garment. Depending on the size of the tiger skin, the price of the chuba ranged from US $3,000 to $5,000. These high prices propelled smuggling of tiger skins into Tibet via Nepal. In 2003 customs officers near the Purang Pass seized 1,392 wild animal pelts, including 31 tiger and 581 leopard skins. Purang is a 12,800-foot-high mountain pass on the Nepal-Tibet border used by Nepalese and Indian pilgrims to visit Lake Manasarovar and Mount Kailash in western Tibet. In 2005 a patrol from Langtang National Park in central Nepal intercepted 240 tiger skins heading to Tibet through Raswua Ghari on the Nepal-Tibet border.

It was both surprising and shocking to see the wearing of tiger-skin garments reemerge not in the West but in the Buddhist state of Tibet. By 2005 wearing tiger skins as a part of their garments had peaked for the newly rich in the TAR. His Holiness the Dalai Lama was alarmed and repelled by this new fashion. In February 2006 he called upon his fellow Tibetans to stop wearing garments made of tiger or leopard skins. He declared that wearing a tiger skin was a sacrilegious act unworthy of Tibetans.

Dalai Lama's decree was widely broadcast over the radio and videotaped for distribution inside Tibet. The videotapes were smuggled into Tibet and shown in monasteries and sites where Tibetan communities assemble. The impact was immediate and positive. Tibetans who once sported tiger skin coats burned their coats in bonfires in towns and villages across the Tibetan Plateau. The Dalai Lama's statement also had a big impact among residents of Tibetan and Buddhist communities in Nepal and India, who also destroyed their tiger-skin garments. Sales of tiger skins started to fade in markets in both Nepal and in Tibet, but the trade did not stop completely.

Investigations launched by the Environmental Investigation Agency (EIA), both overtly and covertly, indicate that the current price for a tiger skin varies from US $11,660 to $21,860 depending upon the quality and size of the skin. Similarly, each tiger tooth fetches US $650. Add to these the price of tiger bones at US $1,900 to $3,000 per pound plus the prices of dried tiger penis, fat, meat, and even the claws, and a dead wild tiger could fetch as high as US $30,000 to $40,000 in the Chinese black market.

Given the profit margins, trade in tiger skins and other body parts is too lucrative to abandon. The secretive trade is controlled by crime syndicates, mostly headquartered in India—a fact that was highly publicized by the arrest of Sansar Chand, a kingpin in the illicit wildlife trade, in Delhi in June 2005.

Chand was called the "Evil Genius" for forming a cartel with Nepalese and Tibetan partners to smuggle tiger skins and bones from India to mainland China via Nepal and Tibet. He earned his infamous title for his part in wiping out all the tigers in Sariska National Park, once a premier tiger reserve in Rajasthan in northwestern India, mostly by baiting and poisoning wild tigers.

Chand is a member of the Kanjar tribe of Rajasthan. Traditionally the Kanjars made their living by hunting wildlife, including snakes, rabbits, jackals, and porcupines, to sell their meat, bones, leather, and other body parts. During the colonial era of the British Raj, they were designated as "despicable groups" for their ultraliberal views on sex and allegedly using their women for prostitution. Consequently they were regarded as among the most abhorrent ethnic groups in India's caste- and creed-controlled society.

After India became independent, the government was very much concerned about the Kanjars' welfare, as they ranked among the poorest of Indian society. To maximize the use of their traditional talents, the government gave them special license to catch and sell rhesus monkeys for export to biomedical research facilities in Europe and America. However, being uneducated and poor, the Kanjars sold their catch through higher-caste intermediaries, who exploited their hard labor and pocketed most of the profit. By 1977 India had banned the catching and export of monkeys. In addition, most hunting and trapping were made illegal under India's wildlife preservation laws.

However, the government's laws didn't prevent the trade from being profitable. Many Kanjars went back to their traditional livelihood of hunting and trapping, even though it was now illegal. Sansar Chand was one of them.

Born poor in 1958, he started poaching and selling wildlife as a child. By age sixteen he had become a criminal mastermind. He was arrested for illicit trade in tigers, leopards, and an assortment of more than 670 other wild animals and sentenced to eighteen months in jail. However, he served only six months before being released as an underage criminal in accordance with the Indian penal code.

This sentence did not deter Chand from further wildlife crimes. By the time he was convicted again in 2003, he had more than fifty cases pending against him in courts that stretched through nine states of the Indian Union. But he escaped a harsh jail sentence through bail, bribery, and brilliant legal representation. Chand also allowed no outsiders to penetrate the core of his organization. His immediate family members formed the inner circle of his crime syndicate. These included his wife, Rani Saini, and his son, Akash.

Though government institutions were comparatively lax in pursuing Chand, a number of NGOs were persistent in their efforts to see that India's most notorious poacher was jailed. Their efforts finally paid off. In June 2005 Delhi police raided Chand's warehouse and confiscated the largest haul of illicit wildlife skins, bones, and other body parts in history.

Indian wildlife conservation organizations hoped that he would receive a long jail sentence. However, in March 2008 the court dismissed his case for lack of evidence. Chand's lawyers used legal loopholes in India's arcane legal system to dispute Chand's tie with the raided warehouse, even though his mother lived there. NGOs still hope that Chand will receive a severe sentence from the more than forty cases that are pending against him in several states in India.

Fortunately, thanks to the efforts of Indian NGOs in assisting law enforcement and publicizing the cases, Chand is currently languishing in jail. Before being released, he was charged again under the Mumbai Control of Organized Crime Act (MCOCA). The provisions of MCOCA were used for the first time in India for a crime against wildlife in March 2008. Unless the act is repealed, it is unlikely that Chand will be released anytime soon. His wife, Rani, and his son, Akash, are also in jail after being arrested in October 2004 for breaking wildlife protection laws.

Another notorious tiger poacher, Abdul Khader Chaudhary, was arrested in the State of Karnataka in southern India in February 2008. Alleged to be a criminal partner with Sansar Chand's son, he is infamously credited for being singlehandedly responsible for smuggling six hundred tiger skins out of India.

As of this writing, at least a dozen tigers had been poached in 2009. Earlier that year, the Wildlife Protection Society of India (WPSI), a New Delhi–based NGO dedicated to combating poaching, reported that at least six tigers had been poached in major tiger reserves in India. Likewise, the Wildlife Conservation Society (WCS) a New York–based nonprofit, reported that thirty-three tiger skins had been seized from an illicit wildlife trader in Sumatra, Indonesia. Although the number of tigers poached in Nepal is not known, the Wildlife Conservation Network (WCN), another wildlife watchdog, reports that poaching of tigers continues throughout the Terai forests of southern Nepal.

The *Hindu,* one of India's national newspapers, reported on October 14, 2009, that, after months of pursuit, a notorious poacher named Paapu had been arrested by the staff of Nagarhole National Park, a major national park in the state of Karnataka in southern India.

The orthodox methods of saving tigers in the wild, largely based on protection and punishment, have been heavily criticized, mostly by social-sector NGOs. They have questioned the practicality of arrests and imprisonment of poachers as a sustainable deterrent to reverse the sinking population of tigers in the wild. These critics have also pointed out that picking a fight with established tiger farmers in China is a futile exercise. Designing innovative programs to prevent poaching of wild tigers on the Indian subcontinent will deliver better results than condemning the Chinese.

The Tiger-Wallahs must rationally address some difficult questions from the Chinese perspective, particularly regarding the farming of tigers to eat their bones and flesh. By trying to dismiss the proponents of the "use it or lose it" principle, are the international wildlife conservation NGOs trying to divert attention from their own failures in bringing back the tiger from the brink of extinction? Is the "eat it to save it" paradigm a prudent strategy—a pragmatic and ethical tactic that equates Asia's largest wild cat with America's farmed bison or Russia's commercial reindeer herds?

13
EAT IT TO SAVE IT

WHEN IT COMES TO MAKING MONEY, POACHING TRUMPS ANIMAL conservation every time. Greed for quick and easy money overwhelmingly outpaces fear of arrest and conviction. For example, a wildlife guard entrusted to protect tigers makes about US $100 to $150 per month, depending upon his rank or years of service. In contrast, a poacher can easily bag about US $1,500 at the minimum, in one night for a tiger skin and at least another US $1,500 for bones and other body parts. Although many wildlife guards are honest, there is a built-in incentive to be corrupt, particularly if one considers the dismal pay scale, sad state of housing, and other facilities provided to these front-line foot soldiers assigned to protect tigers.

Some development experts have stated that unemployment, underemployment, and lack of opportunities for making an honest living are the root causes of conservation woes in tiger countries. They have pointed out that the past forty years of efforts to save the tiger by governments, guns, and guards have failed miserably.

Currently the tiger is restricted to only 5 percent of what used to be its historical range in the wild, which once stretched from the banks of the Caspian Sea to the coasts of the Pacific Ocean in Siberia. Moreover, the tiger's numbers have dwindled from one hundred thousand at the beginning of the twentieth century to only 3,500 today. These experts argue that international efforts to ban tiger farming and trade in tiger parts only helps poachers and smugglers at the national level.

Barun Mitra, president of Liberty Institute and the Julian Simon Centre in New Delhi, India, and a leading development expert, is one who promotes economic incentives to save endangered species such as the tiger. In a provocative op-ed article in the *New York Times* in October 2006, he claimed that the Chinese are on the right track with their approach to making tiger conservation compatible with commercial sales. He proclaimed that farming tigers to meet the growing market demand for tiger parts is a pragmatic approach.

A firm believer in market forces, Mitra argued that there is no incentive for the poor in tiger countries to protect tigers. He also claimed that unlike transparent and free market forces, high-handed government regulations breed corruption that benefits only poachers, illicit traffickers, and criminals. Harsh but unenforceable laws only drive the trade underground and jack up black market prices, building incentives against saving the tiger.

Mitra is not the only one who believes the best option to save endangered species lies in unshackling their commercial potential. Dr. V. Santhakumar, professor at the Centre for Development Studies in India, also champions tiger farming. He recommended that China should not ban but open the market for tiger bones and other body parts through a regulated market mechanism.

These free-market proponents assert that the command-and-control approach of the government and international NGOs fails to recognize the harsh realities of life in developing countries. Some have pointed out that even in the United States, the world's richest country, the American bison was brought back from the brink of extinction through private-sector incentives for farming and ranching. If it is right for Americans to buy bison burgers in the supermarket, why should it be wrong for Chinese to eat farmed tiger meat or drink wine fermented from the bones of captive tigers?

This point was argued vehemently in May 2009 by John F. Stossel, co-anchor of America's ABC News *20/20* special program on tiger preservation. "Sell them and eat them," said Stossel, a writer, author, and investigative journalist. He was reiterating that the best way to save the tigers is to farm them and eat them. "International bans on the trade of rare animal parts (tiger organs, elephant tusks, rhino horns) have been about as successful as the international war on drugs," he added.

A champion of a free and open market driven by supply and demand, Stossel compared tigers to chickens or the bison in America. He argued that private owners should be encouraged to raise and sell tigers for human consumption.

Stossel's comments created a furor among the Tiger-Wallahs, who dismissed him as a right-wing sensationalist who lacked any evidence to back up his opinions. Others, however, pointed out that some endangered crocodiles were saved from extinction by breeding them in captivity and tapping the economic potential of their skins.

True believers in market forces like Mitra, Stossel, and Santhakumar contend that neither national governments nor international NGOs can continue to demand the same thing repeatedly and expect positive results in light of four decades of miserable failure. They claim that despite the unprecedented rate of growth of conservation groups, proliferation of tiger conferences, and hundreds of millions of dollars spent on preservation, the tiger is just as close to extinction as when the World Wildlife Fund launched Operation Tiger in 1972. In short, they want the conservation community not to prohibit but to encourage tiger farming, albeit with an open and transparent set of standards and monitoring mechanisms.

Others argue that it is time to let the tiger go extinct in the wild. Paradoxically one of them is not a development economist but a conservationist. Chris Packman, a prominent British wildlife expert and producer of award-winning wildlife films, appears regularly on British television shows. In September 2009 he created a furor that pitted him against the World Wildlife Fund (WWF) and other conservation groups, arguing that it is time to "pull the plug" on the giant panda—the WWF emblem—and let it die out in its natural habitat. He claimed that the process of evolution has destined the panda to become extinct. Thus, he claimed, it is a waste of resources to spend large amounts of money to save a species that is not strong enough to survive the natural evolutionary processes. He went on to declare the same fate for the wild tiger.

"I don't think tigers are going to last another fifteen years," he asserted, shocking friends and foes alike. "How can you conserve an animal that is worth more dead than alive?" he continued. "You can't."

One person who does not agree with Packman is Canadian wildlife expert Eugene Lapointe. He is a major proponent of captive breeding of tigers for human consumption as the most pragmatic measure to ensure that tigers are preserved in the wild. Surprisingly, from 1982 to 1990 Lapointe served as Secretary General of the Convention on International Trade in Endangered Species of Wild Fauna and Flora (CITES), the very body that is pressuring China to close all that country's tiger farms.

A former Canadian civil servant, Lapointe became an ardent believer that any policy that prescribes a "no-use" model is fatally flawed. He claimed that prohibition of tiger farming is the key factor driving the tiger toward extinction. Lapointe asserts that it is unrealistic in today's world to rely on governments or various international NGOs to save the tiger from extinction, when more than one billion people live, mostly in tiger countries, on less than one dollar a day.

After serving eight years as Secretary General of CITES, Lapointe was fired for his unorthodox views. Several international NGOs revolted against his belief in the market-based approach to saving the earth's endangered wildlife. Undeterred by his dismissal, he founded the IWMC World Conservation Trust in 1994. IWMC, which stands for International Wildlife Management Trust, is a coalition of wildlife managers who believe that sustainable use is the most powerful tool for saving the world's dwindling

wildlife resources, and Lapointe is one of the most vocal proponents of the "use it or lose it" paradigm.

Champions of this paradigm cite several examples to prove
their point. One of them is the caiman, a crocodilian found in
Central and South America. In the early 1970s trade in caimans
was banned under CITES. However, because the ban did not
diminish the highly lucrative illicit trade in caiman skins, caimans
remained an endangered species. In the early 1980s some South
American governments mobilized scientists, conservationists,
traders, and indigenous people to revisit the caiman trade issues.
Based on their recommendations, some South American countries
reversed their policy, encouraging the captive breeding of caimans
and creating mechanisms to regulate their trade. Within a decade,
the caiman populations recovered. According to Lapointe, CITES
has no record of illegal trade in caiman skins for the last decade.

Another example Lapointe uses is the case of the vicuña, a
member of the camel family that lives in the Andes Mountains
of South America. This relative of the alpaca and the llama has
some of the world's finest wool, which fetches from US $1,800 to
$3,000 per yard. Poached indiscriminately for their meat and wool,
the vicuña population had dwindled to fewer than six thousand in
the 1960s. Trade in vicuña was prohibited when CITES came into
force in the 1970s. However, with a man's vicuña wool coat fetch-
ing US $15,000 to $20,000 in European and American markets,
the ban was totally ineffective.

The governments of Chile, Peru, and Argentina took a more
realistic approach. First, they created new national parks and protected areas. Second, they reinforced antipoaching programs. Third,
by the 1990s they had legalized the trade of vicuña wool but only
from animals that were captured alive. The wool could be sheared
and the animal released back into the wild. It was also prohibited to
recapture and shear the same animal for at least another two years.
The scheme is transparent and highly regulated by each country's

government. The program also ensures that a large portion of the profit goes to local villagers who live in and around the vicuña habitat, providing economic incentives to save the vicuña at the local level. Currently the vicuña population is estimated to be near 125,000.

Lapointe asserts that this kind of program is an example of how a commonsense approach to conservation can increase the population of an endangered species by more than twenty times in four decades. However, assertions by Lapointe and other advocates of the "use it or lose it" model of market-based initiatives failed to convince CITES member countries to lift the ban on tiger trade at the fourteenth meeting of the Conference of the Parties of the CITES at The Hague in the Netherlands in June 2007. Despite hard lobbying by the Chinese, 171 member countries of the CITES overwhelmingly voted against domestic and international trade in tiger body parts. However, it is yet to be seen if this ruling will mean closure of tiger farms in China, most of which operate as private zoos or entertainment parks. It is also not clear whether this decision will force the overt sale of tiger meat and tiger bones underground or will create black markets that are even more lucrative.

The CITES resolution at The Hague would not have been possible without an intensive campaign by American NGOs such as the Save the Tiger Fund, the International Fund for Animal Welfare, and the World Wildlife Fund. They worked behind the scenes to forge a strategic alliance between the United States and key tiger countries such as India, Nepal, Bhutan, and Russia. Jointly they killed a Chinese proposal to lift the ban on tiger trade. However, this ban is also subject to interpretation and enforcement by member countries.

As previously noted, captive tiger centers in China are not called "tiger farms" but are officially designated as public recreational centers or even as tiger-breeding centers. Tigers at these centers are legal and private property akin to the private ownership of tigers in the United States and elsewhere in the Western world.

Consequently, some Chinese accuse the Americans of being hypocrites when it comes to developing countries, particularly China. They point out that the United States has more tigers in captivity than any other country on Earth.

The exact number of tigers in captivity in the United States is not known, but estimates range from five thousand to as high as twelve thousand. The most reliable figure is provided by the Trade Record Analysis of Fauna and Flora in Commerce (TRAFFIC)—an integral partner of the WWF and the World Conservation Union. Their best estimate on the number of captive tigers in the United States is five thousand. This disparity in numbers largely stems from the fact that except for facilities accredited by the American Association of Zoos and Aquariums (AAZPA), records of tigers kept as pets or in private preserves are not known.

TRAFFIC's studies of the captive tiger population in the United States indicate that rules and regulations governing captive breeding and private ownership of tigers are haphazard and vary from state to state. There are no federal standards or mechanisms to monitor tigers in private possession. Nine states do not require any kind of permit or registration to keep tigers as pets. Laws in the thirty-nine states that do have some kind of regulatory mechanism are riddled with loopholes. Exceptions to the rules are readily made for a panoply of private bodies such as dealers; breeders; roadside shows; circuses; education, research, and entertainment facilities; and other activities.

It is also not clear what happens to a tiger after it dies in the United States, particularly the tiger's bones, the most lucrative part of the animal's body. Tiger bones can easily be ground and sold in powder form. There is no evidence that powdered tiger bones are being exported from the United States to China; however, given high prices and strong market demand, the possibility cannot be ruled out.

There also is no proof that an underground market for U.S.-bred tiger bone, meat, and other body part exists in the United States. Nevertheless, the lack of uniform laws governing captive breeding of tigers in the United States provides avenues for U.S. critics to cast doubts and accuse Americans of having a double standard. Consequently, global debate related to captive breeding versus in-situ conservation intensifies in worldwide tiger forums, pitting conservation biologists against tiger breeders in the private sector.

In July 2007 the State Forest Administration of the People's Republic of China collaborated with the Cat Specialists Group of the World Conservation Union to organize a workshop on developing a strategy for tiger conservation in Harbin, China. A key item on the agenda of this international gathering was to probe for avenues of reconciliation between proponents of commerce and conservation of tigers.

In addition to members of the World Conservation Union, WWF, and other conservation organizations and both government and NGOs from tiger countries, attendees included proponents of tiger farming such as Mitra and Lapointe. Despite criticism by some Western NGOs, the Chinese government appeared to be genuinely interested in seeing if and how the issues related to captive breeding of tigers could be reconciled in an open and transparent manner with full participation of the global tiger community.

Unfortunately, the outcome of the meeting was mostly rhetoric and the actions proposed were mostly generic and repetitive. Like the International Tiger Symposium held in Kathmandu in April 2007, this meeting did not produce any concrete resolutions. The key issues about how to reconcile market-based initiatives with strict protection were not addressed thoroughly. Supporters of tiger farming argued that prohibition of trade in tiger parts is not a solution but the underlying problem. In contrast, opponents of captive breeding of tigers and their commercial use replied that tiger farmers have no vested interests in protecting tigers in the wild, arguing that tiger farms provide avenues for laundering body parts of wild tigers.

Most tiger experts, particularly the members of the Cat Specialist Group of the World Conservation Union, claim that tiger farming is a recipe for disaster for wild tigers. The Cat Specialist Group, of which I am a member, is a voluntary association of more than two hundred of the world's leading wild cat experts, including scientists, wildlife managers, and conservationists from fifty countries. Its members argue that comparing tiger farming with crocodile breeding, bison ranching, or even the harvesting of vicuña wool is comparing apples to oranges. They say that policies that promote eating, drinking, or wearing tiger body parts as wise use of a natural resource are a falsehood promoted by tiger farmers who are motivated only by greed and have a big stake in protecting their own business. Similar arguments against the captive breeding of tigers have been widely articulated by the WWF, the Save the Tiger Fund, the International Fund for Animal Welfare, TRAFFIC, and other opponents of tiger farming.

I am a long-standing member of the Cat Specialists Group. I have worked closely with TRAFFIC and am a founding member of the Save the Tiger Fund. My opposition to tiger farming is not based solely on my association with these global organizations dedicated to nature conservation. Furthermore, my views are not driven by economics or ecological principles. Rather they are based on my own ethical and moral values.

To me, saving the tiger is equivalent to preserving man-made icons such as the pyramids and other wonders of the world—a part of human civilization and cultural and natural heritage. I believe we must save what we have inherited from our ancestors and leave it behind for the benefit of future generations. I want history to remember my generation not as destroyers but as protectors of the environment. In addition, as a practicing Tiger-Wallah, I do not agree with the views of Mitra, Santhakumar, Lapointe, and Stossel—advocates for free markets for sale of tiger bones and body parts. I can give at least five specific reasons why their arguments are short on facts but long on fallacies.

First, the Chinese have been unable to demonstrate that tiger farming helps save tigers in the wild. Their motive seems to be pure profit and not conservation. Tiger farms have absolutely no value for conservation education or generating awareness to save tigers in the wild. Most of the studies, particularly those undertaken by the Wildlife Conservation Society, WWF, IFAW, TRAFFIC, and the Humane Society, demonstrate that the so-called education centers are nothing but outlets for selling tiger bone wine and tiger body parts.

The "re-wilding" shows at these centers, purportedly used to train tigers how to make a kill when they are rehabilitated in the wild, are little more than an inhumane and gruesome deception, primarily motivated to fleece hard cash from gullible visitors. These shows promote violence and cruelty against animals, not conservation ethics or the need for saving tigers in the wild. They also goes against Buddhist principles of compassion for all living things and the Confucian philosophy of ethics and morality fundamental to Chinese civilization.

Second, there is no evidence that any of the tigers raised in captivity in China have been successfully reintroduced in the wild. In fact, scientists doubt if tigers reared in captivity can survive in the wild.

Third, the tiger farms appear to be nothing more than a way to thwart Chinese regulations and international covenants. At best they create barriers to enforcement of existing laws. Separating wine made from poached wild tigers from wine made from tigers that have died in captivity is virtually impossible. Bones of wild tigers smuggled out of India, Nepal, and other tiger countries can be easily laundered and sold as the bones of farmed tigers. Advertisements on the Internet and covert investigations reveal that tiger bone wine and body parts of wild tigers fetch much higher prices than those of farmed tigers. Well-heeled buyers believe that wild tiger parts are pure, unadulterated, and thus more potent.

Fourth, the medicinal values of tiger bones touted by tiger farmers are misleading. Genuine practitioners of traditional Chinese medicine (TCM) believe that the bones of other animals have properties similar to tiger bones. To protect their own reputation, authentic practitioners of TCM have removed tiger bone or any tiger parts from their lists of medicinal ingredients. The American College of Traditional Chinese Medicine (ACTCM)—a San Francisco based educational and research group—supports the ban on the sale or use of tiger bones for medical purpose. They believe that better and cheaper alternates are available. One such alternative is the bone of the mole rat (*Mysospalax baileyi*). However, it is unlikely that the majority of TCM practitioners, who reside within China, would be willing to substitute mole rat bones for tiger bones.

Fifth, a cursory cost-benefit analysis indicates that the economic argument that tiger farming reduces poaching in the wild is fictitious. Raising tigers in captivity is expensive, costing tiger farmers US $5,000 to $6,000 a year. In contrast, poachers in India, Nepal, and elsewhere are willing to kill and sell a wild tiger for as little as US $50 to $100. Cheap poisons openly available in pesticides and insecticides are used to poison tigers by lacing their kills. Cost and risk are minimal.

For all these reasons, it is not logical to argue that tiger farms will outcompete poachers and kill the trade in wild tigers, particularly when poached tigers can be laundered through unscrupulous tiger farmers.

The debate between "use it or lose it" commercial tiger breeding and "no use is the best use" to save tigers continues unabated. The arguments of the tiger farming proponents lack empirical data. I feel that their views are driven mostly by ideology rather than evidence. Therefore, I do not ascribe to the "eat it to save it" arguments used to justify farming tigers. Tiger farms in China have been around for more than two decades. Yet poaching of tigers in neighboring countries and smuggling their bones and other body parts across the border into China have increased not decreased.

The supply-side argument that tiger farming floods the market, reduces the price of tiger body parts, and thus provides disincentives to poaching is not valid. There is no reliable data to prove otherwise. Comparing American bison to the tiger is akin to comparing apples with asparagus.

I agree with Dr. Urs Breitenmoser, co-chair of the World Conservation Union's Cats Specialist Group, who once remarked that in the absence of reliable data, it is better to err on the side of caution. Even a stalwart of free-market such as the World Bank has debunked tiger farming as a big gamble.

"Extinction is irreversible, so prudence and precaution suggest that the risks of legalized farming are too great a gamble for the world to take," said Keshav Varma, a director and team leader of the World Bank's Global Tiger Initiative (GTI), a new proposal that seeks to double the number of tigers by the next round of the Year of the Tiger in 2022. Varma, hardly a wildlife biologist, but an economist and an infrastructure development expert, made this statement at the fifty-eighth meeting of the Convention on International Trade in Endangered Species (CITES) Standing Committee in Geneva, Switzerland, in July 2009.

I too agree that the risk of making the wrong decision with a critically endangered species like the tiger is too high. Nevertheless, Eugene Lapointe, John Stossel, and other champions of the "sell it and eat it to save it" mantras challenge this premise. They claim that the risk of doing nothing new or radical is equally great. They feel that given current trends, the tiger is likely to go extinct if tiger conservation as usual continues.

While debate on the best option to save tigers in the wild goes on, the fate of the tiger in its natural habitat remains very uncertain. Will the prediction of Chris Packman come true? Will the tiger really be extinct by 2025?

14

THE FATE OF THE TIGER

"DOOMED," DECLARED *TIME* MAGAZINE'S COVER OF MARCH 28, 1994—the alarming headline set over the face of a snarling tiger. Inside, the feature story predicted the tiger's inevitable extinction.

Time was not the only media source to predict the tiger's extinction from the wilds of Asia. Others, including *Asiaweek, India Today,* and the *Far Eastern Economic Review (FEER)*—three of *Time*'s competitors in Asia—published similar prophecies.

By the mid-1990s the media were rife with reports that the tiger would be extinct by the end of the twentieth century. Yet the tiger has survived, proving a more resilient animal than predicted by the pundits of the press. Ironically, a few of the doomsayers themselves vanished in the new millennium. *Asiaweek* folded in December 2001. Three years later, *FEER* was truncated into a monthly literary journal. *India Today* survived, and its team of investigative reporters continues to report on the tiger's inevitable extinction.

Given the magazine's global stature, *Time*'s story was particularly hard hitting. Its report firmly corroborated reports from field experts exposing the harsh realities on the ground in India, home to the largest number of wild tigers in the world. Local media in tiger countries expanded on the *Time* story. Cumulatively they posed a challenge to national and international conservationists, whose efforts since the 1970s to save the tiger had proved less than successful. The media strengthened the belief that the basic threats to the tiger rarely came from inside tiger reserves but from outside the reserve—a hard lesson some of us had learned earlier when we started the Smithsonian Nepal Tiger Ecology Project in the 1970s. At an international symposium on tigers in Minneapolis in 1986, Chris Wemmer, my scientific supervisor; Dave Smith, my American counterpart; and myself from the Smithsonian project vigorously argued that saving wild tigers had more to do with understanding human behavior outside tiger sanctuaries than the biology of the beast inside reserves. The gathering, mostly dominated by zookeepers and wildlife academics, paid only lip service to our concerns.

Similar views resurfaced vigorously by the turn of the twentieth century when the world's human population crossed the six billion mark, with more than half of humanity living in Asia. Paradoxically, it was not ecological or biological data but the social, population, and economic statistics that reinforced understanding of what truly were the key challenges to tiger conservation. In the new millennium, Asia remained home to the largest segment of the poorest people on Earth, many of whom lived on less than one dollar a day and most of them in the tiger countries. Despite phenomenal economic growth elsewhere in the world, most of the tiger countries ranked equal to and in some places even worse than Sub-Saharan Africa in terms of poverty and social inequity. Poverty has been a major cause of degradation of the tiger's habitat and a major motivator for poaching.

Chris, Dave, and I felt vindicated as more global experts repeated the questions we had been asking at the local level: How can sanctuaries such as Chitwan, Suklaphanta, and Bardia in Nepal and Corbett, Kanha, and Kaziranga in India survive as island of tiger survival in a sea of impoverished humanity? What are the odds of the tiger's survival when rising populations of poverty-stricken people are relentlessly crusading against the tiger and its habitat? Is extinction inevitable when a lucrative black market for tiger skins and body parts flourishes? Will the temptation of illicit earnings convert honest wildlife workers into poachers and traffickers?

All these questions intensified after what became known as the "Sariska Shock." In 2004 scientists were dismayed to discover that the tiger was long gone from Sariska National Park, one of India's premier tiger reserves. An intensive survey commissioned by the Indian government revealed that the number of tigers in India hovered around sixteen hundred at the most, less than half the tiger population five years earlier. This revelation created an uproar in India. Many blamed poaching and illicit trafficking. Others questioned the methodology and reliability of data based on counting pugmarks for tiger census. Forestry and wildlife officers in the government were accused by NGOs of fudging the figures to hide the actual loss of tiger population.

More fuel was added to the fire by the national and international media. "The face of a doomed animal" proclaimed the *Independent,* a popular British daily, highlighting the plight of the tiger on October 31, 2007. Other newspapers and in-house journals of international conservation organizations reported that the tiger crisis in India was matched by similar calamity elsewhere in Asia. Some recalled the dire warnings of Dr. Ulaas Karanth, a distinguished Indian scientist who studied tigers for more than thirty years. He had written that it was not only poaching of tigers but also the reduction of its prey species that had caused tiger numbers to dwindle. The tiger occupies the apex of the food chain, and the availability of its food prey is a key factor that regulates its numbers. Thus it was not only tiger poaching but also the poaching of its main prey species, such as deer, and the destruction of their habitat that had caused the tiger population to decline rapidly. Dr. Bhim Gurung, who has studied man-eating tigers in Nepal over the past five years, suggests that lack of prey species also could cause a tiger to kill humans.

For the past three decades, support for saving the tiger has been championed by the Western-educated elite of the tiger countries, often with support from our cohorts in European and North

American nongovernmental wildlife organizations. I am a member of that group.

The Sariska tiger crisis of 2004 triggered loud criticism of our approaches to saving the tiger. Yet I often ponder what would have been the consequences if our efforts to secure tiger habitats and combat poaching through the creation of a network of national parks and wildlife reserves in the 1970s had not been pursued so rigorously? At the very least we bought time. Without these efforts the tiger could have been gone long ago. Nevertheless, these new criticisms strengthened our realization that there were major gaps in global and national efforts to save the tiger. Except in a few attempts by donor-funded pilot programs, no grassroots support had mobilized in the general population.

The majority of humanity living in or around tiger country was rarely engaged in or benefited from efforts to save the tiger. There is sometimes a disconnect between the needs for conservation and the needs of the local people for food, fuel, and fodder. While tourist facilities like Nepal's Tiger Tops provide employment to some local people, it is not adequate to address the needs of the majority that survive on less than a dollar a day on the boundaries of Chitwan National Park. Hidden behind this picture of gloom and doom are a few rare success stories in which the local community did not remain mere bystanders but became active participants in efforts to save the tiger. One of them is Chitwan's Bagmara Community Conservation Program. This program was masterminded by Shankar Chaoudhury, whom I hired in the late 1980s as a field assistant for the Nepal Terai Ecology Project, an offshoot of the Smithsonian Nepal Tiger Ecology Project.

Shankar comes from the Tharu tribe, the indigenous inhabitants of Chitwan. Trained as a forest ranger, Shankar does not have a PhD and was not trained in the West. In fact, he has never been out of Nepal except for short trips across the border into India. Yet he came with up with a brilliant program that became a model for how to strike an intricate balance between the needs of wildlife conservation and needs of the local people. Shankar believed that protecting human interests first would save rhinos and tigers in Chitwan.

Shankar donated his own land to create a forest nursery to demonstrate to me his faith in his program to convert a patch of degraded forest outside the national park into a community-owned and managed wildlife conservation project. As a pilot project, he fenced in a ten-square-mile patch of Bagmara forest near our camp, nurtured seedlings in his nursery, and then planted the plot with sissoo trees. Sissoo is a valuable timber tree prized by furniture makers, but it takes fifteen to twenty years to mature and harvest. Thus it was an investment for the future. However, Shankar's scheme had a hidden agenda that produced quick returns.

The fenced-off area kept the cattle out. Fed by monsoon rains and protected from overgrazing, fodder grass, herbs, and shrubs rejuvenated the degraded landscape with a vengeance. Shankar's project included harvesting the lush fodder for use by the local villagers. It also triggered a livestock-feeding program for the first time in the area. This program saved the villagers time and removed the risk of being penalized when their cattle strayed inside the national park boundary. Later Shankar opened up his fence line and expanded his project to include adjacent degraded forestland that was owned by the government but leased rent free to the local community. Within three to five years, the landscape had improved dramatically and become prime wildlife habitat. Rhinos, tigers, deer, and other large mammals became permanent residents of the restored landscape around Bagmara.

Shankar made his next move to cash in on the burgeoning tourist trade in the Saurah district. He built a watchtower and rented it out to Saurah tourist lodges for a fee. Unlike revenue from tourism inside the national park, the money earned by Shankar's project flowed directly to the local community. Soon local villagers found a new livelihood by offering nature walks and elephant rides and working as tourist guides. Village women had easier, community-regulated access to the vital resources needed for their daily lives. They no longer had to sneak inside the national park to collect fuel and fodder and risk being caught and fined by park guards.

Shankar's Bagmara Community Conservation Program has been very successful, helping reduce conflicts between local people and park authorities. Still in operation, the program has served as a successful model for replication elsewhere.

The success of Shankar's program depended on three key factors: First, it was not the government but the local community that was empowered and responsible for the project. Second, seed money to jump-start the project was provided by the King Mahendra Trust for Nature Conservation, now known as the Nepal Trust for Nature Conservation—the country's largest NGO. Third, any revenue or resources generated did not end in government hands but went to the local community and were used to improve the life of the community with schools, a health clinic, and new employment development. With creative thinking, and doing ordinary things extraordinarily well, Shankar demonstrated how dangerous wild animals and humans could coexist, with little investment and without often-misdirected donor-driven agendas.

As Shankar was quietly performing his duty without much publicity, news erupted with postmortems on why the tiger number had crashed in India. Whom to blame rather than asking why the situation got worse took precedence in the analysis of the tiger crisis in the Indian subcontinent. Media reports of the tiger crisis ruffled a few feathers in the global conservation community as well as in national wildlife departments. They challenged the Tiger-Wallahs to come up with new, practical, and pragmatic solutions.

The global publicity about the plight of the tiger generated by the media led to an increase in the number of NGOs concerned with saving the tiger, both in the West and in the East. They increased from only a dozen in the 1970s to more than a hundred by 2000. Indeed, this was a positive sign that reenergized conservationists and expanded awareness to the plight of the tiger. The diversity of new tiger-saving NGOs also demonstrated that saving the tiger is a complex issue and that solutions are seldom obvious.

Yet problems in the field remain mostly unresolved. With the increase in the number of organizations, administrative and overhead costs also skyrocketed. Instead of collaborating on ideas and resources to reach common goals, national and international NGOs competed aggressively for donor dollars. This created confusion among potential donors and often pitted recipients against one another.

Only lip service is being provided on the needs to have country-led coordination mechanism as each organization functions within its own bureaucratic framework and institutional constraints; most of which stem from pressures to compete in fund-raising. Some have even earned the unflattering title of "Dollar Farmers" for their ability to milk tax-deductible dollars from American donors.

Fortunately independent NGO watchdogs such as Charity Navigator and the American Institute of Philanthropy have proliferated in the United States. In addition, donors, philanthropists, and grant-making organizations, particularly in the United States, have become more savvy. They have started questioning how much of their contributions actually made its way down to the field and how much was spent on overhead and administrative costs.

The diversity of NGOs and hard questions asked by donors raised several questions targeted at people like me: Can we, the enlightened Tiger-Wallahs, hardened in our old beliefs, accept new or unconventional methods to save the tiger? Will we remain suspicious of new ideas or new people outside our fraternity? Can the tent of tiger conservationists be made bigger to accommodate a wider array of players, including those whose visions and views may be radically different from ours?

The gloomy numbers of tigers surviving in the wild has also generated pessimism in national development planning circles. Many people, such as noteworthy British naturalist Chris Packman, claim that the tiger's time has come and that the best option is to let the tiger go extinct instead of wasting resources on futile efforts to save it.

"If we are to prevent the last animals from dying out in this century, then we need nothing short of a miracle," Dr. Mahendra Shrestha wrote about tigers in the *Independent* of London on October 31, 2007. Dr. Shrestha is a Nepali Tiger-Wallah and the director of Save the Tiger Fund, a Washington, D.C.–based nonprofit that funds efforts to save the tiger in Asia and the Russian Far East. His article prompted me to compare efforts to save the tiger in the twenty-first century with twentieth century wars waged between and within nations. Good luck and miracles have been factors in both the hot and cold wars of the twentieth century. Yet, as Dr. Shrestha reiterated in his writing, miracles do not happen in a vacuum. They must be triggered by someone taking action.

"War is too serious a matter to entrust to military men," Georges Clemenceau, prime minister of France, once said. This flamboyant Frenchman was zealously promoting his doctrine of civilian leadership in making strategic military decisions during World War I (1914–1918). Popularly known as the "Le Tigre," or "the tiger," for his fortitude, he tried to engender new ideas beyond conventional thinking during wartime. Clemenceau's words can be paraphrased in the campaign to save the tiger: Is saving the tiger too serious a matter to entrust to conservation biologists alone?

It also seems that Tiger-Wallahs need celebrities on their side to be their spokesperson to generate awareness on the plight of the tiger. One recent spokesman was Hollywood actor Harrison Ford. In June 2009 he teamed with WildAid, an active Asia-focused nonprofit, and made public service announcements to be broadcast on television networks all over the world.

"When the buying stops," expressed the actor of *Indiana Jones* films fame, citing the popular message coined by WildAid, "the killing can too." He volunteered to broadcast this message to assist WildAid's aggressive campaign to halt the trafficking in wild tiger body parts. "Our endangered animals are being destroyed by illegal wildlife trade," added Ford, an active board member of Conservation International—one of the largest Washington, D.C.–based international NGOs. "It's up to us to stop it. Never buy illegal wildlife products."

In addition to using celebrities, we Tiger-Wallahs need to emerge out of our cocoons. We need to communicate beyond our coterie of conservation biologists. Do economists, sociologists, hunters, tiger farmers, and people in other professions have better ideas than the conventional pundits of preservation do?

Sadly, I do not have the answer. Like most of my peers, I too have shied away from meaningful dialogue with those who disagree with my professional judgment or moral outlook. Despite a few pontifications, I have not judiciously probed for a middle ground between eating farmed tigers, shooting problem tigers for cash, and preserving tigers and their habitats in the wilds of Asia. But I know that the best plans for saving tigers formulated by organizations such as the Save the Tiger Fund, Wildlife Conservation Society, and the WWF and the national governments in tiger countries have not been fully implemented or fully tested.

There is no dearth of strategies for saving the tiger. Virtually all major international NGOs and government wildlife department bookshelves are decorated with one or more plans. Well meaning and full of desirable prescriptions, these plans, such as the National Tiger Action Plan, mostly remain undoable. Why? Because governments of tiger countries have neither the financial resources nor the expert capacity to implement them. Dr. M. S. Swaminathan, an eminent Indian scientist and philosopher and former president of the IUCN, once aptly remarked, "Conservation without funding remains only conversational."

Often launched with extravagant fanfare, celebrities, and press releases, these plans succumb to Dr. Swaminathan's predictions. The donors and international NGOs that funded these tiger action plans did not make any long-term funding commitments to implement these plans, most of which were prepared by their own experts. Except for raising false expectations, they proved to be unrealistic without full implementation funding.

Now an aging Tiger-Wallah, I often go on nostalgic journeys of the mind. Like other Tiger-Wallahs of my generation, I have won a few battles for the tiger. But none of us has won the war. A few successes stemmed from the fact that we were fortunate enough to have wise and daring political leaders who challenged our intellectual capacity and also provided us with much-needed political support. Above all, they made unpopular but appropriate political decisions with adamant political will.

At times questions creep into my mind about the real tiger warriors of the twentieth century on the Indian subcontinent. I wonder that if not for Prime Minister Indira Gandhi's efforts, would the tiger have gone extinct from India decades ago, as predicted? Likewise, would we have any tigers left in Nepal without the intervention of our kings and princes?

I also am dogged by the thought that the real cause of the current tiger crisis is neither paucity of scientific knowledge nor shortage of funds but the lack of political will. We cannot bring India's Prime Minister Gandhi or Nepal's King Mahendra or King Birendra back to life. But surely we can use our wits to invigorate new political leadership though hard lobbying and public education. Yet government support is critical. After all, the governments own the forests and grasslands that harbor wild tigers. Furthermore, government-to-government dialogue is needed to

coordinate key issues and formulate the best ways to seek cooperation of tiger-consuming countries like China with a burgeoning
tiger population in captivity.

Thanks to the support of national and international organizations, particularly the Smithsonian Institution and the WWF, I
have earned global recognition as a committed Tiger-Wallah. Yet
I keep searching for pragmatic answers to the three hard questions
frequently asked by my friend Dr. John Seidensticker, an American Tiger-Wallah and chairman of the Save the Tiger Fund:

First, how can we help tigers and humans live as good neighbors and ensure that their relationship is not antagonistic but symbiotic? Second, how can we make a living wild tiger more valuable
than a dead tiger to the local people and the governments that
own the real estate designated as tiger sanctuaries? Third, how can
we make tiger conservation not a barrier but a catalyst to reduce
poverty and generate jobs for a better life in tiger countries?

As I continue to search for answers to John's pointed questions, I have learned the basic lesson that just seeking to do the
right thing is not enough. Doing the smart thing is what is needed.
Being right is not good enough. Being smart delivers results on the
ground to real people. The smart thing dictates that we fight for our
cause holistically with war-quality paradigms. Saving the tiger is a
kind of war. It is a war on poverty and hunger. Indeed, it is a war
on population growth and lack of opportunities to make a decent
living. It is also a war against hangovers from the colonial era of
the past century and a war on the neocolonial mindset. Above all,
it is a war on ignorance and a war on our inability to understand
and change cultural and ethical values in tiger countries.

Like any war, the war to save the tiger is unwinnable without
first boosting the morale of the foot soldiers such as rangers, foresters, and wildlife guards, recognizing and rewarding the warriors
on the front lines. First, they must be well paid and well fed. They
must have assurance that their families will be taken care of if they

become battlefront casualties. Unfortunately, building the morale and welfare of foot soldiers rarely ranks as a high priority in tiger-saving action plans and strategies. People entrusted to save the tiger on the front lines are paid a pittance, a fact never highlighted in donor-driven strategies and action plans.

Except in countries such as Nepal, where a contingent of the Nepalese Army is deployed, most wildlife guards lack adequate uniforms, shoes, weapons, or living quarters. Thus the task of saving the tiger is beyond the realm of pure science. It is more related to government policy, political will, and resource constraints in tiger countries. Driven by demands to combat poverty, unemployment, and social inequality, the governments of tiger countries face a wide range of demands from all factions, each clamoring for preferential treatment. Regretfully, saving the tiger does not rank among the top priorities. Consequently, the task for Tiger-Wallahs is very difficult.

"When the going gets tough, the tough get going" is a common American saying used to motivate sportsmen and businessmen to rise to the demands of difficult and changing times. With the plummeting population of tigers in the wild and escalating poaching, trafficking, and habitat loss, the fate of the tiger is highly uncertain. But, as the American saying suggests, Tiger-Wallahs must become smart realists. Preaching to already ardent or converted conservationists is not enough. The vital challenge for us Tiger-Wallahs is to convert the cynics, the unconverted, and the pessimists into optimistic champions of the tiger. We must move forward with agendas based not on rhetoric but on the harsh realities. We must adopt strategies that have been proven successful.

The Bagmara Community Conservation Program in Chitwan National Park developed by Shankar Chaoudhury is one example of moving beyond rhetoric to successful action. By the end of the 1990s, Shankar's project had caught the attention of three of my former colleagues: Mingma Norbu Sherpa, Chandra Prasad

Gurung of the WWF, and Tirtha Man Maskey of Nepal's Department of National Parks and Wildlife Conservation.

Veterans of governments, NGOs, and international organizations, the three Nepalese were determined to expand Shankar's approach into a much wider landscape rarely imagined by any Tiger-Wallah. Their program, aptly named the Terai Arc Landscape (TAL), was very ambitious. It was a vision that looked decades ahead with a mission to create an environment in which large wild mammals and humans could live in harmony. Their basic philosophy: If you want to save tigers in the wild, you must first help the people who live near the tigers.

The primary agenda of the TAL program was to connect eleven protected areas from Nepal's Parsa Wildlife Reserve in the southeast to India's Rajaji's National Park through reforestation, restoration, and income-generating activities along the Terai on both sides of the boarder. Mingma, Chandra, and Tirtha visualized the TAL project from a traditional coin-necklace often sported by the Tharu women of Chitwan. The coins symbolized protected areas; the beaded strings connecting the coins represented conservation corridors. These corridors would connect all the tiger reserves and enable tigers to move freely and safely from one reserve to the other; expanding their genetic pool and increasing their population. A key element of the TAL was to recover the wild tiger and its prey populations by mainstreaming wildlife conservation with community development—putting poverty reduction and livelihood development at the forefront of conservation.

With support from the Save the Tiger Fund, the WWF, the Nepalese government, and other donors, the TAL project was launched in Nepal in 2001. Chandra, Mingma, and their team identified key bottlenecks to creating the conservation corridor and identified sites where tiger habitat could be restored. They packaged all their activities into one holistic program and raised funds from several donors. The latter was a major feat in Nepal, where donors often jealously defended their turf and rarely collaborated.

To demonstrate that actions speak louder than words, TAL kicked off its program with reforestation and rural development activities in western Nepal by forging partnerships with government departments and local communities. Sushila Nepali, one of the first women to work in Nepal's forestry and conservation sector, spearheaded this program. She worked closely with local villagers to address human needs first. In a short time TAL had created Forest Conservation User groups. They also built biogas plants, tube wells, schools, and health centers and even launched temple renovation activities. These first activities were not chosen or dictated by the government or by donors but were prioritized by the local community.

Sadly, after such a good start, the TAL program soon experienced its first setback. The insurgency led by the Nepal Communist Party (Maoists) climaxed in 2003. Violence engulfed Nepal. Amid the chaos, the government declared a state of emergency. The Terai suffered most. Travels in the region were restricted and dangerous. Tourism collapsed. Most of the rhinos I had reintroduced and then moved from Chitwan to Bardia National Park more than a decade earlier were poached. Donors shied away from the Terai, and most development and conservation projects fizzled out. TAL was no exception.

In 2006 a violent uprising forced the king to give up his power. During the subsequent political bickering over power sharing between the Maoists and the Nepali Congress Party, the Terai slowly returned to normalcy. Then a second devastating event shook not only the TAL project but also the whole conservation program in Nepal.

On September 23, 2006, a helicopter crash in the Kanchenjunga Conservation Project Area of northeast Nepal took the lives of twenty-three of the movers and shakers of Nepal's conservation programs. Three of them were the founding fathers of TAL—Mingma Norbu Sherpa, Chandra Prasad Gurung, and Dr. Tirtha Man Maskey, my band of brothers in Nepalese nature conservation. Nevertheless, the TAL remains a dream that can still come true for Tiger-Wallahs, at least in concept and design. If the plans meticulously developed by Mingma and Chandra can be realized, the Terai corridor across southern Nepal could provide a safe sanctuary for tigers for the next hundred years.

I often ponder the fate of the tiger in the twenty-first century. At this turning point of the new millennium, the odds seem to be overwhelmingly stacked against the tiger. With growing human needs for food, fuel, and fodder; demands to expand roads, power plants, farmland, and factories; and an almost-missionary zeal to catch up with the American standard of living, how long can the tiger survive in the wilds of Asia including Siberia? Will the prophecies of doom come true? Will the prediction that the tiger will be extinct from the jungles of Asia by the next round of the Year of the Tiger in 2022 become a reality?

February 14, 2010, marked the beginning of the first cycle of the Year of the Tiger in the Chinese zodiac for the twenty-first century. Horoscopes that highlight the fate of humans born in that year are ubiquitous, particularly in Chinese restaurants. Yet there is no horoscope prophesying the fate of the tiger.

Four years before the last cycle of the Year of the Tiger in 1998, *Time* magazine predicted that the tiger was doomed. But the tiger is still alive in the wild—reduced in population but not extinct. A few wise and enlightened Tiger-Wallahs argue that with a little help, the tiger could survive in perpetuity. George Schaller, an eminent American scientist and naturalist, is one of them. In the 1960s he pioneered the first comprehensive scientific study of the habits and habitats of wild tigers. Schaller contends that tigers have the resilience to adapt to changing times and changing environments, that they are a tough species that readily adapts to a wide range of habitat disturbance.

The tiger is also a good breeder. It can survive with a bit of cover, a supply of prey species, and water. It has a phenomenal ability to recover from human persecution. But will the tiger continue to have access to these bare minimum requirements for survival? Can it survive an onslaught of poaching for its valuable skins, bones, and other body parts? Can its habitat be protected from permanent damage? How can we protect the tiger from being its own worst enemy when it feeds on domestic cattle and occasionally kills humans?

The answers to these questions will determine the fate of the tiger in these decisive times.

SELECTED BIBLIOGRAPHY

Bright, M. (2002). *Man-Eaters.* New York: St. Martin's Press.

Budhathoki, P. (2004). "Linking Communities with Conservation in Developing Countries: Buffer Zone Management Initiatives in Nepal," *Oryx* 38: 334–341.

Bulte, E. H., and R. Damania (2005). "An Economic Assessment of Wildlife Farming and Conservation," *Conservation Biology* 19 (4): 1222–1233.

Burton, R. G. (2002). *The Tiger Hunters.* New Delhi: Mittal Publications.

Chowdhury, B. R., and P. Vyas (2007). *Sunderbans: The Mystic Mangrove.* New Delhi: Niyogi Offset.

Corbett, J. (1944). *Man-Eaters of Kumaon.* New Delhi: Oxford University Press (twelfth impression 1996).

———. (1996). *The Second Jim Corbett Omnibus.* New Delhi: Oxford University Press (fifth impression).

———. (1954). *The Temple Tiger and More Man-Eaters of Kumaon.* Bombay: Oxford University Press (ninth impression 1996).

Damania, R., J. Seidensticker, T. Whitten, G. Sethi, K. Mackinnon, A. Kiss, and A. Kushlin (2008). *A Future for Tigers.* Washington, D.C.: World Bank.

Daniel, J. C. (2001). *The Tiger in India: A Natural History.* Dehra Dun, India: Natraj Publishers.

Dinerstein, E. (2005). *Tigerland and Other Unintended Destinations.* Washington, D.C.: Island Press.

Dinerstein, E., C. Loucks, E. Wikramanayake, J. Ginsberg, E. Sanderson, J. Seidensticker, J. Forrest, G. Bryya, A. Heydlauff, S. Klenzendorf, P. Leimgruber, J. Mills, T. G. O'Brien, M. Shrestha, R. Simons, and M. Songer (2007). "The Fate of Wild Tigers," *BioScience* 57: 508–514.

Dinerstein, E., E. Wikramanayake, J. Robinson, K. Karanth, A. Rabinowitz, D. Olson, T. Mathew, P. Hedao, and M. Connor (1997). "Part I: A Framework for Indentifying High Priority Areas for the Conservation of Free-Ranging Tigers," *A Framework for Indentifying High Priority Areas and Actions for the Conservation of Tigers in the Wild.* Washington, D.C., and New York: World Wildlife Fund–U.S. and Wildlife Conservation Society, in association with National Fish and Wildlife Foundation's Save the Tiger Fund.

Environmental Investigation Agency (2009). *A Deadly Game of Cat and Mouse: Tiger Criminals Give China the Run-around, A Report on the Findings of an EIA Investigation into the Illegal Trade in Asian Big Cat Parts in China, 2009.* London.

Environmental Investigation Agency (1996). *The Political Wilderness: India's Tiger Crisis.* London.

Government of Nepal, Department of National Parks and Wildlife Conservation, and Ministry of Forests and Soil Conservation (2007). *Tiger Conservation Action Plan for Nepal.* Kathmandu, Nepal.

Gratwicke, B., E. I. Bennett, S. Broad, S. Christe, A. Dutton, G. Gabriel, C. Kirkpatrick, and K. Nowell (2007). "The World Can't Have Wild Tigers and Eat Them, Too," *Conservation Biology* 22(1): 222–223.

Gupta, R. D. (2006). *Jim Corbett: The Hunter-Conservationist.* New Delhi: Rupa.

Gurung. B. (2008). "Ecological and Sociological Aspects of Human-Tiger Conflicts in Chitwan National Park, Nepal." University of Minnesota, Minneapolis (doctoral dissertation).

Gurung, B, J. L. D. Smith, C. McDougal, and J. Karki (2006). "Tiger Human Conflicts: Investigating Ecological and Sociological Issues of Tiger Conservation in the Buffer Zone of Chitwan National Park, Nepal." Kathmandu, Nepal (unpublished report submitted to WWF–Nepal Program).

Hemley, G., and D. Bolze (1997). "Controlling Trade In and Reducing Demand for Tiger Products: A Preliminary of Priority Needs. A Framework for Identifying High-Priority Areas and Actions for the Conservation of Tigers in the Wild." Washington, D.C., and New York: World Wildlife Fund–U.S. and Wildlife Conservation Society, in association with National Fish and Wildlife Foundation's Save the Tiger Fund.

His Majesty's Government of Nepal, Ministry of Forestry (1996). *Buffer Zone Management Regulation.* Kathmandu, Nepal.

His Majesty's Government of Nepal and the World Wildlife Fund (2001*). Terai Arc Landscape Program.* Kathmandu, Nepal.

International Fund for Animal Welfare (2007). *Made in China—Farming Tigers to Extinction.* Yarmouth Port, MA.

Ives, R. (1996). *Of Tigers and Men. Entering the Age of Extinction.* New York: Avon Books.

Jackson, P. (1980). "A Tragic Sequel: A Son of Chuchchi Kills a Villager," *Smithsonian,* July 1980: 107–115.

———. (1990). *Endangered Species: Tigers.* London: The Apple Press.

Joshi, S. (1999). "A Socio-economic Analysis of Residents in the Buffer Zone of Royal Chitwan National Park, Nepal." University of Minnesota, Minneapolis (unpublished master's degree dissertation).

Karanth, K. U. (2006). *A View from the Machan: How Science Can Save the Fragile Predator.* Ranikhet, India: Permanent Black.

———. (2001). *The Way of the Tiger: Natural History and Conservation of the Endangered Big Cat.* Bangalore, India: Centre for Wildlife Studies.

Karanth, K. U., and J. D. Nichols (eds.) (2002). *Monitoring Tigers and Their Prey.* Bangalore, India: Centre for Wildlife Studies.

Linden, E., and Anita Pratap with other bureaus (1994). "ENVIRONMENT: Tigers on the Brink," *Time* magazine, U.S. edition. March 28, 1994. www.time.com/time/magazine/article/0,9171,980409,00.html.

MacCormick, A. (2003). *The Mammoth Book of Man-eaters.* New York: Carroll & Graf Publishers.

MacKinnon, K., H. Mishra, and J. Mott (1999). "Reconciling the Needs of Conservation and Local Communities: Global Environment Facility Support for Tiger Conservation in India," *Riding the Tiger: Tiger Conservation in Human Dominated Landscapes.* J. Seidensticker, S. Christie, and P. Jackson (eds.). Cambridge, England: Cambridge University Press.

Martin, E. B. (1992). "The Poisoning of Rhinos and Tigers in Nepal," *Oryx* 26: 82–86.

McDougal, C. (1977). *The Face of the Tiger.* London: Andre Deutsch.

———. (1987). "The Man-Eating Tiger in Geographical and Historical Perspective," *Tigers of the World: The Biology, Biopolitics, Management and Conservation of an Endangered Species.* R. L. Tilson and U. S. Seal (eds.). Park Ridge, New Jersey: Noyes Publications.

McDougal, C., A. Barlow, D. Thapa, S. Kumal, and D. B. Tamang (2005). "Tiger and Human Conflict Increase in Chitwan Reserve Buffer Zone, Nepal," *Cat News* 40: 3–4.

McNeely, J., and P. A. Wachtel (1988). *Soul of the Tiger. Searching for Nature's Answer in Exotic Southeast Asia.* New York: Doubleday.

Menon, V. *A Field Guide to Indian Mammals.* New Delhi: Dorling Kindersley with Penguin Books.

Mills, S. (1992). "Stars in Stripes," *BBC Wildlife* 10 (11): 32–42.

———. (2004). *Tiger.* London: Firefly Books.

Miquelle, D., L. Nikolaev, J. Goodrich, B. Litvinov, E. Smirnov, and E. Suvorov (2005). "Searching for the Coexistence Recipe: A Case Study of Conflicts between People & Tigers in the Russian Far East," *People and Wildlife: Conflict or Coexistence?* R. Woodroffe, S. Thirgood, and A. Rabinowitz (eds.). Cambridge: Cambridge University Press.

Mishra, H. R. (1982). "Balancing Human Needs and Conservation in Nepal's Royal Chitwan National Park," *Ambio* (Sweden) 11(5): 246–251.

———. (1984). "A Delicate Balance: Tigers, Rhinoceros, Tourists and Park Management vs. the Needs of the Local People in Royal Chitwan National Park," *National Parks, Conservation and Development.* J. A. McNeely and K. R. Miller (eds.). Washington, D.C.: Smithsonian Institution Press.

———. (1982). "Ecology of Chital (*Axis axis*) in Royal Chitwan National Park: With Comparison with Hog Deer (*Axis procinus*), Sambar (*Cervus unicolor*) and Barking Deer (*Muntiacus muntjak*)." University of Edinburgh, Scotland (doctoral dissertation).

———. (1981). "Gnade Fur den Tiger! Wir fingen einen 'Morder,'" *Das Tier* (Germany) 6: 45–51.

———. (1974). *Nature Conservation in Nepal: An Introduction to the National Parks and Wildlife Conservation Programme of His Majesty's Government.* Kathmandu, Nepal: HMG Press.

———. (1990). "National Parks," *Nelles Guides—Nepal.* Munich: Robertson McCarta—Nelles Verlag.

———. (July 1984). "Nepal. Ecologie dans le parc des tueurs d'hommes," *Geo. Un Nouveau Monde: la Terre* (France) 65: 92–93.

———. (1991). "Operation Unicorn: A New Home for the Rhinos of Chitwan," *Shangri-La* (Royal Nepal Airlines in-flight magazine) 2 (4): 52–60.

Mishra, H. R., and E. Dinerstein (1987). "New Zip Codes for Resident Rhinos in Nepal," *Smithsonian* 18: 66–73.

Mishra, H. R., and M. Jefferies (1991). *Royal Chitwan National Park: Wildlife Heritage of Nepal.* Seattle, Washington: The Mountaineers.

Mishra, H. R., and T. M. Maskey (1982). "Zuruck Indie Flusse," *Tier Grizmeks Sielmanns Tierwield* (Germany) 6: 14–18.

Mishra, H. R., and D. Mierow (1974). *Wild Animals of Nepal.* Kathmandu, Nepal: Ratna Pustak Bhandar.

Mishra, H. R. and C. Wemmer (1983, October). "Abenteuer in Nepal's Chitwan-National Park. Auf Nashornfang mit Elefanten," *Das Tier* (Germany) 10: 14–17.

Mishra, H. R., C. Wemmer, and J. L. D. Smith (1987). "Tigers in Nepal: Management Conflicts with Human Interests," *Tigers of the World: The Biology, Biopolitics, Management, and Conservation of an Endangered Species.* R. L. Tilson and U. S. Seal (eds.). Park Ridge, New Jersey: Noyes Publications.

Mishra, H. R., C. Wemmer, J. L. D. Smith, and P. Wegge (1992). "Biopolitics of Saving Mammals in the Wild: Balancing Conservation with Human Needs in Nepal," *Occasional Papers Series.* C. P. Wegge (ed.), 9: 35. Aas, Norway: NorAgric Agricultural University of Norway.

Montgomery, S. (2001). *The Man-Eating Tiger of Sunderbans.* Boston: Houghton Mifflin Co.

Nepal, S. K., and K. Weber (1993). *Struggle for Existence: Park-People Conflict in the Royal Chitwan National Park, Nepal.* Bangkok, Thailand: Asian Institute of Technology.

Ng, J., and Nemora (2007). "Tiger Trade Revisited in Sumatra, Indonesia," *Petaling Jaya* (Malaysia). TRAFFIC Southeast Asia.

Nowell, K. and L. Xu (2007). *Taming the Tiger Trade: China's Markets for Wildlife and Captive Tiger Products Since the 1993 Domestic Trade Ban.* Hong Kong: TRAFFIC East Asia.

Nyhus, T. J., and R. Tilson (2004). "Characterizing Human-Tiger Conflict in Sumatra, Indonesia: Implications for Conservation," *Oryx* 38: 68–74.

O'Neil, E. (2008). "Tigers: Worth More Dead than Alive," *World Watch* 21: 6–11.

Peissel, M. (1966). *Tiger for Breakfast: The Story of Boris of Kathmandu.* New Delhi: Time Books International.

Pye-Smith, C. (1988). *Travels in Nepal. The Sequestered Kingdom.* London: Aurum Press Ltd.

Reddy, E. A. (2004*). Man-Eating Tigers of Central India.* New Delhi: Indialog Publications.

Reza, A., M.A. Islam, and F. A. Nishat. (2004). *Bengal Tiger in the Bangladesh Sunderbans.* Dhaka, Bangladesh: International Union for Conservation of Nature (IUCN).

Ricciuti, E. R. (2003). *Killer Animals: Shocking True Stories of Deadly Conflicts between Humans and Animals.* Guilford, Connecticut: The Lyons Press.

Ripley, S. D. (1952). *Search for the Spiny Babbler, an Adventure in Nepal.* Boston: Houghton Mifflin Co.

Sahgal, B. (2008). *The Bandhavgarh Inheritance.* Mumbai, India: Sanctuary Asia.

Sanderson, E., J. Forrest, C. Loucks, E. Ginsberg, E. Dinerstein, P. Leimgruber, M. Songer, A. Heydlauff, G. O'Brien, G. Bryja, S. Klenzendorf, and E. Wikramanayake (2006). *Setting Priorities for Conservation and Recovery of Wild Tigers: 2005–2015. The Technical Assessment.* New York and Washington, D.C.: WCS, WWF, Smithsonian Institution, and NFWF–STF.

Sankhala, K. (2005). *Tiger! The Story of the Indian Tiger.* Dehra Dun, India: Natraj Publishers.

Schaller, G. B. (1967). *The Deer and the Tiger.* Chicago: University of Chicago Press.

Seidensticker, J. (2008). "Ecological and Intellectual Baselines: Saving Lions, Tigers, and Rhinoceros in Asia," *Foundations of Environmental Sustainability, the Coevolution of Science and Policy.* R. L. Rockwood, R. E. Stewart, and T. Diet (eds.). New York: Oxford University Press.

———. (1996). *Tigers.* Stillwater, Minnesota: Voyager Press.

Seidensticker, J., S. Christie, and P. Jackson (eds.). (1999). *Riding the Tiger: Tiger Conservation in Human Dominated Landscapes.* Cambridge: Cambridge University Press.

Shakya, K. (1996). *Encounter Wildlife in Nepal.* New Delhi: Nirala Publications.

Shakya, M. M. (2004). "Trading for Extinction: An Exposé of Illegal Wildlife Trade in Nepal." Kathmandu, Nepal: Wordscape.

Shakya, M. M., and A. Chitrakar (2006). *Cost of Conflict on Nepal's Conservation Efforts.* Kathmandu, Nepal: Wildlife Watch Group.

Sharma, U. R. (1991). "Park-People Interactions in Royal Chitwan National Park, Nepal." University of Arizona, Tucson (doctoral dissertation).

Shrestha, M. K. (2004). "Relative Ungulate Abundance in Fragmented Landscape: Implications for Tiger Conservation." University of Minnesota, Minneapolis (doctoral dissertation).

Singh, B. A. (1993). *The Legend of the Man-Eater.* New Delhi: Ravi Dayal

———. (1973). *Tiger Haven.* London: Macmillan.

Smith, J. L. D. (1984). "Dispersal, Communications and Conservation Strategies for the Tiger (*Panthera tigris*)." University of Minnesota, Minneapolis (doctoral dissertation).

Smith, J. L. D., M. E. Sunquist, K. M. Tamang, and P. B. Rai (1983). "A Technique for Capturing and Immobilizing Tigers," *Journal of Wildlife Management* 47: 255–259.

Smythies, E. A. (1942). *Big Game Shooting in Nepal.* London: Thacker, Spink.

Stainton, J. D. (1988). *Forests of Nepal.* London: John Murray.

Studsrod, J. E., and P. Wegge (1995). "Park-People Relationship: The Case of Damage Caused by Park Animals around the Royal Bardia National Park, Nepal." *Environment Conservation* 22 (2): 133–142.

Sunquist, M. E. (1981). "The Movements and Activities of Tigers (*Panthera tigris tigris*) in Royal Chitwan National Park." University of Minnesota, Minneapolis (doctoral dissertation).

Sunquist, F., and M. E. Sunquist (1988). *Tiger Moon.* Chicago: University of Chicago Press.

Tamang, K. M. (1979). "Population Characteristics of the Tiger and Its Prey." University of Minnesota, Minneapolis (doctoral dissertation).

Taylor, J. (1959). *Maneaters and Marauders.* Dehra Dun, India: Natraj Publishers (reprint 2008).

Thapar, V. (1986). *Tiger: Portrait of a Predator.* New York: Facts on File Inc.

———. (2004). *Tiger: The Ultimate Guide.* New York: CDS Books in association with Two Brothers Press.

Tilson, R. L., and U. S. Seal (eds.) (1987). *Tigers of the World: The Biology, Biopolitics, Management, and Conservation of an Endangered Species.* Park Ridge, New Jersey: Noyes Publications.

Tilson, R., P. Nyhus, O. Jackson, H. Quigley, M. Hornocker, J. Ginsberg, J. Phemister, N. Sherman, and J. Seidensticker (eds.) (2002). *Securing a Future for the World's Wild Tigers.* Washington, D.C: Save the Tiger Fund, National Fish and Wildlife Federation.

Ward, G. C., with R. W. Ward (2004). *Tiger-Wallahs: Saving the Greatest of the Great Cats.* New Delhi: Oxford University Press.

Wemmer, C., J. L. D. Smith, and H. R. Mishra (1987). "The Biopolitical Challenge," *Tigers of the World: The Biology, Biopolitics, Management, and Conservation of an Endangered Species,* R. L. Tilson and U. S. Seal (eds.). Park Ridge, New Jersey: Noyes Publications.

Wemmer, C., R. Simons, and H. Mishra (undated). "The Smithsonian-Nepal Tiger Ecology Project. Case History of a Cooperative International Conservation Program" (unpublished case study).

Wildlife Trust of India (2007). GTF *Action Tiger. Tiger Action Plans of 12 Tiger Range Countries.* New Delhi: Wildlife Trust of India.

Williamson, D. F., and L. A. Henry (2008). *Paper Tigers? The Role of the U.S. Captive Tiger Population in the Trade in Tiger Parts.* Washington, D.C.: TRAFFIC North America and World Wildlife Fund.

Wood, F. (1995). *Did Marco Polo Go to China?* London: Martin Secker & Warburg Ltd.; an imprint of Reed Books Ltd.

World Wildlife Fund (1998). *Alternative to Tiger Bone Medicine.* Washington, D.C., and Toronto.

———. (2001). "Terai Arc: In the Shadow of the Himalayas. A New Paradigm for Wildlife Conservation." Washington, D.C.

———. (2001). *Terai Arc Landscape Fact Book.* Kathmandu, Nepal: WWF–Nepal Program.

———. (2001). "Terai Arc Landscape Nepal. Proceedings of the Stakeholders' Consultative Workshop on Terai Arc Landscape (TAL) Conservation in Nepal." Kathmandu, Nepal: WWF–Nepal Program.

———. (1994). *Wanted Alive! Tigers in the Wild.* Gland, Switzerland.

INDEX

ABOUT

Hemanta Mishra began his field career in 1967 with the Nepalese government and has worked with the Smithsonian Institution, the World Wildlife Fund, the World Bank, and Asian Development Bank as well as other major conservation groups. He has made extensive scientific studies of large Asian wild animals. He was a key player in the international team that preserved and stabilized the habitat and is credited with halting the extinction of the rhino and tiger populations in Nepal. He lives in Vienna, Virginia.

The author and his wife Sushma pose with a sedated tiger just before the tiger woke up and melted into the riverine forest. *Dave Smith*